D1466213

SCAMORAMA

Eve Edelson

disinformation®

Published by The Disinformation Company Ltd.
163 Third Avenue, Suite 108
New York, NY 10003
Tel.: +1.212.691.1605
Fax: +1.212.691.1606
www.disinfo.com

Library of Congress Control Number: 2006929815

ISBN-13: 978-1-932857-38-2
ISBN-10: 1-932857-38-9

Printed in USA

10 9 8 7 6 5 4 3 2 1

Distributed in the USA and Canada by:
Consortium Book Sales and Distribution
1045 Westgate Drive, Suite 90
St Paul, MN 55114
Toll Free: +1.800.283.3572 Local: +1.651.221.9035 Fax: +1.651.221.0124 www.cbsd.com

Distributed in the United Kingdom and Eire by:
Virgin Books
Thames Wharf Studios, Rainville Road
London W6 9HA
Tel.: +44.(0)20.7386.3300 Fax: +44.(0)20.7386.3360 E-Mail: sales@virgin-books.co.uk

Distributed in Australia by:
Tower Books
Unit 2/17 Rodborough Road
Frenchs Forest NSW 2086
Tel.: +61.2.9975.5566 Fax: +61.2.9975.5599 Email: towerbks@zip.com.au

CONTENTS

PREFACE

YES, IT'S A SCAM

This book is about liars telling lies with compound interest to other liars. A struggle is being waged on the internet, between criminals and pranksters. On one side are fraudsters who con their victims out of hundreds of millions of dollars each year. The basic tool of the trade is email, and the crime is the infamous 419 scam—a form of fraud whose current masters hail from Nigeria and which gets its name from section 419 of the Nigerian criminal code. It begins with an email from a stranger:

From: mrsmariam10@tiscali.dk
Subject: PLEASE SAVE MY SOUL

I apologise for the surprise this mail may cause you. I am soliciting your assistance as to enable my family round up the remains of our life. Following the death of my husband Sani Abacha, former head of state of Nigeria, the new president has turned the country against us. [BLAH...] I will be grateful if you could receive my last $50 million for safe keeping. I will give you 10 percent as a commission and to cover any expenses which may arise ... Our accounts have been frozen... [BLAH BLAH...] My son Mohammed is very sick in prison and his lawyers are ripping us off. We have almost resulted to start begging. I cannot lay my hands on this money due to the fact that our passports has been seized by this government... [BLAH BLAH BLAH...]

It is "advance fee fraud" because the victim sends money first, in anticipation of a great reward. "Expenses" do arise. That is the scam.

There's nothing new or uniquely Nigerian here—this old scam goes on elsewhere in different variations. A strikingly similar scam flourished in post-Revolutionary France. Yet the 419 scam is special in a number of ways.

When advance fee fraud reached Nigeria, it fell on fertile ground. Powered by email, its scope now exceeds anything of which 19th century French con artists could have dreamed. Embrace of technology, virtual companies, globalization, repurposed content—the 419ers applied these "new economy" concepts and made a lot of money doing so. These emails are so pervasive that they have inspired parodies—George W. Bush, Ken Lay, and even First Bank of Gondor versions.

Neither electronic crime, nor corporate scandal, nor the waste and folly of many governments (which dwarfs the scammers' takings) are new. However, most fraud is not packaged in a form that looks remarkably like political satire. 419 scam letters routinely involve impersonations of corrupt bureaucrats and politicians. (The scammers are not exactly underdogs, though; many are rich themselves, they will rob anyone and some have worked within government as well.)

Lastly, the scam's principal delivery mechanism, email, provides the means for its own defeat. On the other side of the struggle, pranksters from around the world are writing back to scammers strictly to waste their time. The resulting literary genre has become known as "scambaiting"—psychological warfare for clowns, or networked guerrilla theater. Some anti-scammers go farther, breaking into scammers' email accounts to warn off their victims, and helping law enforcement. This book documents a weird form of cultural exchange made possible by the internet. It is an introduction to the 419 scam, with correspondences between scammers and the people who love to yank their chains. If you're buying it to scam-proof a loved one and it doesn't have the intended effect, you can always whack the loved one with it until reason prevails.

DISCLAIMER

This book is not a study of Nigerian society, nor am I qualified to write one. There is a large literature on Nigerian politics and a vigorous Nigerian press, much of it online. Ditto for the rest of West Africa.

419 scammers impersonate real people, especially Nigerian political figures, whom they plainly consider corrupt, and therefore fun to impersonate, or actually serious about weeding out corruption, and therefore fun to impersonate. This is not a political tract. In describing any "real people," I stick to reported facts. Anti-scammers also impersonate people and characters, real and imaginary. This book merely chronicles their activities. I do not claim ownership of these characters, or any universes they inhabit. Apologies to any whose (sometimes brilliant) achievements were left out.

Scammers have not condescended to discuss satire with me. They're too busy trying to make money. However, when a scammer sends "her" photo and it's a headshot of actress/model Tyra Banks, that's a clue you're not dealing with an entirely humorless person.

I do not think being scammed is funny. Victims have been financially and emotionally ruined, and even murdered. Victims will not find this book funny, nor does it contain surefire ways to get money back, although there is some advice. Almost no one has ever gotten their money back from 419 scammers through the legal system. This book focuses on comedy because at some point people tune out. Each day brings warnings about new scams, identity theft, dangerous toys, drive-by shootings, cancer, terrorism, ballooning deficits, earthquakes, nuclear weapons in the hands of madmen, and the eventual collapse of our sun into a cold marble. A laugh is one form of self-defense.

I am not a legal or banking expert. Nothing described in this book is an invitation to break laws. Any websites mentioned are for reference only. Be warned that anti-scamming may become an obsession, which alienates your friends, or a literary outlet, which broadens your social circle. Count your silverware. May the farce be with you.

CHAPTER 1

419 ADVANCE FEE FRAUD

ALHAJI D. BAYERO
TEL/FAX: 234 - 90 - 406917
FAX: 234 - 90 - 409188
LAGOS, NIGERIA
21ST JANUARY 1997.

DEAR SIR,

REQUEST FOR URGENT BUSINESS RELATIONSHIP

I AM THE GROUP MANAGING DIRECTOR OF THE NIGERIA NATIONAL PETROLEUM CORPORATION (NNPC) AND A MEMBER OF THE ADHOC COMMITTEE SET UP BY THE FEDERAL GOVERNMENT OF NIGERIA TO REVIEW CONTRACTS AWARDED BY THE PAST MILITARY ADMINISTRATION BETWEEN 1985 - 1993. THE MEMBERS OF THE COMMITTEE ARE INTERESTED IN THE IMPORTATION OF GOODS INTO THE COUNTRY WITH THE FUNDS PRESENTLY FLOATING IN THE CENTRAL BANK OF NIGERIA/ NIGERIA NATIONAL PETROLEUM CORPORATION (NNPC) FOREIGN PAYMENTS ACCOUNT.

OUR REQUEST IS ANCHORED ON OUR STRONG DESIRE TO ESTABLISH A LASTING BUSINESS RELATIONSHIP WITH YOU AND YOUR COMPANY. WE HENCE SOLICIT YOUR PARTNERSHIP TO ENABLE US TRANSFER INTO YOUR ACCOUNT THE SAID FUNDS. YOU HAVE BEEN RECOMMENDED TO US IN CONFIDENCE AND WE WERE ASSURED OF YOUR ABILITY AND RELIABILITY TO PROSECUTE BUSINESS TRANSACTION THAT REQUIRE MAXIMUM CONFIDENTIALITY.

ORIGIN OF FUND

THIS FUND IS PRESENTLY FLOATING IN THE NIGERIAN NATIONAL PETROLEUM CORPORATION (NNPC) FOREIGN PAYMENTS ACCOUNT WITH THE CENTRAL BANK OF NIGERIA (CBN). THIS IS AS RESULT OF GROSSLY OVER INVOICED CONTRACTS WHICH WERE EXECUTED FOR THE NNPC DURING THE LAST ADMINISTRATION IN NIGERIA, AND ARE PRESENTLY UNDER VERIFICATION. TO THIS EFFECT, THE PRESENT ADMINISTRATION IN NIGERIA SET UP AN ADHOC COMMITTEE TO IDENTIFY, SCRUTINIZE AND RECOMMEND FOR PAYMENT ALL VALID CONTRACTS THAT HAVE BEEN FULLY EXECUTED. IN THE COURSE OF OUR ASSIGNMENT, WE HAVE IDENTIFIED A LOT OF MISAPPROPRIATED AND INFLATED FUNDS WHICH ARE PRESENTLY FLOATING IN THE SUSPENSE ACCOUNT OF THE CENTRAL BANK OF NIGERIA READY FOR PAYMENT. THE COMPANIES WHO EXECUTED THIER CONTRACTS HAVE BEEN FULLY PAID. IT IS NOW PART OF THE OVER INFLATED SUM OF USD25,320,000.00 THAT WE INTEND TO TRANSFER INTO THE FOREIGN ACCOUNT.

I HAVE THEREFORE BEEN MANDATED AS A MATTER OF TRUST BY THE MEMBERS OF THE COMMITTEE TO LOOK FOR A FOREIGN PARTNER INTO WHOSE ACCOUNT WE COULD TRANSFER THE SUM OF USD25,320,000.00 (TWENTY-FIVE MILLION, THREE HUNDRED AND TWENTY THOUSAND US DOLLARS) ONLY. HENCE I AM WRITING YOU THIS LETTER. WE HAVE AGREED TO SHARE THE FUNDS THUS:

(1)   65% FOR US (THE COMMITTEE MEMBERS) AND
(2)   25% FOR ACCOUNT OWNER (YOU)
(3)   10% TO BE USED IN SETTLING TAXATION AND ALL LOCAL AND FOREIGN EXPENSES THAT WILL BE INCURED IN THE COURSE OF THIS TRANSACTION.

IT IS FROM THE 65% THAT WE WISH TO COMMENCE THE IMPORTATION BUSINES. PLEASE NOTE THAT THIS TRANSACTION IS 100% SAFE AND GUARANTEED SINCE THE LAW UNDER WHICH OUR COMMITTEE WAS SET UP HAS EMPOWERED US TO DISBURSE ALL THE FUNDS FOUND TO BE FLOATING IN THE CENTRAL BANK OF NIGERIA REDUNDANT ACCOUNT FROM 1985 TILL DATE. WE SHALL COMMENCE THE TRANSFER OF THE FUNDS IMMEDIATELY WE RECEIVE THE FOLLOWING INFORMA- TION BY TELEFAX: 234 - 90 - 406917 OR FAX: 234 - 90 - 409188 VZ:

1.   YOUR COMPANY'S NAME AND FULL ADDRESS
2.   YOUR BANKER'S NAME, ADDRESS, TELEPHONE AND FAX NUMBERS
3.   THE ACCOUNT NUMBER AND NAME OF BENEFICIARY.

THE ABOVE INFORMATION ARE TO ENABLE US PUT UP LETTERS OF CLAIM AND JOB DESCRIPTION TO THE RESPECTIVE MINISTRIES FOR THE ISSUANCE OF THE MANDATORY FUND RELEASE APPROVAL/RECOMMENDATIONS. THIS WAY, YOUR COMPANY WILL BECOME RECOGNISED AND ACCEPTED AS THE BENEFICIARY OF THE CONTRACT ENTITLEMENTS BEFORE THE FINAL REMITTANCE TO YOUR NOMINATED ACCOUNT BY THE CENTRAL BANK OF NIGERIA BEING THE PAYING BANK..

WE ARE LOOKING FORWARD TO DOING THIS BUSINESS WITH YOU AND SOLICIT YOUR ABSOLUTE CONFIDENTIALITY IN THIS TRANSACTION. PLEASE ACKNOWLEDGE THE RECEIPT OF THIS LETTER USING THE ABOVE TELEFAX NUMBERS FOR MORE DETAILS REGARDING THE TRANSACTION.

YOURS FAITHFULLY,

DBayero

ALHAJI D. BAYERO

N. B. THIS LETTER IS BEING SENT BY ORDINARY MAIL FOR CONFIDENTIALITY PURPOSE.

My first scam-o-gram.
Source: A. Scammer

MY FIRST TIME

It came in a brown envelope a long time ago, back when people wrote letters. Exotically (as far as I was concerned) it was postmarked Lagos, Nigeria. Being neither a President nor CEO, I was puzzled by the salutation. It was the first scam-o-gram I ever saw.

A serious effort to parse the writing only confused me further.

Who is this guy? (There is a real Bayero, as it turned out—the Emir of Kano State in Nigeria. The real Bayero had not sent the letter, of course. This was my introduction to the scammers' idea of a joke.) *If it's above board, why the secrecy? Is ordinary postal delivery his idea of secrecy? Do funds "float"? Are decimal points necessary here?* (Head starting to ache.) *Is the money (gasp) embezzled? Then why not waltz into a bank by himself, like other embezzlers? Why write to me? Am I, unbeknownst to myself, a criminal mastermind? If I am, how does he know I will give him back any of this money* (which I haven't yet figured out is imaginary)*? And where did he learn to write?* (Reaching for the aspirin now.)

Within a year, it seemed all my colleagues and friends were receiving such appeals by letter or fax, each one flowery in an awkward style now instantly recognizable to fans. Then the emails started. Progress. Each 419 letter is an attempt to take you for all you've got—a fortune or a small pension—and ridiculous as it may seem, this scam works.

HOW THE SCAM WORKS

An email arrives out of the blue from someone posing as a bureaucrat, banker, royal toady or relative of a conveniently dead dictator, offering the deal of a lifetime. Translated painfully into English, you, dear reader, are asked to help skim imaginary public accounts, or siphon off an imaginary unclaimed inheritance, or in some other way move a lot of imaginary money. In these variations of the story, the whole thing looks like an invitation to embezzle. Quite often though, they are appeals to save a widow or help a cancer patient build orphanages. Your role is always to provide a bank account; your reward, a percentage of the money. *There is no money to be taken, except yours.*

"Forms" must be filled out. The scammer asks for details of your bank account and scanned copies of your passport or driver's license. Although this is generally a red herring—an attempt to impress you and keep you busy—compliance is a bad idea as it exposes you to identity theft. While a bank's security procedures typically frustrate such attempts, criminals *do* succeed in making unauthorized withdrawals. Your ID can also be used to scam others.

Once you're hooked, it turns out that palms must be greased—to bribe imaginary bureaucrats, or pay "demurrage" (storage) charges on imaginary boxes of money. The scammer asks you to send him money with which to do the greasing. Sometimes you are asked to wire money directly to a scammer's bank account, but usually the scammer insists on a Western Union money order. If you send it, you have been scammed. As you await your riches, the excitement turns to worry. Obstacles arise—"anti-terrorism" certificates are needed, "lawyers" must be paid. Your doubts are met with boilerplate responses, or browbeating. Eventually you get wise and retire to lick your wounds. This may not be the end of your troubles, as another scammer may appear, offering to help you recover your losses!

From: ANTI FRAUD UNITS [mailto:antifrauduinitj@yahoo.co.uk]
FROM THE DESK OF RTD.COL.THEOPHILUS DANJUMA.

ATTN SIR,
DUE TO THE HIGH LEVEL OF FRAUD/MONEY LAUNDREY IN NIGERIA BY TOP OFFICIALS, CONTRACTORS, UNPATROITIC CITIZIENS USING FAKE NAME/POSITIONS SUCH AS PASTORS, GOVERNORS, CHIRMAN OF BANKS, PRESIDENT, TOP MEN OF THE SOCIETY AND THE NNPC... THE PRESIDENT MANDATED US TO CARRY OUT A REVIEW OF OVER DUE PAYMENTS TO FORIEGNERS THAT THEIR KIN HAS DIED AND LEFT THEM AN INHERITANCE BY EFFECTING PAYMENT IMMIDIATELY SO AS TO SANITIZE THE IMAGE OF OUR GREAT COUNTRY CAUSED BY THE EMBARRASMENT.

WE ARE FULLY AWARE OF SCAM/FRAUD... IT HAS ALSO COME TO OUR NOTICE THAT YOU ARE COLLABORATING WITH SOME OFFICIAL TO CLAIM THIS FUNDS... BUT YOUR REPRESENTATIVE HERE IN NIGERIA ARE CRIMINALS. YOUR ASSISTANCE IS NEEDED TO PROOF THEM GUILTY UDNER CIRMINAL CODE 419 IN THE NIGERIAN CONSTITUTION. THE ANTI-FRAUD UNIT WILL MAKE SURE THIS FUNDS IS PAID TO YOU. YOU WILL BE REQUIRED TO OPEN A DOMICILARY ACCOUNT WITH ECOWAS BANK IN NIGERIA. YOU ARE ADVISE TO SIEZE COMMUNICATION WITH YOUR NIGERIAN PARTNERS FOR SECURITY REASONS.

YOUR TIMELY RESPONSE SHOULD SAVE YOU UNPLEASANT PREDICAMENT, LIKEWISE YOUR UNTIMELY RESPONSE MIGHT COMPEL OUR OFFICE TO SUBMIT OUR FINDINGS FOR IMMIDIATE ACTION AND CONSEQUENCE PROSECUTION

(The real Danjuma left the military to run a Nigerian oil company.)

The details may vary, but in every case, you part with money up front. Remember? It's called "advance fee" fraud. Victims have borrowed from family to pay the "fees." Others have "borrowed" from company or church coffers, or even become willing accomplices and gone to prison.

The many variations on the scamalicious story are called "formats." One classic format revolves around a Dead Bank Customer, who has died without heir:

...I will like you to stand as the next of kin to Mr. X and claim this funds so that the fruit of this old man's labor will not get into the hands of some corrupt Government officials.

The "dead bank customer" seldom dies a natural death.

A sampling of 385 such letters broke down thus:

Plane Crash	182	(47%)
Car Crash	126	(33%)
Unspecified	40	(10%)

Earthquake/Tsunami/Hurricane	9	(2%)
Illness or Natural Death	9	(2%)
Explosion/Bomb Blast/Oil Blast	8	(2%)
September 11	5	
Assassination	3	
Nautical	2	
War in Iraq	1	
War in Liberia	1	
Kidnapping	1	
Cosmetic Surgery	1	

The last suggests a mean dig at the current president of Nigeria, whose wife died after such a procedure. A spate of letters from her "friends" have since begun to appear. Nobody's death goes unexploited. Some dead bank customers have died repeatedly. Many bear the names of real people who died in real disasters. Nigerian "lawyers" are still looking for the heirs to Paul Wellstone, a US Senator who died in an airplane crash in 2002. The major cause of death to imaginary or impersonated people in fact seems to be air travel:

FOFF FLIGHT 2L8

Airport signage
Credit: Trevor Dykes

Sadly, given the spate of recent tragedies, the adjacent cartoon does not seem to be a wild exaggeration of the state of air travel in Nigeria. Next most dangerous is driving. Perhaps this should not be surprising, as bandits have been said to run cars off Nigerian expressways and loot the wreckage. The phrase "ghastly motor crash" has actually become a standard element in an "official" court document, (opposite).

Other formats include:
- Dictator's widow down to her last $50 million
- You've won a lottery you didn't enter!
- Minister in a refugee camp whose parishioner has a secret treasure
- Former guerrilla doing charitable works
- Save me from a life of prostitution
- Claim this mystery package! (See page 18)

Scammers have even pretended to be Iraqi oil ministers on the lam, but while the body of the letter says Baghdad, the email header says Lagos. Ditto for widows of Serbian militia leaders and Philippine presidents, and secretaries to Russian business magnate (now prisoner) Mikhail Khodorkovsky.

In 2003, I looked at the headers of one thousand emails. Headers, useful things explored in a later chapter, are data attached to emails, which can show their physical origin. Seventy percent came from West Africa, chiefly Nigeria. Nigerians are as wired as they can be in a country with shaky electrical systems, long lead times for telephone lines, and largely satellite-based internet connections. Scammers work out of cybercafés, or use back-office computers; big-time scammers

FEDERAL HIGH COURT OF NIGERIA
HOLDEN IN LAGOS, NIGERIA

PROBATE INHERITANCE FORM: FHCN 295

PROBATE INHERITANCE / AFFIDAVIT OF CLAIM AND FACTS

I ....Female/Male, Citizen of..............................,do hereby solemnly declare that the claim and facts of order contained here in this matter are made in good faith and my free will before this Honourable Court which I hereby swear to an oath as demanded by Section 5(v) cap11 of the Nigerian Civil Code and in relation to the appropriate sections of the 1999 Federal Constitution of Nigeria. That I shall be liable for contempt to the extent of any portion that is false.

1. That I am the above person.
2. That I know..of..............................
   a Citizen of ....
3. That..died in a ghastly motor crash on...........................
4. That before the death..had a total sum of.........................
   with one of the Finance Companies in Nigeria..
   with Account No...
5. That I am.. Next of Kin(Sister/Brother)
6. That this Affidavit is now required for record purpose and re-issuance of the necessary Legal Power and Order to transfer my Late Brother's Fund to me, in line with the requirements of the Nigerian Probate Law of 1976, Cap V Sub Section 2 (i).

....

THUMB PRINT AND SIGNATURE OF DECLARANT

FOR OFFICIAL USE ONLY

Sworn and sealed this day... day.............................20...............

Before me:..

....
Seal of the Supreme Court   **Presiding Judge**

....
Commissioner for Oaths

This Affidavit will only be Validated and Sealed on this Court's receipt from the Applicant, the Statutary Notarisation Levy of US$4,250.00, being Stamp Duty and Processing Fee for Sworn Affidavit by non-resident entities.   xxxxxxxxxxxxxxxxxxxxxxxxxxxxxxxxxxxxxxxxxxx

---

"Ghastly Motor Crash" Probate Form
Credit: Anti-scammer Barnabas Collins

HM Customs and Excise
Freepost SEA9186, PO Box 10, DA20 8BR,
Fax: 0800 528 2014
Email: customs.conf@3xl.net
Attn: The Beneficiary.

Abandoned Diplomatic Trunk Box.
We write to notify you that we have in our custody, a diplomatic trunk
received from Coin Security Company, a London based Diplomatic
Baggage Handling company in line with the British Government /
United Nations laws on world - wide Diplomatic Baggage movement.
The documented information which we have here shows that you are
the beneficiary of the diplomatic trunk which originated from Haiti and
destined to your name and address as the beneficiary. Morover, the
diplomatic nature of the above subject does not empower us to to open
the trunk for examination. However, you are expected to contact us not
later that 72 hours of this notice for your diplomatic trunk to be sent to
you via diplomatic channel.
If we do not hear from you after 72 hours of this notice, we will hand
over both the trunk and the your detailed contact information to FBI in
your country for further investigations on suspected Drug deals and
Terorism. However, if you get back to us and we verify you as the real
beneficiary of the diplomatic trunk, we will release the trunk to you.
Be adviced.

William Smith   4/6/2014
for: HMCS - London.

Mystery package for you!
Credit: A. Scammer

have their own facilities. Others set up shop in nearby Ghana or Togo, Dubai or, increasingly, South Africa. The other emails came from practically everywhere else. Lads from Lagos can be found all over Europe (especially the Netherands, the UK and Spain), North America and Asia. The 419ers also do a sideline in fake Asians, sending many Dead Bank Customer and We Need a Payments Representative letters with pseudo-Chinese names.

Companies have been scammed by individuals posing as civil servants and offering a "request for bid," which requires an escrow fee. Scammers may pose as buyers to obtain invoice forms or stationery for use in fraud. People have started receiving scam letters after making inquiries to legitimate Nigerian business organizations. Nigerian government and bank web sites post scam warnings, which have not stopped foreign victims from suing them. Some victims claim they were taken through government offices by government employees. As far as I know, no one in the US has successfully sued a Nigerian institution. The standard response of a Nigerian agency in American courts is that the victim did not carry out due diligence in confirming the identity of those with whom he was dealing, and that the Nigerian government claims sovereign immunity from prosecution in a foreign court.

HOW 419 SCAMMERS ARE ORGANIZED

Some gangs are large, with offices and "guymen" working in shifts for a cut of the profits. Many others work in ad hoc teams. These can be based on personal or ethnic ties, but members need not even be previously acquainted or on the same continent. The number of hard-core 419ers is hard to estimate. According to Nuhu Ribadu, the head of Nigeria's Economic and Financial Crimes Commission, up to 100,000 Nigerians are involved. A former deputy superintendent of police felt the number is "less than one percent of Nigerians," which would mean 1.2 million people! Anecdotally, 419 seems like a successful business for some and a widespread hobby for others.

There doesn't seem to be any one person in charge—the internet has lowered the barriers to entry. However, loners get stale prospect lists and lack the resources to make big money. At the other end of the scale, in 2005, Spanish police busted a three hundred-member gang pulling in an estimated

$120 million yearly. There are expenses—payments to apprentices, computers, maintaining multiple identities, postage (or the services of forgers), bribes for bank and government employees to obtain official documents, and of course lifestyles must be maintained. Still, top scammers are doing very well, and boast about it (there is more of this sort of thing in the appendix):

I LAUGH AT YOU CUZ YOU ARE THE MOST STUPID AND DUMBEST PERSON I HAVE EVER "KNOWN"... I WANT TO LET YOU INTO A SECRET, I JUST COLLECTED SOME COOL US$9,000 FROM ONE OF MY CLIENTS FROM THE USA. TODAY AND ABOUT THIS TIME NEXT WEEK, HE WILL BE MAKING ANOTHER PAYMENT WORTH US$60,000.

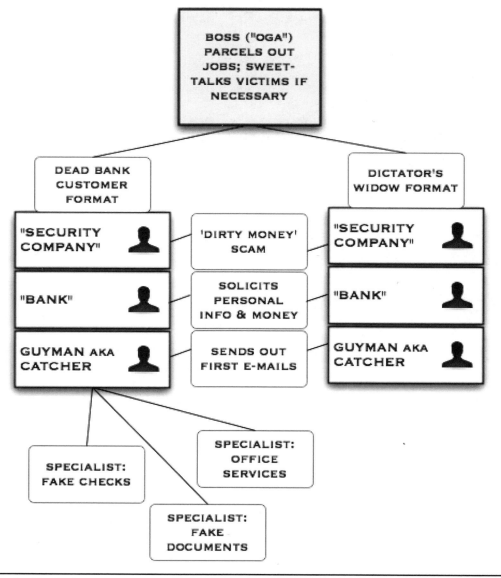

Thinking inside the box
Credit: A. Scammer

If the above is not an empty boast, this scammer has found the perfect victim - a 'client' who will pay, and pay, without the bother risk of a face-to-face meeting.

The preceding chart (page 19) offers a possible rough division of chores in an organized gang, which may have a number of jobs going at once.

"Snail" mail was the main scam vector in the 1980s and 1990s and is still widely used. (Between August and November 1998, the Sydney postal service alone confiscated 1.8 million pieces of 419 letters stamped with counterfeit postage.) Email is cheaper and faster. The initial contact is boilerplate. If a prospect responds, a team assembles to keep up the chatter and mock up certificates. The scammers refer to the victim as a "mugu," which means fool. Victims are induced to meet the scammers in Lagos, Amsterdam or Johannesburg. Some have been held for ransom and even killed. A victim is often shown a box of "defaced" currency, which needs cleaning with surprisingly expensive chemicals. This is the old "wash-wash," known in other countries as the "black money" trick. The victim forks over the payment, is hustled off, and told to await his fortune, which never appears.

Two trunk boxes full of wash-wash money
Credit: A. Scammer

The loot is laundered into legitimate businesses, real estate, cars, industrial equipment, or drugs, and it works in reverse. Nigerian drug dealers, who handle a big chunk of the worldwide heroin traffic, are thought to have moved into 419 fraud because it is cheaper and less risky. (It must also be more pleasant to send out emails than to walk through airport security with a condom in your gut. For a description of how much white powder can be packed into a condom, read Chris Abani's beautiful and tragic novel, *Graceland*.)

419ers are also involved in related crimes such as identity theft, passport fraud, counterfeiting, insurance/health care fraud and credit card fraud. (Merchants are routine targets of credit card fraud from many countries, among which Indonesia, Yugoslavia and Romania rank high, to name a few.) Much of this activity is targeted at the UK and US. One quarter of the major frauds the US Secret Service investigates involve Nigerians. 419 scams cost Americans $250 million a year.

WHY THE SCAM WORKS

It is often said that victims are greedy, and many scam-o-grams *are* bald invitations to embezzle imaginary money. Victims are also dismissed as stupid, which apparently means it's all right to hurt them. Wealthy victims are reflexive objects of scorn—as only other peoples' wealth is despicable. In fact, many victims are not well off at all, but rather financially desperate, poorly educated, unsophisticated and sometimes in failing mental health. They have never heard of General Abacha or the astonishing sums the government is trying to recover from his family. They do not fully understand what is being proposed or grasp its tongue-in-cheek seediness. Overall, though, there doesn't seem to be any obvious profile of a fraud victim—neither age, religion, nationality, gender, social status, profession, nor education seem to make a difference.

Further, many scams do not aim at greed, but at a victim's naïveté—the Latvian pastor who believed his church had won a lottery—or altruism—the American secretary who paid a scammer's imaginary debts to save him from imaginary loan sharks. One English victim shared his experience:

> *My name is XXXXX and I live in London, England. I really wish I'd seen your site before I lost $20,000... I was taken completely and believed I was helping a poor, frightened African girl get out of Ivory Coast, with her father's legacy of $22m that he had left in a security company, when he was mysteriously poisoned on a business trip in France.*

> *I paid for the money to come out of Ivory Coast, where it went to Amsterdam, where I paid more to get it out of customs. This wasn't enough, as the amount kept going up due to the "diplomatic" secrecy of the "consignment"...*

> *I went to Holland, was picked up at the airport by two men in a Mercedes (they were playing gospel music and talking God and Jesus, as they knew I was religious). Then we went to an office, where I was introduced to the manager, who said they would release the consignment to me now, on payment of the customs fee and their charges. I paid $10,000 and they brought in the box. It was opened and it was full of money, secured with pink plastic, which had to remain sealed until it got to the bank. I was then driven back to the airport and told that the money would be in my account soon...*

> *They have a web-site : www.interconfinance.com and if you look at that site, click on "online banking," then click on "accounts" and put in user name xxxxx and password xxxx, you will see an entry crediting my account with $22m.*

> *The next surprise (surprise, surprise!) was that I now had to pay $22,000 to get a license from the Hague, stating it was not drug/laundered money.*

> *At this point, my enquiries saved me. I called the Hague, asking for the price of this form and he said it was a scam. Then I looked up the form name in Google and got straight to your site, where I read the same letters, with variations that I got... they find out your weaknesses, given in confidence and exploit them mercilessly, I was taken in and suffer the financial pressures, as the money was entirely borrowed from credit cards, so convinced was I.*

Other scammers exploit charity—a tailored version was circulating within days of the Asian tsunami of 2004. Some pose as refugees of one or another horrific African conflict, or as managers of funds for Holocaust survivors, or as victims of personal violence such as the Nigerian girl who was (really) attacked with acid by a rejected suitor. Graphic photos are often thoughtfully included.

A sub-genre of the scam involves persuading the victim to act as a check-cashing service for cashiers' checks or postal money orders, which turn out to be forged. The victim may be trying to rent an apartment, or find a job, or sell something:

Showing 1 review

Product Rating: ★ ★ ★ ★ ★

Toshiba libretto U100 (PLU10U-00701K) PC Notebook
by wesere1 new, May 08 '05
(Don't Show)

Pros: d
Cons: d

Hello, I am Steve i LIVE IN NYC, i am urgently ineterseted in the purchase of your item (Toshiba libretto U100 (PLU10U-00701K) PC Notebook)for my cousin, who is working in one of the African countries, As for the payment,I offer you ($2,500.00).with the shipping to nigeria. I will pay you through Western Union Auction Payment (Bid Pay); I would really appreciate it if you can make this transaction fast and quick, as the urgent need of the item. I would want the item ready for shipment and shipped out immediately after you are been notify of the payment Confirmation/Approval. I will like you to arrange for the shipping with one of my courier service (If you dont mind). Kindly get back to mewith your fullnameand address to this Email address(wesere1@yahoo.co.uk) so as to make the payment if you are interested your quick response means alot to me.

Scammer responds to an online ad
Credit: A. Scammer

The scammer sends a check made out for *more* than the requested amount. This is supposedly to cover shipping charges, or (more convoluted) reflects a debt supposedly owed by some middleman to the scammer. The victim is asked to send the scammer a money order for the difference. For job seekers, this is the only job function:

From: SMITH COLE [mailto:global_company010@msn.com]
Subject: REPRESENTATIVE NEEDED.

I represent GLOBAL IMPORT/EXPORT COMPANY based in the UK. My company exports cocoa... Most of our customers pay out in cheques and we do not have an account in your country that will clear this money. It is upon this note that we seek your assistance as our representative in your country. You will receive 10 percent of whatever amount you clear for the company and the balance will be paid into an account we will avail to you. This job is rather easy and does not require a lot of expertise. If you are interested, please email me...

The bad check may actually pass muster with the local bank branch, but not at the central clearinghouse. However, this can take weeks. By then the victim has sent a real money order to the scammer and is dunned by the bank for the bad check.

419ers prepay for hotel reservations with (bogus) checks, then cancel and request a (real) refund. No profession is neglected. A music teacher forwarded this example:

From: mrsloraa@5fm.za.com
Subject: my 2 kids need a music teacher

Good Day,

Iam Dr oliver from holland.iam intrested in bring my 2 kids to your location for you to teach them ... i want my kids to be leactured for 4 weeks which will be $2000. I will arrange for their home stay, guardian and visas to come over to the States for the classes.

...I will instruct attorney in the canadian to issue a U.S certified check in your name. Although the value of the check is more than your charges I think, I should be able to trust you with the remaining balance.The reason why I am doing this is that it would take check sent from over here 60 days to clear over there, whereas a check sent from canadina to U.S would clear tops within 48 hrs. So I will expect that you send my balance to my Personal assistant immediately you recieve payment for your tuition so that my he can be able to arrange for their travelling documents come to the states and accomodation for the programe. ...I would like you to give me your full name,contact address and your phone numbers so that I can instruct my attorney to make out the certified check to you. Pls get back to me as soon as youget this mail so that I can know my stand.

Have a great day.

This is a volume business. A scammer sends batches of forged checks to a middleman, who sends each to an individual victim. In 2004, acting on a tip from British customs agents, US postal inspectors intercepted such a package en route from Lagos to a "Ken Smith" in Indiana. They delivered the package and arrested Ken, also known as Adebayo Adedimila.

Victims of the jobs scam are also used as unwitting accomplices to launder proceeds from crime. (Cases in which the victim simply makes an account available and passively allows transfers in and out are more the hallmark of Eastern European scammers, who use this mechanism to launder money from hacked bank accounts.) Victims are also used to re-ship goods, which were purchased fraudulently.

419ers also make purchases with stolen credit card numbers. Sometimes they use the deaf relay telephone ("tty") service for this purpose, in order to avoid the increasing suspicion vendors feel about foreign accents. This has brought suspicion on the service itself and caused resentment among relay operators, who know what is going on but are not (officially) free to intervene.

Some scammers troll for victims in online chat rooms:

> I was on Yahoo Instant Messanger... someone by the name of "Usman tijani" started to tell me how he/she had 36 million dollars in NIGERIA to invest here in America. I ... decided to play along... he/she kept on asking for information about me and wanted me to transfer the money here ... he started bugging me to pay...

Usman: you know this attorny must be paid his for a fast service
Usman: to enable him produce all the necessary vitals document
Usman: ok/
Usman: he told me 6,500$usd and immediately this money is paid the document will be

passed to the bank for final payment aproval

Me: i dont have any money

Usman: my brother is this how we are going to do this transaction ?

Me: i cant, because i have nothing

Usman: listen am not telling you give me any money but is for the attorny bill

Usman: God will not come down from heven to assist he sent people like you to help people i cant afford the whole what i told him is that when the beneficiary come he will ballance him up

Usman: ok?

Usman: dont be disscourage

Me: what im telling you is that i dont have the money

Usman: i will forward your particulars to the atorny to go to abuja the federal capital high court and start processing the documents tommorrow

Me: i dont have any money to my name, ?I just cant help you there and im sorry. I am in debt up to my ears, and if i had the money i would help you, but i dont.

Usman: MY BROTHER PLS JUST THINK IF YOU ARE IN MY SHOE THAT HAVE SUCH MONEY HANGING SOME WHERE YOU WILL BEG FOR AN ASSISTANCE AS AM BEGING YOU PLS ASSIST ANY THING YOU CAN PLS I PLEED YOU

Me: im sorry but i cannot help you with money. i wish you can understand this, and i understand you if you want to look for someone else.

Usman: MY BROTHER WHAT AM TRYING TO SAY IS THAT THOSE THAT MEAN YOU CANT ASSIST WITH EVEN 1,000$

In none of the above scenarios is the victim asked to do anything illegal or even morally dubious.

Scammers also make cold calls:

Last week, and again this week, I received a phone call at about 7:30 pm EST. The gentleman on the phone had what I believe to be an African accent. I could hear other people in the background talking with the same accents.

The man proceeded to tell me that I had been awarded a Grant from the United States Government. He then said that "your government" often gives out grants to its citizens who need money. It was a special program. He then rattled off my name, my address, phone number to verify the information and said that my grant was to be between $10,000 and $15,000.

All they needed was my Bank name, my bank account number, and routing number and they would deposit my check. At that point I got the giggles. First of all, no government employee is going to call me and be working at 7:30 pm EST. Secondly, I enjoyed how he said "your" government.

The guy could not understand why I would not give him my banking information. I asked him to send me a letter or give me a number I could call to verify his information. He then put me through to his Supervisor. I heard him go "psssst" at someone and tell them I

needed a supervisor. A Supervisor with the same accent told me it was perfectly safe to give him my account number. He informed me that all banks in the US were covered with theft insurance, and that even if I were robbed, the bank would take care of putting my money back in. It was no risk to me at all. In the background I heard someone open a refrigerator, someone else run water, I think they were in someone's kitchen.

I told the guy "nice try" and I hung up on him.

This week's call was funnier. When I answered music was blasting so loud I couldn't hear anyone. Then I heard someone yell "shut-up, I called somebody!" This guy gave me the same speech, same accent, same questions. I told him that they called me last week and it wasn't going to work this week either. He cussed and hung up.

I had not received a letter from anyone in a while asking me to help them get money out of their country, etc. Now I know why... they discovered phones! It struck me as funny until I realized that I know a few Senior Citizens who would give them their account numbers to get the "grant." Don't the crooks worry about caller ID?

Even if caller ID couldn't be faked (it can, and so can voiceover IP, a.k.a. internet telephone), some people will fall for this. Most people delete the emails, but only a small percentage need to be scammed (thought to be around one percent—a response rate a telemarketer would love) to make the business profitable. As long as people fall for it, the scam will go on.

I LOVE LUCY

Sometimes hanging around in chat rooms is a waste of a scammer's time:

Lucyatt27: i need urgent remedy to a tough solution at hand

antiScammer: So, why don't you tell me about it?

Lucyatt27: need to know u ist

antiScammer: I ist what?

Lucyatt27: need somebody good to help my quest

Lucyatt27: have a client, his dead

Lucyatt27: but cant find his next of kin

Lucyatt27: need someone to front as one b4 d govt takes over his monet and properties

Lucyatt27: he s from germany

antiScammer: Not Nigeria?

Lucyatt27: nop nigeria s in africe but germany s in europe

antiScammer: So, what kind of business are you in that you have clients that die?

Lucyatt27: am an attoney to him

antiScammer: What city is your office in? In fact, what is the name of your firm?

Lucyatt27: my name is lucy kudirate am from bamako, mali

Lucyatt27: my firm s lucy chambers am married and 33yrs

antiScammer: Who's Lucy Chambers? And where did you study law?

Lucyatt27: mine

antiScammer: You studied law in a mine? I would think it would be quite dark.

Lucyatt27: a civil lawyer by prof

Lucyatt27: i ve over 21 clients

Lucyatt27: never had a dead one

Lucyatt27: they all big jobs

antiScammer: Hmm....so naturally, the best course of action WOULD be to message random strangers over Yahoo. Ok. Well, I imagine for something as important as this, you'll need my bank records.

Lucyatt27: u sound straight so can u help

antiScammer: I can if your credentials check out. Are the Mandamus forms in order?

Lucyatt27: they are its bout $750,000

Lucyatt27: u ll benefit too

antiScammer: Oh, the things I do, I do with no thought of reward. Can't have a dead guy making all that money.

Lucyatt27: d only problem here is gettih a next of kin

antiScammer: Oh, yes. Now in America, proof of family is required for the legal paperwork. Fortunately, I happen to be a lawyer as well, so in order to avoid the situation of Kirk vs Khan, we're going to need a few items on my end.

Lucyatt27: i ve everythin

antiScammer: Firstly, your fax number, as the Bureau of Kin-Provage will need to send you some documents.

Lucyatt27: he had an accident with his wife and 2 sons

antiScammer: in the case of the death of a whole family, we'll need the Mensrea Certificate stamped by the reporting Constable and the Prime Minister. You have this form ready to fax?

Lucyatt27: let ne have ur no but ull be his next of kin to d bank for me

antiScammer: Ok, so let's start things off with the naked pictures.

Lucyatt27: let me have ur fax no

antiScammer: Our receiving line needs waxing, so I'll have to send you the forms. What is your fax number?

Lucyatt27: 2348033350xxx

antiScammer: If I'm to prove I'm his next of kin, I'll need naked pictures of his wife to prove familial closeness.

Lucyatt27: dats no problem too ill send everything just help

Lucyatt27: we ll pay u just co operate

antiScammer: Hmm...bit of a problem here.

antiScammer: Indians have just stolen our phone and fax. I'm afraid we're stuck, unless...

Lucyatt27: u know we re not too advanced in all in africa

antiScammer: It appears that Shift keys haven't made it there yet. I'm not sure how we can get this resolved unless your firm can front us the money for a new fax machine.

antiScammer: If you can just send me your corporate credit card information, my receptionist will get a fax machine

Lucyatt27: how do i send it pls

antiScammer: Enter the credit card information here and I'll take it down. It'll go much faster if we get one here, because this is America and the Machines roam our streets.

Lucyatt27: our credit card doesnt work in d us

antiScammer: So, I'll need your credit card number, the expiration date, the last 3 digits on the back, and the cardholder's name.

Lucyatt27: ur makin things difficult 4 us

antiScammer: I'll need to get this to the store before they close. It's about to get dark, and the cyborgs will be coming. If you can't show me this much good faith, how can we do business?

Lucyatt27: can see u dont wanna help a lady

Lucyatt27: ill look 4 a ready persom

antiScammer: After all we've been through together? This is how you treat me?

Lucyatt27: we have millions of people connected to d net bye

antiScammer: I'm here ready to give you unlimited access to my account in Switzerland, I just need a little cooperation from you!

Lucyatt27: i ve been ur fool

antiScammer: Well, just answer one thing for me, Lucy.

Lucyatt27: u ll soon be one to somebody to dats nemesis

antiScammer: What law school did you go to that they didn't teach you how to use a Shift Key?

Lucyatt27: bye

antiScammer: Lucy, Baby! Don't go! I can change!!!

antiScammer: Lucy?

antiScammer: o/\ Mem'ries...from the corners of my mind.

antiScammer: Misty water-colored mem'ries...of the way we were! o/\

CHAPTER 2

THE FRENCH CONNECTION

Whether it be that the multitude, feeling the pangs of poverty, sympathize with the daring and ingenious depredators who take away the rich man's superfluity, or whether it be the interest that mankind in general feel for the records of perilous adventure, it is certain that the populace of all countries look with admiration upon great and successful thieves.
– C. Mackay

Widows of assassinated aristocrats, orphaned children of cocoa planters. Is this not new wine in old bottles? Americans will be reminded of Twain's fictional Lost Dolphin of France, conning his way through the South. Some aficionados consider 419 a "Spanish prisoner" scam. This infamous con was an appeal for financial help to free a poor soul from a Spanish prison, supposedly dating back to the Napoleonic wars, or even the English-Spanish wars of the Renaissance. In the 1920s, American Oscar Hartzell was nearly conned into buying a share of the "unclaimed inheritance" of Sir Francis Drake. Deciding to go into the business himself, Hartzell scammed thousands of people. Fleeing to Britain, he lived off the takings until he was deported home and put in prison.

To my ears, however, a modern-day 419 letter sounds most directly like the *lettre de Jérusalem*. The memoirs of Eugene-Francois Vidocq provide a glimpse at this scam of post-Revolutionary France. An adventurer and ex-con, Vidocq worked as a police informant, then rose to become founder of the Bureau de la Sureté, and a pioneer of criminal detection. Vidocq described a scam carried on *within prisons*, by sending a letter to someone with royalist sympathies. It was couched as the confession of a servant whose aristocratic master had hidden his treasure before going to his doom at the hands of the Revolution. The "servant" offered to retrieve the treasure, in return for a modest percentage. My translation follows. A scholar would do a more elegant job, but none of the melodrama is my invention. Vidocq's comments are in parentheses.

Sir, Pursued by the revolutionaries, M. the viscount of ***, M. the count of ***, M. the marquis of *** (care was taken to choose the name of someone well known and recently denounced [by the government]), whom I served as a valet, went into hiding to escape the rage of his enemies; we ourselves fled, but pursued along the way, we were about to be arrested when we came within a short distance of your town; we were forced to abandon our carriage, trunks, even our luggage; we did manage to save a small trunk containing Madame's jewels, and 30,000 gold francs; but fearing to be caught with these objects on us, we moved off a little way from where we had been forced to halt; after having mapped the place, we hid our treasure, then disguised ourselves, entered your town and put up at a hotel ***. We learned of a person to whom one could in need entrust large sums of money; we wanted to charge this person with retrieving our money and sending it to us bit by bit according to our needs, but destiny decreed otherwise. You doubtless know the circumstances surrounding the arrest of my virtuous master, up to his sad end. More happily than he, I was able to make for Germany, but soon, taken with the most awful misery, I determined to go back to France. I was arrested and taken to Paris; found in possession of a false passport, I was clapped in irons and now, following a long and cruel malady, I am in the infirmary at Bicêtre (a prison - lettre de Jérusalem was said to refer to its location near the police Préfecture, in the rue de Jérusalem in Paris). I had, before returning to France, taken the precaution of hiding the map in the lining of a box, which, happily, is still in my possession. In the cruel position in which I find myself, I believe I can, without discredit, take some of the money hidden near your town. Among several names we reviewed, my master and I, at the hotel, chose yours. I do not have the honor to know you personally, but the reputation of probity and generosity which you enjoy in your town is a sure guarantee to me that you will acquit yourself well in the mission with which I wish to charge you, and that you will be worthy of the confidence of a poor prisoner who has hope only in God and in you.

Please be so good sir, as to let me know if you accept my proposition. If I were so happy as to convince you, I would find a way to send you the plan, so that you would have no more to do than dig up the box; you would guard the contents in your hands; you would give me only what would be necessary to alleviate my unhappy state.
I am, yours, etc.

P.S. It is not necessary to tell you that a matter such as I propose must be carried out with the greatest discretion; thus, in your response, which will have to pass the prison clerk before reaching me, limit yourself to replying only yes or no.

The French version endures, as a French victim informed me. Here is a modern example, in English:

Dear Sir,
It is with a heart full of tears and anguish that I call on you to come to my aid.
I am Madame Marie Wambek, the spouse of General Roberto Wambek (deceased) who was formerly the Minister of Defense and Chief of the army of the Republic of Guinea Bissau in the fallen regime of Mr. Bernado Viera. During the coup d'etat mounted by General Ansumane, who succeeded in taking power from Mr. Bernado Viera, my husband was assassinated.

During this turbulence, my family and I, we have taken flight to Cotonou, Republic of Benin, in order to avoid embarrassment and (what might befall us) from the new government, which confiscated all the properties and the bank accounts of supporters of the former President, Mr. Bernado Viera. Finding myself in this unhappy situation, I seek someone reliable in your country who will accept to receive urgently for me, a sum of 15 million American dollars (US$15,000,000.00). This money remains the only thing we have at this time and is still intact in a security company where my husband deposited it before dying.

On that note, I pray you to assist me to urgently safeguard this money in your country. I have concluded all arrangements to obtain all the judicial papers permitting you to reclaim this money as my (executor?) and legitimate beneficiary of the fund. With hope of us meeting in the near future, we are going to discuss our mutual business relation such as the possibility for you to obtain the residence permit for my children and me in your country. We are not at ease in Africa for reasons of security. I must admit our survival depends now on your assistance.

I am prepared to compensate you with the sum of $4 million at the success of this affair. I repose all my confidence in you. Pray do not disappoint me. Pray treat this affair in all confidentiality. I guarantee you that you run no risk in this operation. Help me, help me please.
Thanks for contacting me with my private email.
Hoping to receive your news.

Best compliment.
Mme Marie Wambek

These scam-o-grams generally come from francophone countries such as Ivory Coast or Senegal. Confusingly, when people respond in French, the writers often prefer to carry on in English. Even more confusingly, in some French scam-o-grams, which are obviously the product of machine translation, certain English words are simply left un-translated. 419 letters are floating around in Spanish, Dutch and German but most seem machine translated from English without further review and make about as much sense. Scammers, posing as refugees from other African countries, seem unnerved to receive replies in the local languages:

I received this plea for help in distributing excess funds from the Central African Republic. I'm fluent in the tribal trade language of the country. I don't think he appreciated my attempts to communicate with him in Sango.

First email from him:
My name is Garaba Jean-Mario, a national of Central African Republic... I was a protocol officer to Ange Felix Patasse, the former president of Central African Republic, who is deposed and is now on exile in the republic of Togo. In the event of the rebellion,

I made away with two well-sealed boxes each containing the sum of USD 25,000,000 from a secret vault in the presidential villa. With the help of my friend, who was a courrier, he assisted me in transporting these boxes to Cotonou, in Benin through a diplomatic channel. For security reasons, he assisted me in lodging these boxes with a security company in Cotonou and registerd the boxes in his name as containing FAMILY DOCUMENTS AND FILES... I want you to assist me in raising this claims so that this money will be released for us. No time to waste. Regards. Garaba Jean-Mario.

My reply:
How lucky! you selected someone who used to live in the Central African Republic. I lived upcountry at Yaloke. Ita, mbi ma toto ti mo, mais mbi ye ti hounda mo. tenti nye mo ye ti mgbanzi ginza so kwe? mo hinga, a tanga ti ita ti mo na be afrique a ba mpasi mingi, na mbi pense ayeke njoni ti tene mo mou 65 percent ti nginza so, na mo bata ni pepe, mais mo mou ni na a jo so ayeke na besoin ti kobe, na yoro, na a mbeni ye nde nde. A yeke a mara ti jo tonga so, so a ye ti aide a ita ti ala so fade a mo lege na RCA ti djia lango ti bira na peko ti ala.
ita ti mo na Amerique

(rough translation: I hear your cries, yet I question why you are so selfish with such a large sum of money when your fellow countrymen are in such poverty? I encourage you to give 65 percent of it to the people of your country who need food and other things just to survive. It is people like you, with the power to help their fellow man who can enable the C.A.R. to leave behind the era of poverty and war.
your brother in America)

Jean's second email:
Nice to know you used to live in Central Africa. Where are you from? Where do you live presently? What do you do for a living? Please respond in English.

My reply:
Don't you know Sango?

Jean's final email:
You are not under any obligation to believe me. Forget it. Bye.

Plus ça change.

THE FIELD OF HONOR

"Count Ludwig von Carabos" heard from a scammer:

The Scammer:

> I am mr. Macdonald Dubem,Branch Manager of Zenith Bank, Idumota Branch,delta state Nigeria. I have an urgent business proposition for you.
>
> On December, 1997, a Canadian Oil consultant/contractor with the Nigerian National Petroleum Corporation, Mr. Barry Kelly made a numbered time (Fixed) Deposit valued at US$11,500,000.00 (Eleven Million Five Hundred Thousand United State Dollars). Upon maturity, I sent a notification but got no reply. Finally we discovered that Mr. Barry Kelly died from an automobile accident.
>
> I found out that he died without making a WILL. According to Nigerian Law, the money will revert to the Nigerian Government if nobody applies to claim the fund. I will like you to stand in as the next of kin so that the fruits of this old man's labor will not get into the hands of some corrupt government officials.
>
> I will like you to provide your full names and address so that the Attorney will prepare the documents, which will put you in place as the next of kin. A bank account which you will provide will then facilitate the transfer of this money to you as the next of kin. The money will be paid into your account for us to share in the ratio of 65 percent for me and 30 percent for you and 5 percent be used in settling taxation and all local and foreign expenses. There is no risk as my position guarantees the execution of this transaction. I do urgently await your response or reach me through my confidential and private phone 234 80 xxxxxxxx.
>
> Best regards, mr macdonald dubem.

The astute reader has already pegged this as a classic "dead bank customer" letter.

"Count von Carabos" responded accordingly:

> Dear Mr. Dubem:
> I am Count Ludwig von Carabos, the only brother of the late departed Barry Kelly. He changed his name when he emigrated to Canada.
>
> I am truly shocked and saddened to hear that you are the repository of my dear brother's wealth. After his tragic death, we made vast efforts through the Nigerian government and other modalities to locate my brother's body and his money. They could not find it. Now we learn that you have somehow gained access to this money that belongs to our family. We are shocked and appalled that you have derelicted your duties as a banker and your ethics to rob a dead man's grave. This is a grave insult

to the von Carabos family name and its honor!

The von Carabos family has lived on the same land in Germany for 1,000 years. The von Carabos name is renowned throughout Europe for the excellence of our business, producing police interrogation equipment, which we sell to secret police agencies throughout the world. We are a family of impeccable honor and tradition. Your failure to yield up this fortune to the family at the time of my brother's death is an insult to our honor and tradition!

Therefore, I am sending our family's most trusted emissary, Kommandant Wilhelm Klink, and his aide, Sergeant Schultz, to Lagos as part of my team, which will include the family accountant, Arthur Anderson, the family lawyer, William Kunstler, and our retainers. As my family's representatives, they will get to the bottom of this chicanery and recover our wealth. Any attempt by your organization to interfere with our just claims will result in the strongest sanctions.

While Kommandant Klink recovers our money and the body of my brother, I will recover our family's honor. The von Carabos family has a long tradition of protecting its honor on the field! Therefore, I challenge you to a duel!

Under Code Duello, you may choose the location. As the challenging party, I choose the weapons. I will be bringing a set of Krupp pistols for this very purpose. With my seconds in attendance to ensure there is no chicanery, we will meet on the field of honor and settle honor.

We will meet in Lagos on June 27, at 3 p.m. We will proceed to Zenith Bank to settle the accounts, then to the cemetery to recover my brother's body, and then to the dueling site. You will make yourself known to my team by holding up the following sign:

IAMAS
TUPIDC
ONMAN

That is the von Carabos family motto, and it means, "fraudere est vivere." That is how we shall know you. We will settle this assault on the von Carabos family tradition and this affair of honor. If you do not appear, then you are indeed a coward, a mugu, and a bearer of shame and deceit, and we will attain justice for the family ourselves.

Sincerely,
Ludwig Von Carabos

Strangely, the scammer did not reply.

CHAPTER 3

WHY DOESN'T SOMEONE DO SOMETHING?

This is the period when we started hearing about 419, it is the period we started having drug problems. It is a period when Majors (in the army) started buying property in London.
– Nuhu Ribadu

The more destruction there is everywhere, the more it shows the activity of town authorities.
– Gogol, *The Inspector General*

Law enforcement entities worldwide are quite aware of 419 and prosecute a number of related cases, although these are not always described in 419 terms. Previous Nigerian administrations gave the matter only lip service, except (or even) when pressed by foreign governments. Prosecutions in Nigeria were relatively few, and convictions rare. The situation seems to be changing, although there is much cynical back-and-forth about whether this is the beginning of real reform. While this book is not about Nigerian politics, some well-known facts will help put a 419 letter into context and explain why it looks like political satire.

IN NIGERIA

First, 419 is a crime in Nigeria (under Decree 13 of the Advance Fee Fraud and other Fraud Related Offences Act of 1995). The problem is not a lack of laws. Second, 419 is only part of a larger picture. Nigerians *themselves* are victims of all sorts of fraud, with 419 so common that it is slang for a con of any kind. Transparency International rates Nigeria one of the most corrupt countries in the world. The level of corruption in government and society is widely documented in the published literature, a vigorous Nigerian press, and online, with just a few sources cited here. Bribery is common in everyday transactions, extortion for spare change at police roadblocks being just one example (people have been shot for holding out). Famously, scammers sell peoples' houses while they are away. Bank employees siphon off money from accounts. Nigerian bloggers make it clear, in eloquent terms, what they think about the state of the country. (A number of blogs are listed in the appendix.) Nigerians abroad are not exempt. 419ers intercept their telephone calls home and frighten them into wiring money for operations on relatives who aren't sick. Nigerians wishing to go abroad encounter green card scams.

President Olusegun Obasanjo heads the first civilian government in many years. Since gaining independence from Britain in 1960, Nigeria's leaders seem to have treated the treasury as a personal kitty. General Sani Abacha, president from 1993 until his death in 1998, is accused of having taken $4 billion. Scam letters "from" his widow Mariam and son Mohammed complaining of family accounts being frozen are drawn straight from the newspapers. Most of the $280 billion in oil revenues over the last thirty years were embezzled, or squandered on ill-conceived public works projects. Money coming in as trade revenues or foreign aid went out again in suitcases, which the government is still trying to get back. Nigeria has a lot of oil and fertile soil, and should be rich. Instead, there is widespread poverty, very high unemployment even for technically trained graduates, a crumbling infrastructure, and huge debt. In short, ordinary people have been royally ripped off for a long time, by scammers in and out of government.

On top of this, the military has killed many civilians, with no one brought to justice. The police are widely considered corrupt and brutal. A senior officer himself described the ranks as extremely poorly paid, trained and housed, and they are finding vigilantes serious competition.

Such a situation would corrode civic feeling anywhere, and Nigerians often describe their country as a colonial construct. It is only forty years since a civil war claimed one million lives. Violence is common between religious and ethnic groups, with the smaller groups ground between them like pebbles, or warring for a share of the oil wealth. A number of states have instituted Islamic law, in a challenge to federal authority. Merely holding the country together looks challenging, and yet Nigeria endures. This kind of situation is not unique to Nigeria, nor is it offered as justification for the scam, but it must be understood to fully appreciate the bitter joke that is a 419 letter. General Abacha got his, and the scammers want theirs.

DEAR SIR,
I am Lawyer Ally Johnson, attorney to late MARK, who until his death, was an crude oil consultant with Shell Oil in Nigeria herein shall be referred to as "my client." Sometime precisely may 1st, 2002, he was abducted by irate youths of the Niger-Delta, the oil producing areas in Nigeria, following the riots by these youths over degradation of their community by incessant and frequent oil spillage as a result of crude oil exploration. In the course of these development, Mark and some other oil workers lost their lives. Unfortunately, Mark has no family, because in the attempt to rescue the workers by security operatives, the Irate youths, set the house ablaze and Mark and his family died of burns. I have contacted you to assist in repatriating the money left behind by my client... about 20.5million dollars...

A crime, which is a large source of income, was not high on the government's list of priorities. 419ers are seen by many as Robin Hood figures. The scam spins off jobs for other people nominally outside the criminal enterprise, who provide office services. It probably brings a lot of money to cybercafés. Scammers buy luxury goods, which is nice for car dealerships and retail outlets, and funnel the loot into real estate and finance. Scammers are not necessarily good for the rest of the economy. Corruption has wrecked Nigeria's reputation and discouraged foreign investment (oil excepted). Many foreign vendors will not ship goods there or take Nigerian credit cards. This has driven even legitimate businesses to shift to neighboring countries. Money from all kinds of crime is laundered not only through banks, but also by importing industrial, chemical and pharmaceutical goods, at a rate which floods the market and drives local companies under.

There have, however, been significant developments. President Obasanjo has fired some high-level bureaucrats for financial irregularities, including managers of the Nigerian National Petroleum Corporation, and set up a panel to identify contracts awarded or billed fraudulently during the period of military rule. The number of licensed banks has shrunk drastically as government cracked down on those, which were undercapitalized or suspected of corruption.

The most notable development may be the establishment of the Economic and Financial Crimes Commission (www.efccnigeria.org). Headed by Nuhu Ribadu, the EFCC has arrested legislators and bureaucrats and seized vast amounts of cash and property. Representative Maurice Ibekwe, the first legislator charged with 419 by the civilian government, died in 2004 while awaiting trial. In 2005, the former Inspector General of Police, Tafa Balogun, was sentenced to six months in prison for extortion, and two Nigerians were convicted of defrauding a Brazilian bank, Banco Noroeste, out of $242 million. 419ers have also been made to repay a few individuals with large losses. In January 2006, a Lagos court sentenced a scammer to 376 years in prison for bilking an American out of $1.9 million (one of the few foreigners to have testified in a Nigerian court on the matter). In 2005, the EFCC forced 419ers to return $4.5 million stolen from a Chinese family.

This is not the first administration to promise change. One has to start somewhere. As Ribadu gets close to other senior government figures, some simply refuse to appear before his tribunals and accusing the EFCC of a political vendetta. The dismissive attitude of government officials toward court orders, along with concern about human rights, spurred the Nigerian Bar Association to a two-day boycott of the court system in 2006.

OUTSIDE NIGERIA

There is a lot of law enforcement activity aimed at 419ers, although it isn't always described as such. Many scammers are also involved in other crimes and have been prosecuted outside Nigeria on related charges, such as wire, postal, bank or credit card fraud; visa fraud; identity theft; embezzling; counterfeiting; fencing stolen goods; money laundering; and conspiracy to do any or all of the above. These crimes sometimes make use of knowledge gained while employed in banks or simply dumpster diving (buy that shredder!). A sample follows:

- In 2002, South African police arrested twenty-two Nigerians for running fake bank web sites. The listed telephone numbers forwarded to Nigeria, the UK and US. Victims got a mouthwatering glimpse of the "balances," then paid "processing fees." The millions of dollars in loot were banked in Taiwan and Monaco and laundered into export-import businesses. (The SAPs support a website, www.419legal.org, which seeks cooperation from anti-scammers.)

- In 2003, six 419ers in Amsterdam were sentenced to prison and ordered to compensate their victims.

- In 2004, two Nigerians were arrested in Dubai, United Arab Emirates, for attempting a 419 scam on a Saudi national, and each sentenced to nine months in prison.

- In 2004, Nigerians were arrested in India and Pakistan for running the "wash-wash" scam.

- In 2004, a suspect in a Dublin cybercafé tried manfully but unsuccessfully to swallow a USB memory stick before being hauled off by the gardaí. (This is described in more detail in Chapter 8.)

- In 2004, a Nigerian was sentenced in Wales to twenty months in prison for fraud. He was found with email extractor software, fake Nigerian police stationery, and other information that led to his victims.

- In 2004, the Ghana police arrested two Nigerians who attempted to scam the Bank of Ghana out of $48.6 million. They were also running a 419 scam on a Ghanaian businessman. Police in Ghana and Ivory Coast have arrested a number of scammers over the years.

- In 2005, six Nigerians and two Senegalese were arrested in Dakar for extortion—the "son of Kabila" story.

- In 2005, Spanish police arrested some three hundred 419ers. The gang was spending millions of dollars yearly, to send out 18,000 letters by mail each week.

The British National Criminal Intelligence Service has its own West African Organized Crime group, which works with other police agencies, customs and Interpol.

In the US, the Secret Service is the lead investigative agency in this area. Task forces with local law enforcement have resulted in a number of prosecutions. A sampling:

- In 2004, a Nigerian immigrant in Texas was indicted for buying seventy postal money orders with low face values, and changing their values to larger amounts ("raising"). Innocent dupes may be used to cash altered money orders.

- In 2004, after a bank employee in Ohio triggered an investigation, two Nigerians pled guilty to multiple identity thefts. One had worked in a bank and altered customers' listed mailing addresses and ordered duplicate ATM cards. The two collected Social Security, credit card, and bank account numbers of over one hundred people. Computer forensics turned up evidence of online applications for credit cards under multiple names. After cleaning out their elderly victims' finances, the scammers invested the proceeds in cars, clothes, and gadgets.

The Southern District of Texas, as part of the US Attorney General's Nigerian Organized Crime Strategy program, has worked with a number of potential victims to set up sting operations. An FBI agent based at the FBI's Internet Fraud and Complaint Center in West Virginia traveled to Lagos in

2004 to help train EFCC agents in detecting fraud. As a follow-up the team arrested sixteen people and seized more than $400,000 worth of merchandise ordered with phony credit cards.

Some criminals skip the dumpsters. In 2004, ChoicePoint, a broker of consumer records used in background checks, sold access to thousands of individuals' records, including social security numbers and insurance information, to a group of "businessmen." The "businessmen" then tried to redirect the mail of hundreds of those people, a usual first step toward identity theft. Olatunji Oluwatosin, a Nigerian national, pled guilty to conspiracy and grand theft, refusing to turn in his co-conspirators.

Some online vendors now attempt to block web traffic from entire countries from which a high percentage of fraudulent or "charge-back" transactions originate. Nigeria is only one of many such countries, among them Indonesia, Romania, and others in Asia and Eastern Europe. In 2005, the biggest internet domain name registrar, Go Daddy Software, briefly blocked traffic from Nigeria, keeping owners of domains from administering their web sites.

VICTIMS

The victim has a tough row to hoe. Pursuing a fraud case is not pleasant in any judicial system, and police are typically uninterested unless the loss is huge, or solid related charges can be brought to bear. The odds are especially poor if the scammer is in Nigeria and the victim elsewhere. Scammers routinely operate across national borders (which can hold up investigations), with multiple identities, bank accounts, and phone numbers, which can be routed to a mobile phone anywhere.

Evidence can be hard to collect. Western Union provides fraud warnings on their web site, but a money order is like cash—once a scammer collects it, which he can do at any branch, regardless of where he says he is, he's home free. Email headers are needed to back up requests to ISPs for logs (which many ISPs do not keep). Computer forensics experience needed to preserve evidence on a computer (fake certificates, correspondence) may be lacking. A victim who travels to meet a scammer may be disoriented. Meetings may take place in a hotel lobby, or a borrowed office.

Some victims hide their losses out of embarrassment or fear. Some refuse to admit to themselves that they've been scammed. On the other hand, in 2003, a victimized Czech pensioner shot the nearest Nigerian—the unfortunate consul in Prague, which must have seemed like a pretty sweet posting till then.

Websites listed in the appendix offer some practical help. However, a victim with anything less than huge losses and the resources and intestinal fortitude to pursue them is, I believe, unlikely to be vindicated through the justice system. One German victim, Frieda Springer-Beck, spent twelve years seeking justice in Nigerian courts. She got a settlement, but the scam took over her life—she now lives in Lagos, trying to help other victims. It is far, far better not to be scammed in the first place.

COMEDY BREAK: WHO YOU GONNA CALL?

Professor Thomas Mallory of Miskatonic University (Department of Metaphysical and Paranormal Studies) received a "dead bank customer" letter. Sometimes the scammers are careless in their spelling. The mention of a "ghostly accident" on the Sagamu Express Road caused Professor Mallory to dust off his proton accelerator pack. ("Professor Mallory" annoys large computers at a Southern university in the United States. Miskatonic University exists in the fantasy world of the American writer H. P. Lovecraft—or is it only a fantasy?)

Dr. Idris Ali:

> From: idrisali@voila.fr
>
> IDRIS S. ALI. LAWYER AND SOLICITOR
>
> NO 24 CANAL STREET IKOYI LAGOS NIGERIA.
>
> TEL:234-1-7762xxx.
>
> SIR,
>
> I MUST FIRST APOLOGIZE FOR THIS UNSOLICITED MAIL. MY NAME IS IDRIS S. ALI SOLICITOR AND THE ATTORNEY TO MR. JOHN RYERSON, A CITIZEN OF YOUR COUNTRY, WHO WORKED WITH AN OIL COMPANY IN NIGERIA.
>
> ON THE 21ST OF APRIL 1999, MY CLIENT, HIS WIFE AND THEIR THREE CHILDREN WERE INVOLVED IN A GHOSTLY MOTOR ACCIDENT ALONG SAGAMU EXPRESS ROAD AND LOST THEIR LIVES. SINCE THEN I HAVE MADE ENQUIRIES TO LOCATE MY CLIENT'S RELATIVES, WHICH PROVED ABORTIVE.
>
> I SEEK YOUR CONSENT TO PRESENT YOU AS NEXT OF KIN SO THAT THIS ACCOUNT VALUED AT US$15.5MILLION DOLLARS CAN BE PAID TO YOU AND THEN YOU AND I CAN SHARE THE MONEY 35 PERCENT TO YOU AND 65 PERCENT TO ME. ALL I REQUIRE IS YOUR HONEST CO-OPERATION.
>
> BEST REGARDS,
>
> DR. IDRIS S. ALI [ESQ]

Prof. Thomas Mallory:

> Mr. Idris S. Ali,
>
> Could you please describe in more detail the exact nature of this "GHOSTLY" accident?
>
> Specifically, what haunts, haints, phantasms, apparitions, spooks, shades, ghosts, phantoms, demons, fetches, tulpas, demigods, and/or other supernatural or occult entities were responsible for this accident?

I am Thomas Mallory III, director of the Supernatural and Metaphysical Studies Department here at Miskatonic University. We have searched since last May for a genuine so-called "hostile haunting" site, with no verifiable results. If you can confirm this Sagamu Express Road site as the home of a vindictive or otherwise malicious supernatural entity, my team would be eager to subject the site to a full and thorough investigation.

Sincerely,

Dr. Thomas E. M. Mallory, III

Director

Dr. Idris Ali:

Thank you for replying this mail. It will be a better Idea if you came on your own to the scene of the accident, but if you need a better explanation of this, I will gladly put you through.

Have you ever witnessed a ghost in your life before?.this is somebody who was supposed to be tranvelling with his family to their Station when they had this accident, people saw three corpse as they lay tyhere bleeding, but in a matter of seconds, there were no where to be found. This site remains a mystry till today as these as these people (three ghost believed to be the family that lost their lives) still parade that area. I have gone there myself as a friend and lawyer to the family, waited in the dark, seen them come out in the night at that particular Spot where the accident took place, witnessed for my self.

I happen to be close confident to Mr.John Reyeson, since he had some funds(US$ 7.million)with the Bank, Standard Trust Bank Limited, I wonder if you can assist me transfer the funds to an overseas account. This will only be done if you claim to be his next of Kin, we will then move towards procuring the necessay papers concerning his death before the release of the funds.

Let me know what your plans are and I will profer solutions to them. Regards.

Dr. Idris Ali

Prof. Thomas Mallory:

Wonderful! It appears, sir, that you have a Class IV free-floating vapor on your hands—Dr. Stanz is eager to take readings, as he is convinced that we may soon be witness to a full-force interdimensional flux crossover of a magnitude unseen since the Tunguska Event of 1903!

And, since you've been so kind as to bring this haunted road to our attention, we are pleased to offer you an opportunity to join our Department of Paranormal and Metaphysical Studies as a (PAID) Site Consultant. The pay is, as with most academic pursuits, depressingly low—a mere $2625.50 per semester, with an additional $500 added as a transatlantic altercation addendum.

Are you at all interested in joining our search for the paranormal? I'll send you (via email, for your convenience) a short form to complete. Please respond as soon as possible so that we can get you started as a Site Consultant right away.

(The good doctor discovers a sudden and keen interest in all things paranormal...)

Dr. Idris Ali:

Dear Sirs,

Thank you for this wonderful Opportunity that has been given to me. I will only accept on the condition that it does not in any way affect my believe in the almighty God.

Let us then talk on my terms of payment.

1)I will require a mobilization fee of at least half of the amount agreed to be my salary per semester which is US$1,325 through WESTERN UNION MONEY TRANSFER.

If my terms are Okay, I will require the Payment been done immidiately.

Regards.

Dr.Idris Ali.

Prof. Thomas Mallory:

Dear Dr. Ali,

Wonderful! The Selection Committee will need to see your Application (form attached).

As to your religious concerns—you need have none. We treat our supernatural investigations in a scientific manner—we are keen to probe the occult, but not pat it on the head, read its pamphlets, or get into conversations with it. Just ask Dr. Spengler—he has trapped over two-dozen actualized ectoplasmic free-roaming vapors, but the man still doesn't believe in ghosts!

Here are the papers, Dr. Ali. Please complete them with as much detail as possible. Drawings and diagrams are always impressive!

Sincerely,

Dr. Thomas E. M. Malthus

* * * O N L I N E   A P P L I C A T I O N * * *

SITE CONSULTANT CLASS II (FORM MU-243-LV & WITNESS REPORT):

PRINT, SCAN, AND RETURN TO SENDER.

1) NAME OF APPLICANT:

2) SSN, PID, CITIZEN ID NUMBER, OR OTHER IDENTIFIER:

3) COUNTRY OF CITIZENSHIP:

4) CURRENT MAILING ADDRESS OF APPLICANT:

5) PREFERRED METHOD OF PAYMENT (Check, Western Union cash transfer, electronic funds transfer, Miskatonic University bursar credits):

6) IS APPLICANT OVER LEGAL AGE OF ADULTHOOD?

7) IS APPLICANT ON THE FACULTY OF AN ACCREDITED CLASS A UNIVERSITY?

8) AREA OF SPECIALIZATION (EXAMPLE: GENERAL PARANORMAL STUDIES, POLTERGEIST COUNSELING SPECIALIST, NOCTURNAL GADABOUT RESEARCHER)

PLEASE SUMMARIZE YOUR INTENDED CONTRIBUTION TO THE ONGOING MISSION OF STUDIES:

DESCRIBE THE SUSPECTED SITE, WITH DATES, NAMES OF WITNESSES, CULTURAL RELEVANCE, AND GEOGRAPHY:

PROVIDE THE EXACT LOCATION. INCLUDE DRAWINGS IF NECESSARY:

DESCRIBE WHAT YOU SAW, HEARD, OR EXPERIENCED AT THE SITE. PLEASE BE SPECIFIC:

DRAW ANY APPARITIONS, GHOSTS, SPIRITS, VAPOROUS FORMS, FREE FLOATING TORSOS, PERSISTENT OPTICAL ANOMALIES, AND/OR OTHER UNUSUAL OR APPARENTLY SUPERNATURAL OBJECTS, BEASTS, OR OTHER ETHEREAL FORMS OBSERVED BY YOU AT THE SITE:

—— end of application forms ——

Dr. Idris Ali:

Dear Sirs,

Thank you for this reply, I have expended so much money in this trabnsaction so far, I am going to send this as the last information until I receive some funds as commitment/mobilization before any other information that you will require.

Prof. Thomas Mallory:

Dr. Ali,

Please, just send what you have! Scribble a few notes, draw the phantoms as best you can, and get the papers back to me! Funding like this doesn't come around often. Speed is of the essence. You need only provide a two-paragraph history of the hauntings, or draw a Class II Torsal Apparition!

(At last, the Lawyer coughs up completed official whiz-bang Miskatonic University form!)

**** DR. IDRIS ALI ****

1. **NAME OF APPLICANT:** KALOMO IDRIS ALI (DR)

2. **SSN,PID CITIZEN ID NUMBER,OR NUMERIC IDENTIFIER:**

 NIGERIA BAR ASSOCIATION MEMBERSHIP IDENTIFICATION CARD NO.042

3. **COUNTRY OF CITIZENSHIP:** NIGERIA

4. **CURRENT MAILING ADDRESS:** 24 CANAL STREET, IKOYI LAGOS-NIGERIA

5. **PREFERED METHOD OF PAYMENT :** WESTERN UNION MONEY TRANSFER, US DOLLARS

6. **IS APPLICANT OVER LEGAL AGE OF ADULTHOOD:** YES

7. **IS THE APPLICANT ON THE FACULTY OF AN ACCREDITED CLASS A UNIVERSITY?:** I ATTENDED THE UNIVERSITY OF LAGOS AND NIGERIA LAW SCHOOL.

8. **AREA OF SPECIALIZATION OF APPLICANT:** COMPANY LAW.

PLEASE SUMMARIZE YOUR INTENDED CONTRIBUTION TO THE ONGOING MISSION OF STUDIES:

MY INTENDED CONTRIBUTION TOWARDS THESE IS TO ASSIST OUR SCIENTIST AND OTHER SUPERNATURAL BEING PERFORM THEIR ACTIVITIES TO HELP OR ASSIST THE HUMAN RACE IN ANY WAY POSSIBLE.ALSO TO CONTRIBUTE TO THE DEVELOPMENT OF THE PSYCHIC ANT OTHER SUPERNATURAL POWERS IN EVERY POSSIBLE WAY.

DESCRIBE THE HISTORY OF THE SUSPECTED SITE:

THOUGH THAT AREA HAS BEEN KNOWN FOR THIS KIND OF DEVILISH ACT SINCE 1954 AND SINCE THEN, PEOPLE HAVE BEEN KNOWN TO DIE AT THAT AREA,AND AS SOON AS THEY DIE,THEY ARE NOTICED ARROUND THERE FREIGHTNING PEOPLE.IT SEEMS AS IF THERE EXISTS SOME KIND OF MISTIC POWERS ARROUND THERE.THERE IS NO CULTURAL RELEVANCE AS THAT PARTICULAR AREA HAS BEEN NOTICED FOR THAT,BUT PEOPLE WHO BELIEVE IN GHOST GO THERE TO OFFER SACRIFICES TO THEIR ANCESTORS AND ALSO TO APPEASE THEM AND EVEN ASK THEM FOR OTHER MERCIES.

PROVIDE THE EXACT LOCATION OF THE SITE:

I CAN NOT GET THE DRAWING OF THE AREA AS IT WILL COST ME A LOT MONEY TO GET THE TOWN PLANNERS AND ARCHITECHS TO GET THAT ARRANGED. IT IS ALONG SHAGAMU EXPRESS WAY AS IF YOU ARE COMING INTO LAGOS FROM OGUN STATE.THE RULER OF THAT AREA,CHIEF OLUKOYA AKAMBI IS A LIVING WITNESS AND HIS COUNCIL OF CHIEFS ARE A LIVING WITNESS TO THIS DAY.

DESCRIBE IN YOUR OWN WORDS WHAT YOU SAY, HEARD OR OTHERWISE EXPERIENCED AT THE SITE:

I SAW SOMETHING THAT LOOKS LIKE HUMAN CREATURES BUT SPEAKING IN VERY STRANGE LANGUAGES WEARING CLOTHINGS THAT THEY WORE ON THE OF THE ACCIDENT. I COULD NOT SEE THEIR FACES CLEARLY BUT THEY WERE FOUR IN NUMBER THE SAME NUMBER THEY WERE ON THE DAY OF THE ACCIDENT.THEIR MOVEMENT WAS ALMOST ABNORMAL BECAUSE I COULD NOT SEE THEIR TOES BUT THEU APPEAR TO BE IN A VERY SAD MOOD AS IT COULD BE NOTICED FROM THEIR ACTIONS.

Prof. Thomas Mallory:

Dear Dr. Ali,

I feel confident that I can procure funding approval.

We are off to investigate an alleged haunting in Mordibund Manor. Dr. Spengler's readings indicate a bi-polar lunar reciprocating spectre, and at least two low-level thermal poltergeist nexi. You can imagine our excitement, as a fellow student of the supernatural. Mordibund Manor promises to exceed even the Amityville Apartment 3-G site for arcane infestation, and I don't need to tell you how many deep-reach IR cameras we ruined there! Wish us luck!

Prof. Thomas Mallory:

Well, sir, what an amazing investigation we conducted!

Mordibund Manor was positively seething with electrokinetic and parapetroleoid energy vortexes. Why, at one point, Dr. Stanz was conducting a high-frequency RF sweep of what appeared to be Eric the Red, and Dr. Spengler found himself confronted by a contingent of rare microwave poltergeist flagella! You could hardly see the PK meters for all the ectoplasm in the air. We'll be analyzing that data for many days to come.

Prof. Thomas Mallory:

Sir, I am outraged. It seems you have attempted to defraud Miskatonic University! Were it not for the vigilance of Dr. Harold Ramis, Professor of Ancient Languages, who is also on the Application Approval Committee, your scurrilous attempt might well have succeeded.

Dr. Ramis inquired as to how you and I met. I noted that I received an email from you, in which you described the ghostly death of your former client on the Sagumu Express Road. Imagine my surprise when Dr. Ramis went on to describe, nearly verbatim, the rest of your original email!

Shame on you, sir. It was after re-reading your first email that I realized your use of the term "ghostly" was a typographical error. Why, a quick internet search for "Sagamu Express Road" revealed that it is mentioned as the site of a "ghastly" crash in hundreds of scam emails just like yours! I see now that you merely wished to trick some foreigner into travelling to your country so that you might rob them. To think we nearly assembled a team and traveled to Nigeria! Dr. Spengler, heartbroken but still convinced of your goodwill, called the University of Lagos. The person at the University broke into laughter and told him "you are being fooled."

I should have known you were a fraud. Your description of the Sagamu Road haunting should have revealed to me that you know nothing of supernatural matters. Sir, it is painfully obvious now that you have never seen so much as a Class I Partially Materialized Low Emission Spectral Afterimage, much less a Class IV Actualized Free Ranging Self-Aware Spectre.

That, perhaps, shall soon change. I have notified the Legal Branch of Miskatonic University. I do not know what action they shall take. I do know that Dr. Spengler, a gentle soul unless provoked, remained in his laboratory all night. I also note that, as of this morning, our main containment facility is short one Class VI (Variously Solid) Perpetually Regenerative Hostile Spirit Entity. I recall the circumstances under which we trapped this Entity, and its particularly foul and malign nature. Such an Entity would be happy to exchange its freedom for the completion of, say, a favor. I do not know what promise Dr. Spengler may have extracted from this creature, nor will I ask. But if I were you, Dr. Ali (or whatever your name is), I would be wary of dark places, and bumps and scratchings in the night. Perhaps that sound was just the wind.

Then again, maybe it wasn't.

Thomas Mallory

CHAPTER 4
THE MANY, THE PROUD, THE SCAM-BAITERS

I have always been wily and clever
At deceiving and swindling and such,
And I feel just as clever as ever,
But I seem to be losing my touch.
Yes, I'm clever, but where does it get me?
My employer gets all of my take;
All I get is my daily spaghetti,
While he gorges on truffles and steak.
What's the use? What's the use?
There's no profit in cheating. It's all so defeating
And wrong, Oh, so wrong!
If you just have to pass it along.
– Candide (the operetta)

SAY KIDS, LET'S PUT ON A WEB SITE!

My taxonomic impulse having been roused, I began to collect and classify what I came to think of as scam-o-grams. The Scamorama web site began as a simple re-posting of the first 125 in the collection. They had subject lines like these:

- Request for urgent business relationship
- Trust fund for alms and ammunition
- Urgent business execution
- We did over-inflate the contracts
- I was a moslem until the master Jesus met me
- I am only trying not to be noticed by my government
- Very urgent, please self my soul

Armed with a standard story line, there is no narrative pothole out of which the scammer cannot clamber and no cliché he cannot mangle. (It's been claimed that this is a deliberate device to make the victim feel superior, which never made sense to me.) No tragedy is left unmined for material—massacres in Liberia, suicide bombings in London, pipeline explosions, plane crashes, September 11, the Asian tsunami. He is hardworking, running as many scams as possible, color-coding the telephones (if working in a superior facility) so as to remember who he is pretending to be from day to day.

Scamorama was meant to amuse friends. At the time, there were few other web sites on this subject, almost all angry. This was long ago in internet time—Google's creators were still in grad school. I didn't expect much attention. Then emails began arriving from people all over the world who'd received similar letters. Some of these people were hard up and desperately wanted to believe they'd been left money by a mysterious relative. It was sad work talking them down. Some had been scammed and were heartbroken. In some the nerve impulse was still traveling up to the brain. Others feared for a loved one about to fall victim. I felt like a lonely-hearts columnist.

Ultimately, a collection of letters would be dull and make no impression on people who want to believe. Making fun of poor spelling would also be appalling. Then the thing happened which elevated Scamorama to the level of psy-ops. Pranksters began to send in correspondences. To my astonishment, they were writing back to scammers—*for fun*. That is the sport of scam-baiting—if you can't beat 'em, then laugh at 'em, wind them up, and waste their time. Every moment a scammer is trying to scam Harry Potter, Lord Imhotep, Bart Simpson or Joseph Stalin, he isn't scamming someone else. I posted the correspondences, and more kept coming.

RACISM, COLONIALISM, ETC., ETC.

The topic of racism floats below the surface of many discussions of the scam, and sometimes breaches loudly. The rare submission from obvious white racists, which I rejected out of hand, showed an assumption that I was white, and the type of white they would be comfortable with, that no white person had ever pulled a scam, and that no black person would resent scam letters. 419ers are racist too, and sometimes rather whiny. Race, however defined, is part of the picture, but not the point. 419ers will scam anybody and rationalize it depending on who you are (or who they think you are). You needn't be white. Being from a different ethnic group, or simply being un-scammable, is offense enough.

A 419 scammer who thinks you are white may hold forth on colonialism:

> ... I am a 419 guy and have riped the likes of you with the same technology that you stupid asshole evented to manipulate we african. What we do down here is nothing to make us ashame as we are only trying to get back what you fucking bastard took from us way back. I guess you people call it reparation.
>
> Just for one fucking moment, you probably would have thought that we Africans are set of crazy fool that are no way near your self belief intellegence but oh no, you white monkeys(Micky Mouse if you like) are even more stupid for all we care as we are really moer original than you lazy white cheap and greedy beings that would want to claim what you are not part of just about the same way you bastards riped our continent. Let me tel you this for once, have you ever sat your ass down to ask yourself what colour is the devil? Must probable you like and the likes of you would say that He was a black man. But today be it know to your sorry ass that the devil was an angel of God that was thrown down to earth. What colour does the angels have? White right? Then cann't

you see how you maniacs out there tried to change what we believed in? A wolf in sheep clothing is simply a wolf and nothing more. Go fuck your mother fucking asshole that has being infected by the same atificiary beliefs that has beclouded your vision as a young man that is surpposed to be asking us how did we acquire our bank of knowledge. Be true to your self and give us a little tumbs up for our intelligence dommy.

Another scammer put it more concisely:

Tell your fellow whites that the reparation due to Africa for 300 years of rape and violation will be paid in full either by hook or by crook, from this generation or the next. And unless the white man confesses and takes a positive proactive action for restitution, he can never be free. This is the idealogy of the scammers. Would you want to know how Europe and America underdeveloped Africa? Would you want to know more about the perenial debt burden of the third world countries and the refUSl of the so called Industrialised Nations to accept debt repayments intead of insisting on debt servicing? What do you call this? A scam of international scale or is it international politricks?

Whether scammers have an ideology beyond lining their pockets is doubtful. They spare other Africans the political lecture. A Kenyan shared the following ("Below is ... what the fellow replied when he discovered that I knew he wanted to con me."):

MUGU ["fool"]
YOU SHOULD THANK YOUR GOD THAT YOU LATTER DISCOVERED, IF NOT MAYBE BY NOW YOUR SMALL EARNED SALARY WOULD HAVE BEEN IN MY BANK ACCOUNT. YOU ARE STILL A MUGU FOR WRITING AND LET ME ASSURE YOU THAT YOU ARE NOT YET FREE BECAUSE I HAVE MORE THAN 82 OTHER WAYS TO DEAL WITH FOOLS LIKE YOU.
IDIOT.

African-Americans get special treatment:

YOU ARE A BUSH MAN I DONT HAVE FUCKING TIME FOR POOR GUYS LIKE YOU ...WELL YOU ARE ONE OF THE AFRICAN SLAVES IN AMERICA WE WILL SOON GET YOU PEOPLE BACK TO FATHER LAND.
NOMATTER HOW MUCH THEY BUY YOU GUYS WE MUST PAY THEM BACK AND PICK OUR BROTHERS...
YOU DONT EVEN GO TO SCHOOL .CANNOT EVEN SPEAK GOOD ENGLISH AMERICAN LATINS IS NOT ENGLISH GO BACK TO SCHOOL SLAVE...
TO HELL WITH POOR PEOPLE LIVING IN AMERICA.SO SORRY YOU DONT KNOW YOUR FATHER LAND IN AFRICA MANY HAVE COME BACK AND WE GAVE THE LAND TO BUILD HOUSE YOU NOWAY ANY TIME I SEE YOU IN AFRICA I WILL JAIL YOU.YOU BETTER STAY THEREIN UNTIL YOU DIE OKAY.
YOU MUST BE A SLAVE THERE OKAY IAM BETTER THAN YOU IAM IN MY FATHER LAND OKAY.

RICH SLAVE.

The subject of Asians hasn't come up in these heart-to-hearts, but 419ers scam them too.

Not one African correspondent found scam letters funny (reactions ranged from bemused annoyance to fury), although some found scam-baiting amusing. Imagine living next door to a scammer. Imagine being taken for a criminal because of your nationality. Imagine trying to do business in such a climate.

A correspondent from Sierra Leone responded thus to a scam-o-gram from "Dr Ahmed Abdullah, CEO of the Sierra-Leone national Gold & Diamond Mining Corporation":

> Hey Ahmed,
> Where and how did you get my email address??
> I was born in Sierra Leone you dipShit, i will not be scammed by you.
> Sincerely,
> your worst nightmare!!!

A Nigerian shared some thoughtful comments:

> First, as a Nigerian am giving you guys kudos for the job you are doing, though I believe you could do better by making people realize that genuine business people still exist in Nigeria.
>
> I stumbled on your site and it was like a rude awakening for me. And I ask myself, have things got so bad? I never felt that way before. Not even on the day a strange but curious western fellow asked about my country of origin (actually am a graduate student in Canada), and upon my response, he echoed the same thing you've been highlighting. But I must say that singular experience, with what I read on your site never took a bite of my self-esteem as a Nigerian. I can still remember growing up in a society where honor and glory was bestowed on honest and hardworking people. Years of military dictatorship have changed that, especially from 1985 under Ibrahim Babangida rulership. This leader himself is a crook, and it was during his rule that the so-called "Lads" started having a field day. But don't be surprised if I point it out to you that many of these "Lads" are merely secondary school dropouts roaming the street of Lagos or elsewhere.
>
> But what is intriguing to me is how any honest businessman from the west could have fell for these comics. In fact, many of the correspondence were so funny. How could people fell for this until now. So my first point is that there are still some greedy westerners out there still in search of the "loots" their own "direct forefathers" might have forgotten in Africa during the years of slavery.
>
> Please, in as much as you are trying to alert innocent people out there. I would not want you to make the same mistake that people from this part of the world (West) always

make. Here, people tend to generalize easily. In nature it's never that way. Not all Nigerians are con. There are still models in our own society that we are imploring our youths to look up to.

The country is only in a passing phase. We are still trying to find ways of redirecting the "artistry" and skills and energy of these "Lads" towards activities that's going to benefit them and the larger society.

Please inform the reader of your website that there's the Nigerian Chamber of Commerce and also the consulate of Nigeria (and other responsible sources) to seek information on any business opportunities. It is only sane for any business minded individual to make the right effort. And people in the west should be aware that the government is making effort to weed out these fraudsters, apart from the private efforts of well meaning individuals.

Lastly, the people from the west will be doing their "horizon" a lot of good if they learn more about other nations and culture, especially in Africa. I have to tell you that we know more about you than you know about us, in that way we are always aware of what to expect in your society (West). In the west the number 1 may always be 1, but in Africa it may be leaning sideways just because a gale is blowing.

THE FUNNY PART

But seriously, folks—there's a funny side to all this. Scam-baiting is not only a literary genre but a weird form of cultural exchange. Anti-scammers reach into their own cultural grab-bags for material with which to build their personae, and often display a keen sense of national self-mockery. I am convinced that some 419ers know perfectly well their time is being wasted, but carry on anyway, because it amuses them. Anaïs Nin wrote porn to pay the bills. Maybe a future novelist or playwright is hunched over a computer in Lagos right now, concocting another "cocoa orphan" story.

Meanwhile, some scammers have corresponded with potential victims for over a year, to find their correspondences posted on web sites for the amusement of the world. Sometimes a 419er is carrying on multiple exchanges with what turns out to be one anti-scammer, or a team on three continents. Along the way, scammers have been talked into doing some pretty silly things. "Micheal Ofori" went into the chat rooms and tried to scam "Mandy," a beautiful girl from Los Angeles (actually a guy from Sweden). Mandy had unusual tastes, and wanted a token of Micheal's sincerity (photo right).

Scammer poses for lady pen pal
Courtesy: "Mandy"

Captain Pike of Starfleet, despite his infirmities, managed to persuade a Lad to join the Church of the Holy Pineapple. As part of the initiation, a snap was demanded:

Scammer joins church of the holy pineapple
Courtesy: Captain Christopher Pike

The Unkindly Contributor (a noted anti-scammer with a scathing wit) orchestrated a sixteen-month encounter, which produced the most unlikely document ever to come out of a scambait. The Lad tried the classic "wash-wash" approach:

the currency is defaced with an inscription ,,united nations high commission for refugees (unhcr) ... i found a bottle containing chemical for cleansing the money with an instruction booklet on how to use the chemical right....

No American born since the passage of the Clean Water Act can abide an unknown chemical! The Unkindly Contributor brow-beat the scammer into preparing a Materials Safety Data Sheet for "wash-wash" chemicals (see reproduction, right).

While some scam-baiters are content to indulge their literary leanings, others go further. A scammer may ask a victim to fly to Amsterdam or Lagos to hand over the money. What if? What if the "victim" makes an imaginary reservation on a real flight, arriving at three a.m. scammer time? What if the "victim" insists on being met with a sign guaranteed to make arriving passengers do a double-take? One Lad dutifully constructed a welcome sign which said "here, grab my nuts" in Bahasa, Indonesia. Other Lads have posed unwittingly for webcams. They looked glum in the wet Amsterdam weather.

For many small-time scammers, coaxing money orders out of retirees is a sideline to more serious aspirations. A British prankster kept his scammer on the hook by posing as a scout for Manchester United.

Some have persuaded scammers to send them gifts as tokens of good faith. "Bart Simpson" of Quebec got a Lad to send him US$5. "Pierpont" received a sample of actual, analyzed gold dust.

Chapter 8 contains advice from master scam-baiters, whose achievements are proof that humor knows no borders. (Some of the funniest English-language material posted on Scamorama, by the way, comes from people whose first language is not English.) The most important thing, however, is to scam-proof yourself and those around you, as covered in the next chapter.

ZUDUS CHEMICAL PRODUCT

Zudus chemical product is specially designed to cleanse deface bills.do not use or handle this chemical until you have read and understood the material safety data sheet (MSDS) and label for the chemical.

RULES

The following are rules that apply for persons using the zudus chemical product.
use locally exhausted workplace for operation when their use is prescribed in the standard operating procedure.note.as a general rule ,a hood or other local ventilation device is needed when working with volatile substances.
brief intense inhalation of solvent can produce a high brain concentration and syptoms such as dizziness and nausea.

use of gloves ,aprons and chemical goggles plus face shields as splash protection is needed when handling the zudus chemicals product as it can affect the skin or eyes.

APPLICATION

Use at least a minimum of four litres of zudus chemical product and pour into an empty bowl.activate the chemical with ten teaspoonful of salt.wait for about fifteen minutes,then pour the bills into the water and wash gradually for thirty minutes.pull the bills and try in the sun or heat related motivator for a period of thirty minutes,you will finally discover that the defaced print on the surface of the bill is no more.

PREVENTION(ref.material data safety sheet)

1,Promptly flush eyes with water for at least 15 minutes if the chemical contact the eyes,seek medical attention if needed.

2,Promptly flush skin with water if the chemical contact skin and seek medical attention if symptoms persist.

3,Inspect goggles before use,wash them before removal,replace them periodically ,and use the type of gloves specified in the standard operating procedure.remove clothing and gloves upon contamination.

4,Do not eat,drink,smoke,chew gum or apply cosmetics when using the zudus chemical product and wash hands before conducting the activities.

5,Beware of overly simple rules such as storing like chemicals together e.g this may put concentrated nitric acid with acetic acid,a combination of oxidant and fuel that will combust immediately and violently.

6,do not use damaged glassware.

7,Use equipment only for its designated purpose.

8,Promptly clean up spills,using appropriate protective equipment and disposal procedures described in the standard operating procedure.

9,Always wash face,hands and arms with soap and water before leaving the work area.this applies even if one has been wearing gloves.

10.No smoking is allowed around the chemical.

COMEDY BREAK:
SOCCER CHAT AT THE FOREIGN OFFICE

Lady Agatha Bristol, CBE, of the Foreign Office, and her special agents are a team of Britons who turned their multiple personality disorders to good use. Several ex-KGB operatives, including Mikhail Stroganov, have also found homes at the FO. Their sketchy understanding of the post-colonial world has not prevented them from outflanking many scammers. In this adventure the staff were approached by yet another Mrs. Mariam Abacha and lawyer "Richard Williams," her legal advisor and possibly alter-ego.

Mrs. Mariam Abacha:

> Dear Friend,
>
> I am Mrs Mariam Abacha, widow of Sani Abacha the late Nigerian Head of State. You were introduced to me through the Chamber of Commerce.
>
> I am presently in distress while my son Mohammed is undergoing trial. The government has frozen all the family account and auctioned all our properties. To save the family from bankruptcy I have managed to ship to Europe the sum of $US20.000,000.00 kept by my late husband.
>
> The money was disguised to beat the Nigerian security and it is deposited in a security company in Europe. I want you to receive the money into your account for the family safely. I am offering you 30 percent for assisting me secure this money before it is located by the Nigerian Government Agents. Contact me so I can forward to you all necessary details. Best Regard
>
> Mrs. Mariam Abacha

Mikhail Stroganov:

> MADAM
>
> HOW YOU FOUND MY CONFIDENTIAL EMAIL ADDRESS IS AS BIG A MYSTERY AS HOW YOU HAVE THE NERVE TO CONTACT ME WITH SUCH A SCHEME_HOWEVER I AM IN FINE FETTLE THANKS TO MY BOWDEN CUSTARD AND SCONE COMPANY SHARES ACCRUING_YOU HAVE MY INTEREST NOW LET US SEE WHAT CAN BE DONE_PLEASE GET BACK TO ME SOON_GREETINGS FROM MOSCOW
>
> STROGANOV
>
> Stroganov Publishing (Pvt) Ltd
>
> 4402 Bowdinskaya Street
>
> Moscow 0169 Russia

Mrs. Abacha:

I THANK YOU IMMENSELY ON YOUR WILLINGNESS IN ASSISTING ME ON THIS TRANSACTION. PLEASE CONTACT MY ATORNEY WHO CAN UPDATE YOU ON HOW TO RECEIVE THIS FUND.

NAME:LAWYER RICHARD WILLIAMS

EMAIL:richardwilliams_associates1999@yahoo.com

MOBILE NUMBER:234-803-7121xxx

MY WARM REGARDS.

Mikhail Stroganov:

THANK YOU FOR YOUR NOTE_WHILE IT IS MY NATURAL CAUTION THAT HAS MADE ME A BILLIONAIRE I HAVE TO ADMIT THAT YOUR PROPOSAL HAS A SEMBLANCE OF LOGIC ABOUT IT_ I WILL BE BACK IN TOUCH OVER THE NEXT FEW DAYS AS I AM VISITING MY NEW SCONE AND CUSTARD FACTORY IN ST. PETERSBURG THIS WEEKEND

Mrs. Abacha:

HOW ARE YOU AND YOUR BUSINESS I PRESUME ALL IS WELL WITH YOU.HAVE YOU CONTACTED THE LAWYER LIKE I ASKED YOU TO.

Stroganov:

THANK YOU_I AM IN FINE FETTLE EVEN THOUGH RUSSIA LOST AT EURO 2004_ LET ME KNOW THE NEXT STEP_ AT ONCE IF YOU PLEASE

Mrs. Abacha:

PLEASE DO CONTACT THE ATORNEY.SORRY FOR THE EURO 2004 CHAMPIONS I PRAY GOD WILL MAKE YOU WIN.MY COUNTRY ARE REALLY PLAYING GREAT.

Stroganov:

I DID NOT KNOW YOU WERE A FOOTBALL FAN_THIS PUTS AN ENTIRELY DIFFERENT SLANT ON OUR RELATIONSHIP_WHICH TEAM DO YOU SUPPORT??_I WILL ESTABLISH CONTACT WITH HIM SOON

Lawyer Richard Williams:

RICHARD WILLIAMS & ASSOCIATES

NO. 2, FALOHUN STREET, SURULERE LAGOS.

EMAIL:richardwilliams@ny.com

ATTN: Mikhail Stroganov

REGARDING MY CLIENT MRS ABACHA:

FIRST AND FORE MOST I NEED YOU TO SEND A POWER OF ATTORNEY BECAUSE DOCUMENTATIONS SHOULD BE MADE ON YOUR NAME SO I NEED A POWER OF ATTORNEY TO DO THIS.

Stroganov:

MR WILLIAMS

I AM RATHER PREOCCUPIED WITH MRS. ABACHA AT THE MOMENT_SHE SAID THAT SHE ENJOYED FOOTBALL AND THIS IS SOMETHING I INSIST ALL OF MY BUSINESS PARTNERS DO SO THE WAY IS SMOOTHED FOR ALL CONCERNED_ WHICH TEAM DO YOU SUPPORT?

Stroganov:

WILLIAMS _I DO NOT KNOW HOW YOU CONDUCT BUSINESS IN THE THIRD WORLD BUT HERE IN MOSCOW TIME AND TIDE WAITS FOR NO MAN MY FINE FRIEND _HOWEVER I AM PREPARED TO MAKE ALLOWANCES _NOW GET GOING_IS THAT CLEAR???

PS DID YOU SEE HOLLAND V GERMANY???

Lawyer Williams:

DEAR SIR, I NEED YOU TO SEND A POWER OF ATTORNEY TO EMPOWER THE SECURITY COMPANY TO RELEASE THE ORIGINAL AND CERTIFIED CERTIFICATES.

I AWAIT YOUR SPEED RESPONSE.

Stroganov:

_THIS IS RATHER AMATEURISH BUT IT HAS A LOGIC OF SORTS_NOW LET US MOVE FORWARD TOGETHER MY DEAR FELLOW

PS DID YOU SEE SPAIN V GREECE???

Stroganov:

> MRS ABACHA
>
> I HAVE CONTACTED WILLIAMS AND ALL IS IN HAND_HAVE YOU BEEN WATCHING EURO 2004??? UNFORTUNATELY YOUR PRAYERS WERE NOT ANSWERED AS RUSSIA WERE KNOCKED OUT LAST NIGHT_ I AM VERY DEPRESSED_WHAT IS A BILLIONAIRE PUBLISHER TO DO??? BUT I AM HOPING THAT A PROFITABLE END TO THIS TRANSACTION WILL CHEER ME SOMEWHAT_DO YOU THINK ZINEDINE ZIDANE IS THE BEST PLAYER IN THE WORLD AT THE MOMENT??

Mrs. Abacha:

> DEAR MR STROGANOV, IT WASN'T MY PRAYER FOR YOUR COUNTRY TO LOOSE THE GAME MAY BE ALLAH HAS SOMETHING IN STOCK FOR YOUR COUNTRY.PLEASE MY GOOD FRIEND /PARTNER IN PROGRESS ASSIST ME SO I CAN USE MY SHARE FOR INVESTMENT FOR MY CHILDREN.

Stroganov:

> WE ARE DOING EVERYTHING IN OUR POWER TO ASSIST YOU IN THIS COMPLEX TRANSACTION_HOWEVER I CANNOT HELP BUT BE CONCERNED AT RUSSIA'S LACK OF AGGRESSION DURING EURO 2004_DO YOU THINK WE SHOULD HAVE PLAYED WITH THREE STRIKERS??? THESE QUESTIONS ARE RACKING MY BRAIN AND YOUR OBVIOUS EXTENSIVE KNOWLEDGE OF INTERNATIONAL FOOTBALL WOULD HELP ME GET MY THOUGHTS IN ORDER

Lawyer Williams:

> Dear Stroganov,
>
> iasked you to send a power of attorney but all to no avail. i am really very sorry about russia losing the tornament.let us look forward for a better tomorrow.

Stroganov:

> I DO APOLOGISE FOR THE DELAY_I HAVE BEEN AGONISING OVER WHETHER RUSSIA SHOULD HAVE PLAYED A 4-3-3 FORMATION LAST NIGHT_HOW DO YOU WANT THIS POWER OF ATTORNEY DOCUMENTED???
>
> PS ARE YOU GOING TO WATCH ENGLAND V SWITZERLAND??

Lawyer Williams:

Please do give me a call on my direct mobile number:234-803-7121xxx.I am highly sorry on the out come of the match russia tried their best but i guess the coach has to look to this.i await your call we can discuss on the transaction and foot ball as well.

Stroganov:

YOUR MOBILE NUMBER IS ENGAGED ALL THE TIME_ HOWEVER I AM SURE WE CAN DISCUSS TACTICS AND FORMATIONS FOR THE REST OF EURO 2004 ON EMAIL IF YOU WISH_I THOUGHT THE FRANCE V CROATIA MATCH WAS SUPERB BUT IT ONLY DEEPENED MY DARK MOOD OVER RUSSIA BEING KNOCKED OUT_STILL I KNOW WE HAVE BUSINESS TO ATTEND TO_HOW DO YOU WISH TO PROCEED???

PS DID YOU SEE ENGLAND V SWITZERLAND???

Lawyer Williams:

Dear Stroganov ,

indeed they were all great matches, especially the match between france and Groatia.It was quiet unfortunate that your country lost out but there is always another tournament to show case the stars of Russia football,I can still recall the great game between Nigeria and russia in suadi 89.

Let us disscuss bussiness. I need the $4300 canadian dollars for the securing of the original documents time never wait for no one.

Stroganov:

THANK YOU FOR YOUR NOTE_I CERTAINLY ENJOYED FRANCE V CROATIA WHERE ZINEDINE ZIDANE SHOWED IN THE FIRST HALF ESPECIALLY THAT HE REALLY IS THE BEST PLAYER IN THE WORLD AND WILL BE REMEMBERED AS AN ALL-TIME GREAT WHEN HE RETIRES_DO YOU THINK HIS BEST POSITION IS BEHIND THE STRIKERS OR MORE WITHDRAWN??? IT SEEMS THAT THIERRY HENRY IS BEING PLAYED OUT OF POSITION BUT A PLAYER OF THAT CALIBRE WON'T STAY QUIET FOR LONG_HOW DO YOU WANT THE MONEY PAID???

Lawyer Williams:

dear friend,

I am very pleased with your respond ,it is true that a striker like henry will not be kept out for longer i expect him to score more goals in the tornament. I want the money{$4300} sent today via western union money transfer to:

MR. Steven Obi,

address:lagos nigeria,

question: id code.

answer:LSR1135AA4

Stroganov:

I DO HOPE YOU ARE RIGHT MY FRIEND_I HAVE INVESTED A LOT OF MONEY IN
THIERRY HENRY BECOMING TOP SCORER AT EURO 2004_SPECTATORS AND
PUNDITS ALIKE THINK HE IS THE BEST STRIKER IN THE WORLD BUT HE DIDN'T
DO IT IN ITALY LIKE BATISTUTA, CRESPO AND SHEVCHENKO_HOWEVER NEITHER
DID BERGKAMP AND HE IS OBVIOUSLY A GOOD PLAYER WHILE CRESPO HAS
SCORED IN THE PREMIERSHIP BUT HAS NOT SET IT ALIGHT DESPITE MAKING IT
IN ITALY_IT IS AN INTERESTING DICHOTOMY DO YOU AGREE??? AND WHAT TEAM
DO YOU SUPPORT??? THE LOCAL WESTERN UNION OFFICE HAS BURNT DOWN
WOULD YOU BELIEVE_CAN YOU ACCEPT A CHEQUE???

Mrs. Abacha:

HOW ARE YOU TODAY? WHAT IS THE CURRENT DEVELOPMENT REGARDING THIS
TRANSACTION.

Stroganov:

I AM WORKING MY HARDEST TO COMPLETE THIS DEAL_ THERE WAS A PROBLEM
WHICH I AM DISCUSSING WITH MR WILLIAMS_HOWEVER I AM SURE WE CAN
OVERCOME IT ESPECIALLY AS THE CZECH REPUBLIC OVERCAME HOLLAND IN ONE
OF THE GREATEST MATCHES IN EUROPEAN CHAMPIONSHIP HISTORY_DID YOU SEE
IT??? AND AS FOR CROATIA V FRANCE IT WAS A THRILL A MINUTE BUT GERMANY
WERE PATHETIC IN THEIR TUSSLE WITH SO-CALLED MINNOWS LATVIA_WE SHALL
SEE WHAT WE SHALL SEE

PS ARE YOU WATCHING ENGLAND V CROATIA???

Lawyer Williams:

this issue of cheque is totally not accepted.i will like you to try money gram.

Stroganov:

WHILST CONSULTING WITH THE LOCAL MONEYGRAM OFFICE IT TURNS OUT THAT
IN THEIR OPINION YOUR SCHEME IS A 419 SCAM_ I THOUGHT I WAS DISAPPOINTED

WHEN RUSSIA WERE EJECTED FROM EURO 2004 BUT NOW I AM SHOCKED AND DEEPLY SADDENED_EXPLAIN YOURSELF MAN BEFORE I CALL MY EX-KGB COLLEAGUES TO HUNT YOU DOWN LIKE THE DOG YOU ARE

PS DID YOU SEE FRANCE V CROATIA???

Lawyer Williams:

this transaction is 100 percent hitch free nothing like scam. you can call me on my mobile number for more explanation:234-803-7121xxx

Stroganov:

I AM PREPARED TO GIVE YOU ONE MORE CHANCE TO PROVE THAT YOU ARE NOT A SHOULDER-PAD WEARING SHYSTER _DO YOU THINK ITALY WERE UNLUCKY OR VICTIMS OF A CONSPIRACY BETWEEN DENMARK AND SWEDEN???

Lawyer Williams:

How on earth do you think i involve my self in scam? i am getting tired of your question it is just a matter of yes or no.

Stroganov:

DID YOU THINK THAT A SEMI-LITERATE SCAM EMAIL IS GOING TO FOOL ANYONE WITH AN IQ HIGHER THAN A CABBAGE LET ALONE ME??? _NOW GET LOST BEFORE I REALLY DO CALL MY EX-KGB COLLEAGUES AND ENSURE THAT YOU STOP SCAMMING FOR GOOD

Lawyer Williams:

Dear Stroganov,

hope your not the same mood you were yesterday.As I said before this is not a scam not a means to take money from you.Indeed my country is know for scam, that does not say there are no honest people in the country.The Russian team played badly intheir first two matches on the championship but that does not mean that they were no good players in the team. Atlist the gave a good account of themselves inthe last match.I am not trying to misdirect you with words but let us examing this all over. If it were not the event which took the life of the husband of my client i believe you wont besounding like this if you really new him.This family use to be very rich before democracy came to Nigeria. The present government has frozen their swiz account and all the account they have outside Nigeria. I agreed to work for them because I know that after the BUSH ADMINISTRATION IN THE states This account will be defrozen. There is a saying in my country that when the mighty fall there is the tendercy that they will rise again because of the investment an the connection they have.As longer as you are a billioneer you have all the resources within you to hunt me down if this is a scam . YOU JUST SEND THE MONEY.

Stroganov:

IF YOU ARE A LAWYER THEN I AM A MONKEY'S UNCLE_FOR GODS SAKE_ HOW CAN YOU FIT MILLIONS OF DOLLARS INTO THREE TRUNK BOXES??? I AM PREPARED TO GIVE ANYONE A SECOND CHANCE BUT I AM BEING ADVISED TO STEER CLEAR OF THIS DUBIOUS BUSINESS_HOWEVER MAYBE A HEAD-TO-HEAD MEETING TO CLEAR THE AIR WOULD BE IN ORDER_CAN YOU GET TO MOSCOW???

PS DID YOU SEE CZECH REPUBLIC V HOLLAND???

CHAPTER 5

CHECKLIST FOR THE SCAM-O-CHALLENGED

I seen my opportunities and I took 'em.
– George Washington Plunkitt

While the internet is handy for comparing notes, it can't think for you. The following checklist will help you decide whether that exciting email offer from a stranger is legitimate or not. When the count reaches one, it's a scam. The checklist can be copied and stuck to your refrigerator for use the next time an exciting business proposal arrives, or given to scam-o-challenged friends. If it does not resolve your issue, proceed to the next chapter, *Answers to Frequently Asked Questions.* Do not stop at the Comedy Break, do not collect $20 million in imaginary money. You need the FAQ.

❍ Does the proposal come from a stranger who found you "through the internet," or in a "business directory," or among the files of his father (a murdered cocoa merchant), or scribbled in the diary of the Sultan of Brunei?

❍ Is the email From: and To: the same person?

❍ Is the letter addressed to "CEO" even though you're a retired dentist or truck driver?

❍ Does the writer claim to be the wife, son, lawyer or banker of a General, Chief, or Prince?

❍ Do the words "secret" or "confidential" appear?

❍ Do other addresses appear in the "copied to": section of this "confidential" email?

❍ Does the writer use a free email service (Yahoo, Rediffmail)?

O   Does he prefer a reply to a different account than that from which he sent the initial email?

O   Is he in a refugee camp—with a dedicated internet line?

O   Has a mysterious relative died without a will?

O   Do kickbacks need laundering?

O   Is the money being stored at a "security company"?

O   Does he send you a picture of the money?

O   Are you asked to email back a scanned copy of your passport or anything with your signature?

O   Are you asked for your bank account details?

O   Does the writer ask you to call a phone number in West Africa or the Netherlands, or a satellite phone (often begins with 874)?

O   Are you invited to visit a web site and view a "bank account" set up for you?

O   Does the writer cite published stories about well-known people, hoping that, because these people exist, you will believe he is connected to them?

O   Is the writing of this senior bureaucrat (or junior aristocrat) simultaneously poor and pompous?

O   Does he mention his conversion to whichever religion he thinks you practice?

O   Does he talk about "coming over" or "coming down" to your country to get an education, or raise his orphaned sister, or invest under your guidance (even though you're fourteen years old, or in prison for burglary)?

O   Is a "bank" certificate attached which looks like an invitation to a child's birthday party?

O   Does the writer send "family" photos obviously snipped from a magazine?

O   Does he promise to reimburse expenses when there weren't supposed to be any expenses?

O   Do any of the following appear: "risk-free," "security reason" or "modalities"? ("Modalities" is worth two points.)

O   Do the words Western Union or Money Gram appear?

- Does the writer start calling you "Mummy" or "Daddy"?

- If you Google his "name," do you see scam letters he's sent to other people?

- When you read his letter to your friends, do they laugh? (Have you felt too embarrassed to read the letter to your friends? Can you read it *out loud* to yourself without snorting?)

- Last, but really first: Do you believe that someone who claims to have embezzled millions of dollars is someone you want to know, can't figure out how to launder it or will send it to a stranger (you) in hopes that you will nicely return eighty percent of it? (If yes, re-read this book out loud in a harsh voice, while sneering at yourself in a mirror.)

COMEDY BREAK: THE CENTER FOR RESEARCH INTO ADVANCED PHARMACEUTICALS

Dr. Billy Rubin was approached by the Son of Someone Important.

In real life, "Billy" is a doctor (general practitioner) in Adelaide, Australia.

James Mobi Kabila:

> Dear,
>
> I am James Mobi Kabila son of the late Democratic Republic of Congo President Laurent Desire Kabila of the blessed memory. I know this letter might come as a surprise but I do not intend to surprise you.
>
> I write in respect of my intention to invest US$35M(Thirty Five Million) with you. I inherited this money from my mother. This money was got through the sales of Diamond and Timber when my father was head of state. My mother though not her legal wife used her privilege position to engage in the business of Diamond and Timber since she knows her survival will depend on how much she can get out of the privilege situation. When my father was assassinated on 16TH Jan. 01 through the conspiracy of army officers that wanted to topple him I escaped to Athens-Greece because of the fear that I might be arrested by my half brother Lt. General Joseph Kabila the present head of state. Actually his mother and my mother are not in the best of relationship because of who among them will be the first lady tussle.
>
> Considering the relationship between Athens-Greece and Congo, my mother advised me to leave for Athens-Greece for security reason, while the funds were deposited with a Security Company in Athens-Greece. On getting to Athens-Greece where I have been living since then as a refugee I am seeking for a foreigner who can assist me in moving this money out for investment. I don't want to invest this money in Athens-Greece due to my status as a Refugee. And I wouldn't want to take risk

because this money is all that I and my Mother is depending on because My half brother has seized my father's assets and left I and my mother empty handed so investing this money abroad should be the best investment.

I expect you to be kind enough to respond to this distress call to save my mother and I from a hopeless future. I agree to compensate your effort with 15 percent of the money and 5 percent for expenses. The remaining "MONEY" will be invested in your business and deterrents sectors in your country. Whatever your decision is please keep this letter tight secret for the interest of my family.

Best Regards,James Mobi Kabila.

Prof. Billy Rubin:

What is the meaning of this?

Our rich multinational firm stands ready to do business, but you must reply otherwise you will find yourself in gladiator school very quickly.

Best Regards

Professor Billy Rubin

Centre for Research Into Advanced Pharmaceuticals, Australia

James Mobi Kabila:

Dear Professor Billy Rubin,

Please I do not understand your mail. Kindly inform me if you are willing to assist my mother and I.Thanks as I wait for your otherwise.

Regards,James.M.Kabila.

Prof. Billy Rubin:

Dear Mr. Kabila,

We are ready to help you and your mother in any way we can, because God knows you need help.

My apologies for the delay. Here in Australia our night is your daytime, and your day is our night. This is very confusing sometimes as not only do we walk around upside down, we also have to work all night and sleep all day if we want to transact international business.

Our company has called an emergency board meeting. Dame Edna Everidge has rushed away from the Melbourne gladioli festival and Lord Henry has been prised away from his weed research in the smoking room.

It seems you need to move a large sum of money out of the country. We may be able to spare the use of our private plane (the Concorde). This plane has a special compartment made by Drinkwater Corporation, which would be just the right size for your money trunks.

The best way to move money is for you to become a shareholder in our company. This will enable us to move the money and avoid Australian taxes. Becoming a shareholder is easy you just have to fill in a form and email it back. Are you willing to do this?

Warmest regards,

Professor Billy Rubin

James Mobi Kabila:

Dear Professor Billy Rubin,

How are you and your business? Received your email and the content demands explanations, thanks again for your interest in this business which is of mutual benefit to both parties involved if build on trust, honesty and promptness. Secondly I will be very greatful to be a shareholder and again I must solicit your strictest confidentiality because of some reason.

I need you as a foreign partner who will receive this consignment on my behalf because of some security reason, as the attitude we are getting from my step brother Joseph (who is the present head of state) is nothing to write home about, and you can see from the demonstration in my country about his system of government, if you listen to world news. For this transaction to progress I will require your address, your direct phone/mobile and fax numbers, your religion and marital status, and your occupation to facilitate the transaction.

Upon the receipt, I will proceed for the change of the name of the consignment to your name and you are expected to receive this consignment here in Athens-Greece and open a bank account where these funds will be lodged in for transfer to your account and most important thing is you being honest to me when this money comes into your care.

So you have to send the above contacts for more briefing. I hope that you have understood what the business is all about, if you have any question do not fail to ask. Finally, I want to assure you that this transaction is hundred percent risk-free and legal.

Prof. Billy Rubin:

Dear Mr. Kabila,

Our transaction will be built on trust and integrity and honesty and will be concluded entirely to our own satisfaction.

1) My contact details are:

Professor Billy Rubin

The Center for Research into Advanced Pharmaceuticals

14 Woolloomoloo Street

Smiggins Holes

NSW Australia

Phone 61+3+5554 xxxx

Fax 61+3+4444 xxxx

Occupation: Managing Director

Marital Status: Married with three children (lymphocyte, neutrophil Phil and globulin)

Religion: God Fearing Christian

2) I have attached two files. One is our share price, which as you can see has been

---

The Center for Research into Advanced Pharmaceuticals

Share Application and Prospectus Form 3b

To be used for the application for Ordinary Shares in accordance with the Australian Stock Exchange Hallux Valgus Act 1936.

Name:

Address:

Suburb and City:

Phone Home: Phone Business: Email:

Number of Shares: 48,611,111

Current Share Price: US72c   Total Cost: US$35,000,000

Please attach a passport photograph here

I hereby do agree to purchase the above shares for the agreed price, and to abide by all company rules as a loyal servant and shareholder.

Signed: _____

Date: _____

CRAP share application and prospectus form
Courtesy: Center for research into advance pharmaceuticals

going up a lot recently.

The other is a share application form. Can you please print this out on your computer, fill in your name and a photograph, scan it and send it back.

Can I ask that the photograph be one of you holding a sign saying "Center for Research into Advanced Pharmaceuticals." That way, we will know the photograph really is you.

3) I have been working with our financial adviser Ms. Martha Stewart who works for the Accounting Firm Quick Turn and Partners. This is a company with utmost integrity and will not disclose our transaction. Once you have completed the forms they can arrange for the purchase of shares in our company through our Athens office. These shares are then moved offshore to Tasmania where we purchase a quick drying inkwell Savings and Loans series of debentures. These are then transferred back into the holding company, rolled over and offset against the original purchase, which then pays out dividends in US dollars. This money is then converted to cash in any country of your choice.

I must say, my friend and business partner, that I don't fully understand all this financial talk, but it has worked well for us in the past. With our rising share price, you should expect a healthy profit of a few hundred thousand dollars! Our company has been researching new medicines to help the sick. We look forward to a profitable relationship. As we say here in Australia, you scratch my nuts and I'll scratch yours!

Give my regards to your mother.

James Mobi Kabila:

Dear Professor Billy Rubin,

I am in receipt of your mail and every content well noted. Please I cannot fill the share application form now because we have to conlude one before moving on to another. I am promising you as soon as this transaction is concluded, we will then talk about the shares.

Please Billy I want to know if you can be able to come to Athens-Greece by next week in order to claim this consignment. Thanks as I wait for your immeadiate response. My mother is extending her greetings to you and your family.

Prof. Billy Rubin:

Dear Mr. Kabila,

I will not be able to come to Athens, but our company can send one of our field operatives Lord Henry Thompson Fotheringham-Smythe. Lord Henry is in the US catching up with an old lady friend of his called Agent 99, but he stands by ready to travel to Athens at a moment's notice.

We will get the paperwork for the shares so that you can purchase these once the consignment has been transferred. If it is not too much bother, we do require a photograph of you so that Lord Henry will know what you look like.

James Mobi Kabila:

Dear Prof. Billy,

I am in receipt of your mail and please I will like to know if Lord Henry will be coming to Athens by this week so that I can inform the security company. Please should I effect your own name or Lord Henry's name as the beneficiary of the consignment and how trusty is he. As I told you before this money is our only hope and future.

Please Prof. Billy I will not use the whole money (US$35M) to purchase shares because I understand that your company wants me to buy shares worth of US$35M, which is not what we wanted. I attach my Int.Passport and as well I will like to have yours and that of Lord Henry so as to know each other well.

Thanks as I wait for your immediate response.

Prof. Billy Rubin:

Dear Mr. Kabila,

Thank you for your photo. Dame Edna says you are a fine looking fellow and she said something about wanting to have your babies. Unfortunately I don't think that will be possible as she is 85 years old, but Dame Edna does remain young at heart!

To Business: Please put my name on the consignment documents. Lord Henry can come over at a moments notice. He has purchased a fine wooden hand carved chest for transporting the money. Lord Henry has been a loyal Number Two for our company for many years. Once you have sent the documentation, let me know when Lord Henry needs to fly over. Can you let me know where you are staying in Athens?

James Mobi Kabila:

Dear Prof. Billy,

Thanks for your mail and my greetings to Dame Edna. I will love to have babies but that will be when am settled and from a younger girl.

I have effected your name as the sole beneficiary of the consignment and please Lord Henry will take the money to your country for the investment purpose. For now I have nothing to do with my country. I will be very glad if Lord Henry will be in Athens by this Friday so that both of us will go together to the security company. Please contact me with this number 306946086xxx so we can discuss more. I also awaits for the pictures (You and Lord Henry).

Thanks and my greetings to every one as I wait to hear from you.

Prof. Billy Rubin:

Dear Mr. Kabila,

What a delight to hear from you.

Lord Henry has fuelled the Concorde, and he will be flying in to Athens on Friday. I trust you will be able to meet him at the airport and transport him in the style to which he is accustomed.

There is one small matter that is most urgent. The Concorde needs a long runway, so Lord Henry needs you to find out how long the runway is at the Athens airport. Perhaps you could ring them and find out. If they won't tell you, perhaps you could walk along the road next to the airport and measure it in feet. If you can also give us your shoe size we can work out if the runway is long enough. You see, if the runway is too short the plane will go off the end and crash!

I have attached a photograph of myself.

(It was a picture of Professor Julius Sumner Miller. His specialty was putting boiled eggs into bottles. When the flame burns it uses up oxygen, and then atmospheric pressure does the work. He was big in the 1980s and at the time it drove the milk board crazy as they couldn't recycle all the bottles with eggs in them!)

Lord Henry:

From the desk of Lord Henry Thompson Fotheringham-Smythe Esq CMG GCMG BSC SSC

Field Operations, The Center for Research Into Advanced Pharmaceuticals

(Re: Lord Henry's qualifications: CMG and GCMG are from the TV show *Yes Minister*—they mean "Call Me God" and "God Calls Me God." BSC and SSC are from the TV show Red Dwarf, meaning "Bronze Swimming Certificate" and "Silver Swimming Certificate" respectively. Lord Henry is a bit over-qualified for this sort of caper.)

My Dear Mr. James Kabila,

I will be concluding this transaction in Athens, and I look forward to seeing you soon.

Professor Billy Rubin has told me all about you.

1) I look forward to concluding this business. You did not say if I would need any money for unexpected expenses, but I have brought some anyway.

2) I attach a photograph of myself so you will recognize me at the airport.

(Picture of Rolf Harris, a great Australian. Not that this Lad would know.)

3) Will you be meeting me yourself at the airport?

4) I do need to know the length of the runway at the airport. This is most important, because we have had problems where runways have been too short, and we have bumped the nose of the Concorde plane at the end of the runway. It takes ages to hammer the nose back into the proper shape. Do let me know as soon as possible, there's a good chap.

5) I will be arriving at exactly 9:18pm on Friday. I look forward to meeting you and your wonderful mother.

Yours in friendship,

Lord Henry

James Mobi Kabila:

Dear Prof. Billy,

Thanks for your mail and your picture looks good. Please ask Lord Henry to contact me with the phone number I gave you (306946086xxx) so that both of us can discuss. I have also sent him mail asking him to contact me immediately.

James Mobi Kabila:

Dear Lord Henry,

Thanks for your email. You looks so cool in the picture. Please contact me immediately.

Lord Henry:

Dear Mr. Kabila,

I must know the length of the runway before Friday night.

I look forward to seeing you then. Will you be at the airport?

Prof. Billy Rubin:

Hello Mr. Kabila,

I have tried calling your number but someone keeps answering in Greek. I don't speak Greek. Is it you speaking in Greek? Maybe you should answer in French or English or a more widely spoken language like Latin or Esperanto.

Lord Henry needs to know how long the runway is. I have suggested he replace the metal nose on the Concorde with a rubber one so it won't get bent. But he insists it is too dangerous to risk bumping the nose at all.

Give my regards to your mother.

James Mobi Kabila:

Dear Prof. Billy,

Please confirm your phone number for me (61-3-5554 xxxx) because and please I will like to have your mobile number if any.

Thanks as I wait to hear from you.

Dame Edna:

From Dame Edna Everage to James Kabila

Hello there my shy little possum! I've heard that you want to be the father of my babies. Im so excited!! Don't tell Lord Henry, but I've stowed away on his Concorde. That means I'll be meeting you in person on Friday. I don't want to rush you, but when we get married, do you prefer pink or a milder shade of purple for the wedding outfits? And what about the flowers in the church? I've attached a photo of me. I'll see you soon.

All my love xxx,

Edna

(For the record, Dame Edna is a drag queen played by Mr. Barry Humphries, who is, of course, male)

Lord Henry:

From the expensive office of Lord Henry Thompson Fotheringham-Smythe Esq

Dear Mr. Kabila,

Our plane is about to take off. I expect the next time we talk will be face to face at Athens airport. I hope you have been able to arrange a limousine. I brought some money in case any unexpected expenses come up.

Prof. Billy Rubin:

Dear Mr. Kabila,

Lord Henry has told me he will be arriving at Athens airport at 9:18pm. He is expecting you to be meeting him. I look forward to a smooth business transaction.

James Mobi Kabila:

Dear Dame Edna,

How are you? Hope fine. You look pretty in the picture and I am just imaging how beautiful you will be when you are young. Please I will be happy to meet you when the transaction is concluded and I am not in a hurry to be a father or have babies now until am settled.

James Mobi Kabila:

Dear Lord Henry,

Actually I do not know the length of the runway but I will assure you that it is okay because Greece is hosting Olympic Games by August. As to ask them or measuring the runway will bring all eyes on me as regards to this terroist activities. They might think that I am planning some evils. Thanks as I wait for your call.

James Mobi Kabila:

Dear Prof. Billy,

Please call me may it is the operator that is answering you. I don't speak greek, I only speak english and my native language. Kindly ask Lord Henry to replace the metal nose with the rubber one but I beleive that the nose will never got bump. You know that they will be hosting Olympic Games around August so their Airport run way is okay.

NB: Dame Edna send me mail and I have replied her. Please inform her that I am not ready to have babies now.

(What is a Lad's worst nightmare? Another Lad stealing his mugu. So let's arrange for that to happen.)

Mugu Stealer:

FROM MR MUGU STEALER

HA HA HA I HAVE GOT INSIDE YOUR COMPUTER AND READ YOUR EMAILS.

I AM GOING TO STEAL YOUR MUGU LORD HENRY WHEN HE GETS TO THE AIRPORT!!! I AM GOING TO TAKE ALL HIS MONEY!!

I AM THE MUGU STEALER!!!

Prof. Billy Rubin:

Dear Mr. Kabila,

Lord Henry and Dame Edna arrived safely at the airport, and they have been most impressed with you. Lord Henry tells me that you met him with a black stretch limousine and took him to the security company where he says he has seen the money. He has been most impressed by the hotel you have provided and said it was a very nice touch making available the unmarried lady.

Lord Henry says that he has had to pay some consignment release fees and legal documentation processing fees. He says they have only come to a few thousand dollars so I see no problems there. He expects to have your money safely out of the country very soon.

It is a great pleasure doing business with someone as professional as yourself.

Mugu Stealer:

FROM THE MUGU STEALER

HA HA MR KABILA

I MET YOUR MUGU AND HIS LADY FRIEND AT THE AIRPORT AND GAVE THEM RIDE IN NICE CAR. THEN I SHOW THEM LOTS OF MONEY. IT IS ALL FAKE MONEY BUT THEY DONT KNOW!!! THEN I PUT THEM IN HOTEL AND GIVE THEM CHEAP PROSTITUTE.

THEN I CHARGE THEM FEES. I HAVE ALREADY MADE OVER $3000US.

HA HA. THANKYOU FOR SENDING ME SUCH GOOD MUGUS.

DO YOU WANT THEM BACK?? WELL YOU CANT HAVE THEM UNTIL I HAVE TAKEN ALL THEIR MONEY THEN YOU CAN HAVE THEM.

I AM THE GREAT MUGU STEALER

Prof. Billy Rubin:

Dear Mr. Kabila,

I am most concerned for Lord Henry. I haven't heard from him for several days. He sent a message saying he was going back to the security company, and we haven't heard from him since. Do you know where he is?

CHAPTER 6

ANSWERS TO FREQUENTLY ASKED QUESTIONS

Q: **I received a letter much like the ones in this book. Do you think it's a scam?**

A: Yes.

Q. **How did the scammer get my (email) address?**

A.   From employee or membership directories, online classified ads, online bulletin boards, job websites and chat rooms. An odd-looking posting on a bulletin board such as "Mugu guyman keep off" or "I'm here ooooo," means a scammer has staked out the board and warned other scammers away. One scammer staked out a support board for victims of brain tumors. Really. Scammers buy lists from other scammers. These lists can be very poor quality, to judge by those which the scammers carelessly attach to emails—many addresses are those of automatic services rather than people. Sometimes other recipients appear in the plainly visible "cc:" (copy-to) field. This is an actual example:

CC: wafl@phonebusters.com, voorlichting@klpd.politie.nl, info@cenbank.org, fipo@rkp.police.se, mediarelations@saps.org.za, hq.commercial@saps.org.za, postmaster@scamorama.com

The reader will quickly see that these are not likely prospects.

Some use email extractors: computer programs, which troll through web pages, carving out email addresses from the text. Lists can also be generated through directory harvesting. This means sending an email to every-name-possible@someISP.com. Whatever doesn't bounce back is a working address.

Q: **My letter came from "MUS Bello," not "Idris Bello," do you still think it's a scam?**

A: Yes.

Q: My letter promised ten percent of $32 million, not twenty percent of $16 million—scam?

A: Yes.

Q: He offered me his telephone number. Could a criminal have a telephone?

A: Yes.

Q: But he addressed me by name!

A: Yeah, so?

Q: He sent me a certificate. Could he print up phony certificates?

A: Yes. Here's one:

"Death Certificate"
Courtesy: A. Scammer

Q: He says he's a minister and one of his flock is in a refugee camp. Scam?
A: Yes.

Q: Am I obliged to answer?
A: No.

Q: I answered. Am I obliged to go on corresponding with him?
A: No. Just stop answering. You've been more ruthless about breaking up with people, you know you have.

Q: He hasn't asked me for money. Just a scan of my passport.
A: Not yet. And don't send it. The signature can be used to forge documents, and the passport can be used to scam other people.

Q: But he says the passport is required to process my visa.
A: Visas are issued by embassies before going to countries, which require them, or at the airport on arrival. Were you planning to visit your scammer? Don't! In any case, Nigeria requires visas. If your scammer invites you to travel there without one, beware. Beware anyway. Be very wary. If you are let in without a visa, the scammer has bribed an official and may blackmail you for entering without a visa. People have died going to meet scammers.

Q: He wants my bank account number. Must I give it to him?

A: No. You mustn't.

Q: **I gave him my bank account number. Can he get at my account?**

A: It does not appear to be the main goal of most 419 scams, but as an unfortunate victim informed me, it *can* happen. At the very least, an account number should not be enough—a signature is needed. (Remember that passport you scanned? That "form" you filled out?) Even if you have nipped a potential scam in the bud, the scammer may attempt a transfer of funds from your account. *Go to your bank.* This is too important for embarrassment.

Q: **I stopped emailing him, but not before I emailed him my scanned ID card. Am I at risk?**

A: Possibly. Certain measures can help prevent identity theft. Notify the police (and get the case number). Alert your bank and find out what protections it has in place against unauthorized wire transfers. In the United States, alert the major credit information companies—Equifax, Transunion and Experian—and ask to be notified of any credit applications placed in your name. The US Federal Trade Commission (www.ftc.gov) can provide further information and referrals to appropriate government agencies.

Q: **Can a money order be cancelled?**

A: Only before it's picked up. Western Union has no protections or insurance against such losses, and will release the money to anyone whose ID (real or not) matches the name on the money order. Many Western Union agents are small shop owners without training in spotting fraud.

Q: **Couldn't someone in a refugee camp (with internet service) have chosen me, out of 100 million people with email, to receive great wealth, through a divine plan?**

A: No.

Q: **You mean he's lying?**

A: Yes.

Q: **Could scammers have important-looking stationery and web sites?**

A: Yes. They bribe bank and government employees for official blank forms and stamps. They create web sites for companies, which don't exist, and copy web sites of companies which do.

Q: **But their web site has a login feature, which shows an account full of MONEY! for ME!**

A: It's just text, there's no money behind it.

Q: **Could scammers impersonate officials if I went to meet them (which I know, in a cognitively dissonant sort of way, is dangerous)?**

A: Yes. They can set up fake offices or borrow real ones from corrupt employees.

Q: **I got scammed. I was trying to sell my camera. The scammer sent me a check for more than my asking price. He asked me to send him a money order for the difference. Confusing, but I did it. Then his check bounced. The bank is dunning me for it! What should I do?**

A: A bank fraud investigator offered this advice: Fill out a *fraud affidavit* at your bank. If the bank's local branch held the check, then cleared it, and THEN their central clearinghouse said the check bounced (which could take weeks), perhaps you need not be held responsible. Note, this is not presented as qualified legal or financial counsel. This is an OPINION. Banks may resist responsibility for such incidents. An attorney may be of more help.

Q: Can a bank help me get my money back?

A: Try them. Banks do not like being scammed. Their fraud examiners know examiners in other banks. Scammers have to bank somewhere.

Q: I got scammed and the scammers say I can "earn" the money back by helping them scam other people. Should I do it?

A: Are you really asking this question?

Q: The scammer keeps calling me at home, what should I do?

A: That's creepy. Ask the phone company and the police for help.

Q: He leaves messages, what should I do?

A: Add some good beats and podcast them.

Q: He wants me to meet him somewhere. Should I?

A: No!!

Q: But he's not asking me to go to Nigeria—only the country next door—

A: No, no!!

Q: But he wants to meet me right here in the good old (name your good old nation).

A: No, no, no!! Even worse. Call the police.

Q: If I am scammed, am I guilty of a crime?

A: No, the people who scammed you are guilty of a crime.

Q: But what if I agreed to do something criminal?

A: You are only a criminal (in my non-binding, non-legal opinion) if you commit a crime. Embezzling from a business to pay a scammer *is* a crime. Agreeing to help transfer funds which you are assured are "100 percent legal and risk-free" is *not* a crime. Agreeing to help a "widow" is not a crime. Responding to an apparent business proposal is not a crime.

Q: What if scammers are threatening me?

A: If they are far away (check the *header* to see how far), don't worry. If they threaten to sue, have a good laugh. In what court? If they say they will unleash the thunder god on you, it's your call. If they are near you, or contacting your home, or appear to have personal information about you or to have broken into your email account, go to the police.

Q: Aren't Nigerian officials sick of this scam?

A: They certainly seem sick of hearing about it. Many officials have spoken out against the scam and government agencies and banks post warnings about it. It has also been claimed that many officials are themselves scammers. The Nigerian government set up a commission to deal with fraud, and have arrested and prosecuted some of these officials. Nigeria also has other problems to deal with, like preventing civil war. While Nigeria may someday make a dent in fraud, scam-proofing yourself and your social circle is the best defense.

Q: Is there a "Sani Abacha"?

A: Yes, General Sani Abacha was a president of Nigeria. There also was (and is) a President Kabila of Congo (formerly Zaire, formerly Belgian Congo) (his son is now president). The Lads are great name-droppers.

Q: Is there a "Charles Soludo"?

A. Yes, Charles Soludo is Governor of the Central Bank of Nigeria, which hosts a forum on the scam. Scammers like to sign off as Soludo.

Q: Is there a...?

A: Very likely. You can look him up, you know.

Q: How many wives, sons, and toadies have the Abacha, Kabila, and Savimbi families got?

A: If you believed all the letters, hundreds, but you don't, do you?

Q: My letter is not from Nigeria, it's from Ghana, or the Philippines or Serbia.

A: Maybe. Check the header. Anyway, Ghana is next door to Nigeria. While people in other countries are perfectly competent to carry out their own scams, Nigerian fraudsters (and ordinary Nigerian businesses) work out of those countries. Anyway, it doesn't matter where the letter comes from. It's a scam.

Q: The letter isn't so badly written, heck, I don't write so well myself. Could these guys be legitimate?

A: No, and it doesn't matter if the grammar is flawless.

Q: This week's letter is a bit different from last week's, could it be legitimate?

A: If you've received more than one, what does that tell you?

Q: But his email address is different.

A: It doesn't MATTER. There *is* no legitimate version of a scam letter. How many times must your mother and I tell you it's a scam?

Q: But he mentioned God.

A: They're great name-droppers.

Q: **After I was scammed that other time, a second stranger offered to help me recover my money! He seemed to know all about it. He says he's with an anti-fraud squad!**

A: Sigh...

Q: **What is "phishing" and are the 419ers doing it?**

A: Phishing is fooling someone into supplying personal information. An email is a common means to this end, stating that the recipient's bank account has been compromised. Clicking a hyperlink in the email leads to an Evil Web Site with a prompt to enter the login name and password of the account. If provided, these can be used for theft. Phishing as traditionally defined lacks the 419 angle of trying to convince a victim to send money. 419ers have been known to email keystroke loggers, and they can try to exploit personal information. However Eastern Europeans seem to dominate the field in "traditional" phishing.

Q: **Do you think this is a threat to national security? Are the 419ers terrorists?**

A: No, I think they're old-fashioned crooks, but my opinion is based on cynicism, not inside knowledge. I think 419ers are probably more comfortable in Armani than khaki.

Terrorists probably have easier ways of making money, like asking rich supporters for it or selling drugs, or committing credit card fraud (Imam Samudra, convicted for the Bali nightclub bombings of 2004, wrote a jailhouse manifesto urging Muslims to take up "carding" for the cause). Electronic means include credit card fraud, identity theft, phishing and outright breaking into insecure bank systems (which did happen to a Nigerian bank). It is, however, convenient to exploit insecure and unregulated networks to pass information. Femi Oyesanya, who writes on Nigerian IT issues, calls Nigeria the "Wild Wild West of Internet Crime." An Al Qaeda suspect arrested in Pakistan in 2004 confirmed that the organization uses web sites and email addresses in Turkey, Nigeria and Pakistan to pass messages. Scam-o-grams have reportedly been used to transmit coded plans for assassinations in West Africa. "I am the son of Jonas Savimbi" = "Fly, all is discovered"? Or perhaps a barrage of spam would go out, but only the intended recipient would know what it meant. Darned if I know. So where does the 419 loot go? I think it goes where it seems to go—into the pockets of crooks, who enjoy spending it.

SCAMANALYSIS: THE DEAD BANK CUSTOMER LETTER

Received: from PC2 (**[193.220.212.23]**)

From: "paulkings2006" <paulkings2006@walla.com>

To: <paulkings12k@yahoo.com>

Subject: Your Assistance Needed

CONFIDENTIAL

ATTENTION:

I HAVE THE COURAGE TO ASK YOU TO LOOK FOR A RELIABLE AND HONEST PERSON WHO WILL BE CAPABLE FOR THIS IMPORTANT BUSINESS BELIEVING THAT YOU WILL NEVER LET ME DOWN EITHER NOW OR IN FUTURE.

PLEASE READ CAREFULLY AS THIS IS VERY IMPORTANT.

I AM **DR. PAUL KINGS**, THE EASTERN DISTRICT BANK MANAGER OF UNITED BANK FOR AFRICA PLC (UBA). THERE IS AN ACCOUNT OPENED IN THIS BANK IN 1980 AND SINCE 1990 NOBODY HAS OPERATED ON THIS ACCOUNT AGAIN. I DISCOVERED THAT IF I DO NOT REMITT THIS MONEY OUT URGENTLY IT WILL BE FORFEITED FOR NOTHING. THE OWNER OF THIS ACCOUNT IS MR. **SMITH B. ANDREAS**, A **FOREIGNER**, A CHEMICAL ENGINEER AND **HE DIED SINCE 1990.**

NO OTHER PERSON KNOWS ABOUT THIS ACCOUNT, THE ACCOUNT HAS NO OTHER BENEFICIARY AND MY INVESTIGATION PROVED THAT THIS COMPANY DOES NOT KNOW ANYTHING ABOUT THIS ACCOUNT AND THE AMOUNT INVOLVED IS (USD $126 MILLION DOLLARS). **ONE HUNDRED AND TWENTY SIX MILLION** US DOLLARS. I WANT TO TRANSFER THIS MONEY INTO A SAFE FOREIGNERS ACCOUNT ABROAD BUT I DONT KNOW ANY FOREIGNER, I AM ONLY CONTACTING YOU AS A FOREIGNER BECAUSE THIS MONEY CAN NOT BE APPROVED TO A LOCAL BANK HERE, BUT CAN ONLY BE APPROVED TO ANY FOREIGN ACCOUNT BECAUSE THE MONEY IS IN US DOLLARS AND THE FORMER OWNER OF THE ACCOUNT IS MR. SMITH B. ANDREAS IS A FOREIGNER TOO.

I KNOW THAT THIS MASSAGE WILL COME TO YOU AS A SURPRISE AS WE DONT KNOW OUR SELVES BEFORE, BUT BE SURE THAT IT IS REAL AND A GENUINE BUSINESS. THIS MONEY WILL BE TRANSFERRED IN BITS AND PIECES UNTIL IT IS CONCLUDED, I WILL APPLY ON YOUR BEHALF IF YOU AGREE TO WORK WITH ME, IMMEDIATELY YOU CONTACT ME, I WILL GIVE YOU ALL THE MODALITIES FOR THE TRANSFER OF THE MONEY INTO YOUR NOMINATED BANK ACCOUNT, FOR THE MUTUAL BENEFIT OF BOTH OF US.

I ONLY GOT YOUR CONTACT DURING MY SEARCH FOR A VIABLE INVESTMENT OPPORTUNITY IN YOUR COUNTRY, WITH BELIEVE IN GOD THAT YOU WILL **NEVER LET ME DOWN IN THIS BUSINESS** YOU ARE THE ONLY PERSON THAT I HAVE CONTACTED IN THIS BUSINESS, SO PLEASE REPLY URGENTLY SO THAT I WILL INFORM YOU THE NEXT STEP TO TAKE. I WANT US TO SEE FACE TO FACE OR SIGN A BINDING AGREEMENT TO BIND US TOGETHER SO THAT YOU CAN RECEIVE THIS MONEY INTO A FORIEGN ACCOUNT.AND I WILL FLY TO YOUR COUNTRY FOR WITHDRAWAL AND SHARING AND OTHER INVESTMENTS.

I AM CONTACTING YOU BECAUSE OF THE NEED TO INVOLVE A FOREIGNER WITH FOREIGN ACCOUNT AS FOREIGN BENEFICIARY. I NEED YOUR CO-OPERATION TO MAKE THIS WORK FINE. BECAUSE THE MANAGEMENT IS READY TO APPROVE THIS PAYMENT TO ANY FOREIGNER WHO HAS CORRECT INFORMATION OF THIS ACCOUNT, WHICH I WILL GIVE TO YOU LATER IMMEDIATELY, IF YOU ARE ABLE TO HANDLE SUCH AMOUNT IN STRICT CONFIDENCE FOR OUR MUTUAL BENEFIT

BECAUSE THIS OPPORTUNITY WILL NEVER COME AGAIN IN MY LIFE.

WITH MY POSITION I CAN TRANSFER THIS MONEY TO ANY FOREIGNERS ACCOUNT WHICH YOU CAN PROVIDE WITH ASSURANCE THAT THIS MONEY WILL BE INTACT PENDING MY ARRIVAL IN YOUR COUNTRY FOR SHARING. I WILL DESTROY ALL DOCUMENTS IMMEDIATELY WE RECIEVE THIS MONEY LEAVING NO TRACE TO ANY PLACE. YOU CAN COME TO DISCUSS WITH ME FACE TO FACE AFTER WHICH I WILL MAKE THIS REMITTANCE IN YOUR PRESENCE AND TWO OF US WILL FLY TO YOUR COUNTRY AT LEAST TWO DAYS AHEAD OF THE MONEY GOING INTO YOUR ACCOUNT.

I WILL APPLY FOR LEAVE TO GET VISA IMMEDIATELYI HEAR FROM YOU THAT YOU ARE READY TO RECEIVE THIS FUND. I WILL USE MY POSITION TO EFFECT LEGAL APPROVALS AND ONWARD TRANSFER OF THIS MONEY TO YOUR ACCOUNT WITH CLEARANCE FORMS OF THE MINISTRIES AND FOREIGN EXCHANGE DEPARTMENTS. AT THE CONCLUSION OF THIS BUSINESS, YOU WILL BE GIVEN 35 percent OF THE AMOUNT, **60 percent WILL BE FOR ME**, WHILE 5 percent WILL BE FOR **EXPENSES** INCURED DURING THE PROCESS OF TRANSFERING.

I LOOK FORWARD TO YOUR REPLY BY EMAIL OR CALL ME ON TELEPHONE.

TELEPHONE: **+234-8030-884xxx**.

Email: paulkings00@walla.com, paulkings001@walla.com, paulkings002@walla.com

YOURS TRULY,

DR. PAUL KINGS.

---

* [193.220.212.23]—Apparently from an ISP in Enugu State, Nigeria

* The proposition is "confidential," despite being a "blind" copy of an email he is mailing to himself—and possibly many others.

* It is VERY wordy (and I have edited it down).

* He suffers from CAPSLOCK.

* Paul Kings—Goofy attempt at Anglo name is possibly revenge for the silly islanders' dance in the original *King Kong* movie.

* I am somebody responsible or important.

* "Smith Andreas" has died many times at the hands of many scam-letter writers.

* $126 million—Spelled out in case you didn't understand.

* "And he died since 1990"—In English this sounds as if he is still dying.
Apparently a carryover from French, in which it would make more sense.

* THIS MONEY ... CAN ONLY BE APPROVED TO ANY FOREIGN ACCOUNT BECAUSE THE MONEY IS IN US DOLLARS—Apparently no *other* bank account in Nigeria can accept US dollars.

* "This massage will come as a surprise"—Most definitely!

* "Modalities"—Apparently a carryover from the French; seldom used in English outside of massage therapy textbooks.

* "Never let me down in this business"—Are *you* honest enough for this deal?

* Although the writer does not know you from Adam, he trusts you to take this money and give him back most of it.

* Twelve uses of the words "foreign" or "foreigner."

* Whoa, expenses?

* The writer finds it necessary to assure you that there is no risk.

* TELEPHONE: +234-8030-884xxx. Often the numbers are "repossessed" by the telephone company for nonpayment, and re-assigned to new, innocent parties.

* A total of five email accounts, useful if some are cancelled due to spam complaints.

SCAMANALYSIS: THE FAKE ID

AI Analysis complete… Report: WARNING; Fake identification. Probability of 99.6%

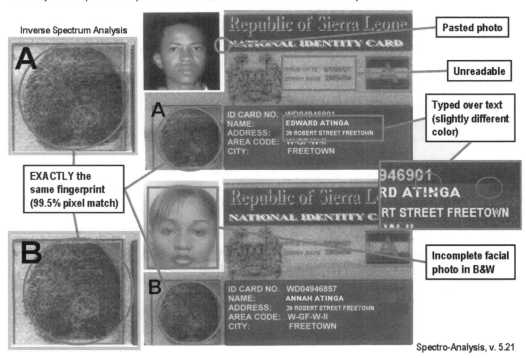

Sophisticated artificial intelligence analysis of a fake ID.

Courtesy: Jack Le Grandeur

COMEDY BREAK: THE INCREDIBLE VOYAGE

While the team at the Foreign Office did not succeed in their ultimate goal of persuading this scammer to send them an X-Box, they did manage to waste six weeks of his time and extract a Loyalty Oath.

Cast of characters:

HRH Princess Margaret—no, not that one, a relative
Lady Agatha Bristol, CBE, of the Foreign Office
Sir Marmite Luny-Binns, chamberlain to HRH
versus
Jonathan Mokoena, scammer du jour, posing as an official of the OAU

Jonathan Mokoena:

From: "Jonathan Mokoena" [joe_mok66@africamail.com]

Subject: PLEASE I NEED YOUR HELP.

Attn: The President,

Dear Sir,

My mail may come as a surprise, but sincerely this is a proposal for a business deal that will benefit both of us. I am contacting you after a frantic search for a person who will be trustworthy and capable of handling a business of this dimension.

My name is Mr. Jonathan Mokoena, the Under-Secretary in charge of Intergration at the Specialized Technical Committee of the African Union (AU), formerly Organization of Afriacn Unity (OAU). You may be aware of the transformation of the OAU to AU, and the mandate to build a new united Africa modelled on the pattern of European Union (EU). For this therefore, the African leaders inaugurated the New Patnership for African Development (NEPAD). NEPAD is to streamline Africa towards achieving a common market, defence, currency, foreign policy, judiciary etc. For the above, the African countries have made whosoever contributions in hundreds of million dollars. We have equally received grants/aids from the EU, US and other international governments and agencies.

As the officer in charge of managing these funds and executing the projects for which they are ment for, I have received all the money expected. However, some international bodies remitted to us amounts in excess of what they pledged. The money in excess and which I have kept out with only me having knowledge of it, is in the turn of Two Hundred and Thirty-Five Million United States Dollars (US$235,000,000.00).

I am therefore contacting you to assist me with the movement of this fund. I cannot openly put this money into any bank here in Addis Ababa, Ethiopia, the AU headquarters where I am now, or in any other part of Africa. This will surely raise eyebrows and expose me. I have therefore concealed this US$235M in four metal trunk boxes, and declared them as artefacts belonging to a foreigner. I deposited the boxes with a Security Company in Accra,Ghana.

This transaction will however be hitch-free. So, I would want you to be in Ghana for the claiming of this fund. I have decided to give to you 40 percent of the total amount involved.

Also, you have to assure me of confidentiality in this transaction.

Thanks in anticipation of your valued co-operation.

Mr. Jonathan Mokoena.

Princess Margaret:

My Dear Mokeona

Your charming and forthright letter has caught all of us here at the Palace by surprise. At first I felt your approach was somewhat forward, but after reading through the details I realized that yours seemed a genuine offer.

Recent developments at the Palace have meant that we have need of financial assistance for the refurbishment of Tode Hall. Once we are reassured as to the security aspects, we look forward to taking things further. I am copying this message to Dame Agatha Bristol CBE, Royal Chambermaid and Holder of the Bedpan, who will be in charge of the details. It may also be necessary to involve My equerry, Sir Marmite Luny-Binns, who is in charge of My security overseas.

With very best wishes

MARGARET

Her Royal Highness Princess Margaret VC

Duchess of Tesco

Room 101 The Royal Les Dawson Suite

Kensington Doss House

Buckingham London FU2 G1T

Jonathan Mokoena:

Dear Her Royal Highness,

First and foremost, I apperciated your acceptance to be my partner while you go home with the 40 percent at the successful conclusion of this transaction.

Secondly, this business requires an utmost secrecy, therefore, you do not have to let any body know about this business.

Third, you will taking care of the claiming of the consignments. You have to start recording whatever your expenses will be, I am assuring you that whatever your expenses amount to, will be given back to you. Already, I have stsrted spending money as the reault of depositing the four consignments, thus your assistance is highly needed.

Expecting to hear from you soonest.

Regards,

Jonathan.

Princess Margaret:

My Dear Mr. Mokeona

It is a pleasure to deal with such a scrupulous gentleman as yourself.

Do not worry about Sir Marmite and Lady Agatha. Their discretion is assured. Sir Marmite is captain of the Buckingham Bingo Team and has had a gallant record serving with the Asda Hussars in our Northern Toxteth territory. Lady Agatha or Lord Luny-Binns will be able to make decisions on My behalf.

May I take this opportunity to thank you for your kindness and to say what an inestimiable help you have been to the Royal Family in these dark days.

Kind regards

Margaret

Jonathan Mokoena:

Her Majesty,

I wish to know whan you are making the trip to Africa for this business. Can you furnish me with your contact phone lines.

Sir Marmite Luny-Binns:

My Dear Mokeona

Her Majesty has asked me to answer your message. How gracious of you to expedite matters. Princess Margaret and I can fly to see you under assumed names of course. The name normally chosen for Her Majesty is Edna Everidge, and for Myself, the name Larry Flynt. I hope this is convenient.

It is not Palace policy to release telephone numbers until full confidence is assured. However we do have a fax number, although it is in the office of the Archbishop of

Canterbury John Leslie, and may not be secure. I apologize for this awkwardness. Some public reserve is necessary. We would otherwise receive a lot of mad calls from socialist activists like the RSPCA.

Sir Marmite Luny-Binns DFC

Her Majesty's Chamberlain-at-Arms

Room 69 The Fred West Rooms

Jonathan Mokoena:

Her Majesty,

I am in touch with the security company by name "African Security." They will send to you a Deposit Document. The Deposit Certificate will be send to you from a friends office. Secrecy muct be maintained. You should not let the Government of England and Gambia to have knowledge of this business. Again, I will want to confirm when Her Majesty will be travelling.

Princess Margaret:

Very well, Mokeona,

We have not yet received back from you the statement of allegience. Prince Clyde is eager to accompany Me on any flight to see you; I trust this is alright? Can you recommend a good 5 star hotel for the royal party in Ghana? Although we will be travelling incognito, we appreciate a good spread, fresh flowers, an X-Box for Prince Clyde, a limousine etc etc.

Sir Marmite Luny-Binns:

Mokeona

Royal custom deems it necessary that you swear a temporary Oath of Loyalty to Her Majesty's interests, to which I am sure you will have no objection. Please read the following out loud, then sign it and return electronically before we can proceed.

"I Jonathan Mokoena, being of sound mind and body, do swear humble merkin and fey feasiance to the service of Her Gracious Majesty Princess Margaret, to the test in all Her issue and dominion, pursuaint in this moment of our right royal business."

(signed) J Mokeona   (date)

Jonathan Mokoena:

Her Royal Highness,

I have studied the Oath. I am going to sign this in utmost good faith (Ubrimae Fidei), and I trust in your person and capacity. I am making arrangement to be in Ghana tomorrow. I hope to rent a phone so we can talk. I will always be travelling to Ghana incognito all the time.

What is the meaning of x-box?

Princess Margaret:

My Dear Mokeona

I am glad that you have agreed to sign and return the oath of allegiance to Ourselves.

We await the details of the hotel. Let it be suited to our station, but not too conspicuous. I remember once when the Queen Mother went to Nairobi for a quiet safari with Sir Harry Secombe, she was entered by mistake into the hotel billiards competition, which brought unwelcome publicity to an otherwise peaceful vacation.

Sir Marmite has twisted his ankle during the Palace croquet tournament, but will take things further when out of traction in a few days.

An X-box is a computer games console currently favored by the young Princes, especially Wayne and Darren, and I trust these are available in Ghana?

Jonathan Mokoena:

Her Majesty,

May you live long. I am in Accra, Ghana now. I am going to send the Oath of Allegience but not on my official letterhead, as this matter does not have any official connotation. I need your understanding here.

I hope you realise you need a visa to Ghana. Please inform me of when you will be in Ghana.

N/B: I am sorry to learn of the injury sustained by Sir Marmite.

Princess Margaret:

Dear Mr. Mokeona

Thank you for this Oath. Can you add a passport photograph? Just a blank sheet of paper is not ideal. Please oblige us, dear chap. There is a great deal of excitement amongst the very few in the know here at the palace at the important business to come.

Jonathan Mokoena:

Her Royal Majesty,

I have confirmed from the director of African Security about the custody of the boxes containing the money. Apart from the clearing charges stated on the Deposit Agreement, there is also a VAT of 12.5 percent on any consignment deposited, before taking delivery.

I have searched around Accra for a hotel that meets your specification, especially in the area of shielding your identity. I can only suggest La Palm Royal Beach Hotel.

Frankly speaking Her Royal Highness, I was taken aback when I learnt that other people are aware of this. Like they say, two is a company, while three is a crowd. I cannot furnish you a phone number, and I would not want to talk to you on a public phone. Well I guess we will restrict all correspondence to email.

Princess Margaret:

My Dear Mokeona

We trust that you are well. Do not worry about unwanted ears. I have a tightly run retinue of trusted retainers and we are very security conscious. Sir Marmite insists on personally vetting all the new ladies-in-waiting in his Royal Caravan at Royal Windsor by the Sea.

The hotel sounds very reasonable. Please ensure that the limousine has fresh flowers inside and a champagne bucket. The extra charges will not present a problem. I will look into the Palace petty cash cupboard. Some has been spent on dance lessons for Princess Candy, but there is some left.

We await your further messages with enthusiasm.

Jonathan Mokoena:

Her Royal Highness,

With every sense of respect, I wish to make an observation. I am beginning to feel that your request might eventually be more than what I can provide. In your request for a Limousine, you asked for fresh flowers and I do not know how this can be organized. You have to know that here in Africa, flowers does not mean much to us and as such, no significance is attached to it as such. Since you are traveling incognito, it will be better you make do with what can be got for you. What about good investments that I will put my money into? I count on your advise in this area.

Princess Margaret:

My Dear Mr. Mokeona

We appreciate the efforts you are making. So do not worry if little things here and there are unobtainable. I remember once on a trip to Korea I had to make do without My daily face massage, but somehow got through it. Although a limousine, we now realise, may prove conspicious, perhaps we can have a good taxi, preferably one with a vetted driver?

In terms of investments, the best person to ask would be the Minister for Oversea Finance, Sir Ronnie Biggs, but he is enjoying a long vacation at Her Majesty's Pleasure at Wormwood Scrubs, and may not be easily contactable.

Jonathan Mokoena:

Her Majesty,

I do not see any need for a taxi or an external Driver. Ghanaians are docile and as a result petty,that getting a taxi Driver close to what we do will amount to pouring oil into fire.With a taxi driver there is a likelihood that we can be exposed. My recipe is to come in with my Personal assistant who can do the driving. We need to keep our jobs after this business,don't we?

Can you tell me where the funds will be wired to? Confirm if there is a telephone number youcan be reached.

I am quite impressed on the queenly manner and dexterity with which you handle this matter. My regards to Sir Marmite and I hope to hear from you soon.

Princess Margaret:

My Dear Mokeona,

The suggestions concerning transportation will be sufficient, I suppose, although please supply nothing too damp or smelly, as I have rheumatism and a dress line to consider.

I have a private account with Bonkers Bank PLC in London, ideal for the transfer of funds.

Jonathan Mokoena:

Her Royal Highness,

May you live long. When am I expecting you in Ghana?

The clearing and handling charge plus 12.5 percent VAT will have to be paid in cash before the boxes could be released to us. As a public servant, I have stretched my purse to a limit and have been able to foot the bill of moving the boxes to Ghana. I would ask you to help settle African Security and you will be reimbursed.

Please tell me about your travel plans. I am hearing of Bonkers bank for the first time.

Princess Margaret:

My Dear Mr, Mokoena,

Sir Marmite has now recovered and may contact you separately. Please forward on the Oath. I will get the travel details in hand. I imagine the Royal Jet will be too conspicuous. The clearing and handling charge should present no problems. I assume £100 notes are acceptable? As far as phone numbers are concerned Sir Marmite is still wary. May we continue by email. Security at The Palace, and at our Winter residence at Gormenghast, is uppermost in our minds.

Prince Darren has asked about the X-Box again. What games do you have?

Jonathan Mokoena:

Her Royal Highness,

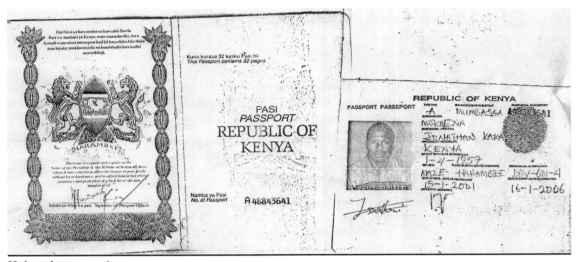

Mokena's passport
Courtesy: A. Scammer

I am attaching to you here my Passport.

Princess Margaret:

Dear Mr. Mokeona,

Thank you for your attachment, which fulfills the conditions of the Oath. May I take this opportunity to say that you are a remarkably handsome man, which allied to your formidable business sense no doubt makes up a remarkable package.

Jonathan Mokoena:

Her Royal Highness,

Greetings to you.

Please, below are my contact address both in home land Kenya and in Ethiopia.

122 Kebele Avenue GRA Addis Ababa Ethiopia, or 140 Standard Street Nairobi Kenya.

I can arrange for a clean and comfortable Mercedes Car. You seem to have doubts, but Ghana has good and beautifully furnished hotels for visitors.

I am not sure of x-box, but in such big hotels you can find all sorts of computer games especially ones that the international community appreciates. I also assume that Pounds Sterling should do. Can you send to me copies of your International passport, as a confidence building measure. You already have mine, dont you?

I have fulfilled every obligation towards you. I hope you are working on finalising this matter. I will be travelling back with you to England after the funds have been wired to your account abroad, disbursement and initial talks for profitable areas of investment.

Princess Margaret:

My Dear Mr. Mokeona,

Poor Sir Marmite has had a relapse after slipping at Brixton Palace during the recent rave pageant, and so it is all up to Me I am afraid at the moment, and I trust you will bear with Me.

The hotel sounds tip-top. Would you make reservations for four for the nights of December 14,15,16. We will use the names of Dame Edna Everidge, Marty Feldman, Bertie Wooster and Lady Macbeth to allay suspicion.

Prince Darren is still asking about his X-Box can you please check what is the situation?

I appreciate your need to have some proof that We are whom We say we are. Unfortunately Palace protocol means sending My official passport is out of the question.

Jonathan Mokoena:

Dear Margaret,

I pray that Sir Marmite bounce back fast. Will you be travelling with Sir Marmite?

As per hotel, I will make a reservation, but could you inform me how your spreading will be. I mean, are you all ladies? And will you be occupying separate rooms? Am I dealing with only you in this business or with four of you?

I still would want to hear your voice, can't you get a mobile phone I can call you on. Let us chat even for once, this is natural for a venture of this magnitude.

I need to have details of your flight.

Princess Margaret:

My Dear Mr. Mokeona,

Once the final technicalities are agreed I am indeed hoping to travel with Sir Marmite. However if he proves too unwell then I will make a substitution from My personal staff.

The two princes may share a room, as they currently do at Castle Popadum, but naturally separate rooms will be required for Sir Marmite and myself. In the absence of Sir Marmite it will be Myself with whom you should be dealing. I don't anticipate being away from the Palace now until the start of the hedgehog shoot, in January.

I don't have a mobile phone (Her Majesty has forbidden such things as not befitting Her court) but I will endeavour to find a number you can use. I will be able to confirm flight details shortly, and will appreciate if you can get the hotel end sewn up nicely for Us, there's a good chap.

Princess Margaret:

My Dear Mokeona

It seems that Sir Marmite will be away from duty for some time. The best person to assist Me will be Dame Agatha Bristol CBE, the Royal Chambermaid and Holder of the Bedpan.

Her involvement will be welcome as the Princes will no doubt need a firm hand during our sojourn. Once they heard that an X-Box is likely to be available, they grew very excited. Prince Clyde is old enough to look after himself, but Darren and Wayne can be rather a problem if not kept occupied. Perhaps you have some nieces I can introduce them to during our stay?

We still await the finalizing of all travel details from your end. Please note that I require the Daily Telegraph each morning, air conditioning, and plenty of face wipes to hand should your peculiar climate prove awkward.

Lady Agatha Bristol:

Your most Gracious Royal Highness,

I have, by your command, spoken to the Staff of the Royal Flight at the base in Wankershire. Every aeroplane is available, ma'am, and I respectfully suggest you select one, and I will make sure that it is prepared according to your specification.

Will Mr. Mokeona be requiring tea?

Yours ever,

Dame Agatha Bristol, CBE

Royal Chambermaid and Holder of the Bedpan

Princess Margaret:

Agatha,

Best let Mr. Mokeona speak for himself on the delicate matter of tea. Good work with the Wankershire flight, by the way, but I think We need to be discreet on this one and will be travelling under disguised identity.

Lady Agatha Bristol:

Your Most Gracious Royal Highness,

As ever you are correct.

We are preparing flight plans for Zaire, ma'am. Sir Arthur Daley has a house there, which could be convenient.

Princess Margaret:

Lady Agatha,

We are NOT travelling to Zaire, but Ghana for goodness sake. Please stay on the ball with this one, and remember it is your last chance to make good.

Lady Agatha Bristol:

Your Highness,

I have reserved a flight on BA Flight 332 to Mogadishu, in Somalia.

Somalia, I believe, is close to Ghana. I am trying to find out if there's a bus service to take you to Ghana from there.

Your Highness, Mr. Mokoena has not informed us of which tea he prefers.

Jonathan Mokoena:

Dear Sir/Madam,

I do not understand what is happening. This whole thing is confusing to say the least.

For christ sake there is a direct flight to Ghana on a daily basis on BA.I do not have to be in london to know this. Margaret should get back to me,ASAP.

Lady Agatha Bristol:

Dear Sir,

Please forgive me. I was looking at the map of Africa the wrong way.

I am pleased to say that I have booked a flight for the Royal Party to The Congo.

I trust this is in order, ma'am?

Mr. Mokoena, sir, I still do not know which type of tea you favor.

•

Jonathan Mokoena:

Dear Margaret,

Please do not be discouraged by what I am about to write, but this has been bothering me.

The Princess Margaret I know is late and died at the age of 71. All necessary search I have made about you and the Castles you mentioned came to nill, even your Duchess of Tesco produced no results. I have made extensive search and could not lay hands on any tangible information about your person.I asked for a phone number and copies of passport ,but these were tactically avoided for reasons I see as flimsy .I am afraid of working into the hands of International Security Agents especially now there is money lundering laws here and there.I will only be rest assured when you can give me added info,period.

You have to understand my apprehension. I am a top notch in the AU and cannot allow myself to walk into murky waters,my job and position is enviable that any slip will land me into trouble that could consume me for life. Put yourself into my shoe then you can understand the way I feel.

With all respect Madam,tell me whom you are and I have promised to keep this to myself and so shall it be.I sent my passport to you,why can't you send yours to me,there is always an exception to the rule.

Princess Margaret:

My Dear Jonathan

My Aunt Margaret was laid to rest some months ago as you rightly observe, a sad event reported around the world. I am still in mourning. I am clearly not to be confused with the dearly departed.

Castle Popadum goes under the offical name of Windsor Castle. The name Popadum is a traditional family one, used out of habit as the facade of that ancient and venerable pile reminds the viewer of a particular kind of English cake, the lemon popadum. There is no mystery about this but I can see how how it has become confusing.

As far as supplying confirmatory documents, my actions are circumscribed by concerns over security. It was only a few years back since the Queen Mother was mugged down the Fulham Road. However I have obtained a phone number: 00 906 403 07xx which should serve to allay your doubts. This must never be divulged to your friends or tribe members.

I feel you are growing less serious. Perhaps it would be best after all to end it now, as Sir Marmite intimated over a bunch of grapes at the royal Ken Dodd Hospital. I am afraid he takes a very cynical view of your intentions.

Margaret

Jonathan Mokoena:

Her Royal Highness,

May you live in interesting times and how are you? I send you my belated heart felt condolences on the death of your beloved Aunt. May her soul rest in perfect peace, Amen. I was not informed fully on your background. Please tell Sir Marmite that there is nothing ulterior about my motives or intentions. Take it from me Margaret, we shall prevail. Having worked in high places I have come to know what it takes to keep matters discreet and confidential.

I did not like the way Lady Agatha Bristol addressed me as a colonial fellow.I take exception to that.I am no less human,and have gone ahead to catch the golden fleece.

Thanks for your co-operation and my regards to the Royal Household.

Princess Margaret:

My Dear Mokeona,

Lady Agatha has been reminded to treat you with all the dignity and respect you deserve.

What news of the X-box? Prince Darren was very insistent this morning and quite spoilt My morning walk with the corgis over Toxteth Heath.

Jonathan Mokoena:

Her Royal Highness,

I must reiterate that I am delighted to have you as partner, since your background has formed a facade through which this money can be assimilated into your country's financial system without any complications. Now I beleive you, that you and I form a formidable package.

I have made up my mind to travel to Ghana come Sunday 8th Dec,2002,so I can facilitate the issue of reservation myself.I will also be in Ghana till your arrival on the 14th.

I spoke with the banker,and told him that we shall meet him on the 16th. Dear Margaret, considering the work this man is doing for us,is it possible to buy three Bvlgari wristwatches(with chronometer)for the banker and his colleagues.The banker is the first individual to run a private bank there, so it has to be something worthwhile.

Can you give me a code that I can be using to communicate with you in due course.

Princess Margaret:

My Dear Mr. Mokeona (or may I be permitted to call you Jonathan?)

Lady Agatha will have confirmed the travel arrangements very shortly for Our travel outwards on the 14th. I was perturbed that your banker is so casually involving other people. Is that wise?

I will delighted to find some watches for you when I next visit Knightsbridge. There will be quite a bit of room in the diplomatic pouch! I wonder if by a similar good favour you are able to provide some items for our little party when We arrive? I rashly promised Sir Marmite a tribal headress to cheer him up. I will offer most any asking price to make the old gentleman happy.

Any news on the X-Box by the way? Prince Wayne has been greatly taken by the new game "Sucker Time 2," and wonders if this is available in your country?

Lady Agatha Bristol:

Your most Gracious Royal Highness,

Sir Hugh Janus, the Chancellor, contacted me this morning. He was blunt, to say the least, ma'am. Not only does he feel that Mr. Mokoena is a conman, he is greedy as well, because he wants the Bulgari watches.

Princess Margaret:

My Dear Lady Agatha,

This is indeed disturbing news. I have grown quite attached to the little fellow. I suggest that I allow Mokeona to defend his reputation against such grave allegations.

Jonathan Mokoena:

DEAR AGATHA,

I AM NOT A CONMAN AND NEVER WILL BE.I TAKE EXCEPTION TO THIS STATEMENT.

Lady Agatha Bristol:

Your Highness,

If I have offended Mr. Mokoena, I do apologise. But I am duty-bound to point out Her

Majesty's Government's concerns. Sir Hugh Janus also wishes to see more evidence of these funds.

Jonathan Mokoena:

Dear Margaret,

Thanks for your last mail. I wonder who is wrong on the spelling of bvlgari. Yes you could call me Jonathan.I must say that I am not comfortable with the way this new lady you introduced write.I have received subtle insults from her.

I only suggested something for the banker Nana kwame Boateng and his colleagues. Boateng was only told that the money came from the sale of real estate in Ghana (which incidentally is a hot area of business there).

I do not understand what brought about a conman.Is it because I made a suggestion? That I did not get the spelling right does not make me one(though I know I got it right).,afterall in your mails some spellings are got wrongly(due typographic),and like wise mine to you.Does this make us semi-literate?I do not need it,as i do have some.I do nt intend to write much,a suggestion is optional and does not confer anything on anyone.I beleive in moderation in all I do,and you can sence it from the way I write.

Regards Jonathan

Princess Margaret:

My dear Jonathan,

Excuse the nagging doubts of My servants. It is essential that I am protected from any disgrace. Some time ago, we had problems with a Mr. Albert Schweitzer who claimed he was doing charitable work in Africa. We soon saw through his yarn and sent him packing, I can tell you!

I am satisfied that you are a thoroughly reliable and responsible fellow...

Please proceed with the reservations, using the secret names. I will be coming with Lady Agatha and two of the Princes. There will also be Fergie, our dog.

Jonathan Mokoena:

Dear Madam,

I hope I am not been misunderstood on the issue of the gift.I personally do not need any.I thought that a gift would be heart warming to a gentleman whose assistance to us is immeasurable at the moment. I am talking of a Bvlgari wristwatch.Thats all.Unless you have other ideas.

With this I hope I am understood.Thank you.

Regards Jonathan

Lady Agatha Bristol:

Dear Sir,

I am but a conduit; a messenger for others' views. My own opinions, on your integrity or what kind of watches you want, are totally irrelevant.

What kind of tea do you favour?

Jonathan Mokoena:

Dear Margaret,

I bought my flight ticket to ghana already.Once I get in I will call you. Please advise on a convenient time frame to call.

There are African masks in the arts shop in the Hotel,I am sure of this. Since the colour and carvings of these masks are varied and diverse in concept,it will be advisable to make choices from the range, rather than restricting the choice to mine.

Princess Margaret:

My Dear Mr. Mokeona,

I have found a lovely Bvlgari item for you. Its diamonds shine quite lovely as it lies on the desk in front of Me, next the picture of my dear husband Count Monte Cristo.

I am more likely to be in the office 9 - 5 GMT. Outside of these times I may be walking the corgis or attending the state bingo sessions at the House of Lords.

I think it will be a pleasant gesture to exchange the paperwork over a glass of sherry, or whatever passes for such, in Ghana when we finally meet, my dear chap.

I look forward to hearing how our travel itinerary has been formed, just to put Sir Marmite's mind at rest. I was with him last night at his sick bed, and he was very nervous about the business despite my reassurances.

Lady Agatha Bristol:

Your Highness,

We have prepared the Royal Flight to fly to The Congo. Is this correct?

Jonathan Mokoena:

Dear Agatha,

You are flying to Ghana and not Congo. There is a direct flight from London to Ghana daily. How come up to this moment you are still looking at the map of Africa wrongly, this is disturbing to say the least.

Lady Agatha Bristol:

Dear Mr. Mokoena,

I'm terribly sorry. My knowledge of the colonies only extends to the Isle of Wight.

Is Ghana the country next to Sudan?

Jonathan Mokoena:

Dear Agatha,

Let me hear from Her Royal Highness on the arrangement you are making for the trip.

Staying just in the hotel till Saturday is boring to say the least.

Lady Agatha Bristol:

Dear Mr. Mokoena,

Security concerns prohibit me from telling you the Royal party's travel arrangements.

I am not sure of your "boring" comment but Her Highness will not be pleased.

Perhaps Sir Marmite was correct about our colonial subjects after all.

Jonathan Mokoena:

Dear Margaret,

For Christ sake you are with the deposit documents and you are repository of this whole matter. It took a lot of courage to write you, because I feared someone turning my offer down and my inadvertently exposing it. You have a duty to relax the old man on this. I cannot harm you neither do I harbour any ill intention. All the enormous amount of money we hear on foreign magazines that are taken out to foreign accounts did not just get there, it was facilitated by people. You and I can do it, only if agree. We should protect each others interest, in this way we can stay united and achieve success.

Jonathan

The wristwatch is for Mr. Boateng and Co.

Princess Margaret:

My dear Mr. Mokeona,

Please do not take such a tone with Myself or refer to Sir Marmite so casually. He has been a loyal retainer to the crown, having fought with distinction at Agincourt.

This is all irregular to say the least. I have half a mind to cancel this business and spend the 14th December at the Brixton Country Dance Championships instead. Control your manners, young man, or I shall cast you aside.

Jonathan Mokoena:

Her Royal Highness,

If by Saturday night(14th Decmber)I do not meet with you,I will get back to Ethiopia.

I am sure that you all will embrace and appreciate me when you see the money with you two eyes. Afterall money has moved out of Africa in various means and through the help of Foreigners like you.Why then should an oppurtunity be scuttled by a mere doubt.

I regret that Sir Marmite is sick, I am a christian and I do appreciate my fellow human beign.

The ball is now in your court,I am waiting for news from you.Take Care and God bless.

Princess Margaret:

My dear Jonathan,

Thank you for putting the reservations through. I assume the agreed secret identities have been used? Lady Agatha is clearly confused on Geography. You will excuse this blip caused by her former reliance on Laudanum. This is no longer the case but has occasional effects on her faculties.

Any news on the X-Box?

Jonathan Mokoena:

Her Royal Highness,

I have tried to call your number and it was not connecting.

You can reach me on 233-24-xxxxxx,this phone is in my room,i requested for it from the hotel for security purposes.

I thought it wise to send this picture, for you to know that I mean no harm. I know that this will make the difference between doubt and reality.

Let me know your final itineary.

Do have a nice day.

Jonathan

Princess Margaret:

Dear Jonathan

Alas, this is all I get:

Content-Type: image/jpeg; name="copy percent2Oof percent20Dollar.jpg"; name="copy of Dollar.jpg" Content-Disposition: attachment; filename="copy of Dollar.jpg" Content-Transfer-Encoding: base64 /9j/4AAQSkZJRgABAQAAAQABA

Which is not much help as you will appreciate. At his bedside, Sir Marmite suggested that perhaps it was code. We both thought of contacting Sir Sexton Blake, the retired MI5 code breaker, for help but decided this would be unnecessary.

If you are not serious I will cease all communication, and draw solace from knowing an embarrassing incident has been thus avoided. There are other matters also requiring My regular attention, such as flower arranging classes in the Abbey.

Jonathan Mokoena:

The Money again
Courtesy: A. Scammer

Her Royal Highness, I am truly amazed that the attachment did not come this time around. I will try again.

Princess Margaret:

Jonathan,

Thank you so much for the lovely picture of the money. I will confirm My travel arrangements shortly. Will it be possible to have cars waiting for us at the airport?

Jonathan Mokoena:

Dear Margaret,

Let me know flight details. The hotel will be picking you up at the airport.

Lady Agatha Bristol:

Your Most Gracious Royal Highness,

I have grave news.

Young Prince Jordan walked into my study to discuss his Royal engagements for the day (the roller-skating dance in the Royal County of Bounds Green) and he saw the email sent by Mr. Mokoena. Prince Jordan feels the picture is a mocked up, indeed amateurish depiction of money that does not exist. On top of everything, Mr. Mokoena still won't tell me which tea he favours.

Princess Margaret:

Lady Agatha,

This is very disconcerting. I will have contact the Prince to stress the faith and trust I have in Mr. Mokeona. However I know that ever since his accident with the badger baiting ceremony, the Prince has been liable to fits of temper, which make reasoning with him difficult.

I believe Orange Pekoe will be sufficient for our friends, or perhaps Pizzle.

Princess Margaret:

My dear Jonathan,

Sir Marmite (now slightly better, thank you) has asked what security measures will be in place at the hotel. He feels such issues must be resolved, especially after the dreadful taunting and bottle throwing from the Welsh separatists given to Lord Winalot yesterday at Asda. While Lady Agatha will be happy to patrol the corridors (she has a small Walther PPK and special forces training) she can't do everything on her own.

Has the La Palm Royal Beach got a policy on dogs? Fergie can be rather a handful and tends to nibble at curtains and things if excited by new sights and sounds.

Lady Agatha Bristol:

Your Most Gracious Royal Highness,

Prince Jordan is adamant that Mr. Mokoena is (in His Highness' words) "a filthy swine, a scam artist and a ne'er do well." The intelligence reports on Mr. Mokoena from MI6 are inconclusive.

I await your instructions.

Jonathan Mokoena:

Dear Margaret,

The hotel says you will have to take care of your pet,feed it and bath it. another is that you will not be allowed to come with it,except you have a quarantine document.

I am amused when i read Lady Bristlo's mails.Why do you condone such utterances?

I doubt your seriousness if you can be asking question of terrorist barely two days to your earlier schedule. Lady agatha has rained abuses at me with reckless abandon since you brought her into this,how does she intend to shake my hand?

Princess Margaret:

My Dear Jonathan,

Please accept My apologies about the sentiments expressed by Lady Agatha. Please try not to be so touchy, there's a good chap.

Now, concerning my arrival on the 14th. Lady Agatha has made the reservations. Visas have been obtained from The Duchess of Duke Street at the Foreign Office. I suppose Lady Agatha will just have to be extra vigilant. This of course brings its own dangers: I remember vividly the trouble we had when she brought down a Hare Krishna collector at Luton Airport, fearing his friendly overtures were a terrorist advance.

Where and where shall we meet and how will we know each other? I have a ginger wig and a splendid pair of Armani lemon jeans which will surely make Me stand out in the crowd, while allowing a casual anonymity. Please advise.

Lady Agatha Bristol:

Your Most Glorious Royal Highness,

The arrangements have indeed been made with the hotel. I am taking the following equipment:

Glock 9mm

2 x Heckler & Koch MP5

2 x Remington 12 gauge pump-action shotguns

4 x Sig Saur .357 automatics Pro-Series 10X Sniper Rifle with night-vision scope

6 x Uzi 9mm sub-machine guns

Smith and Wesson .45 pistol

Twin .44 Desert Eagle pistols

12 x TakeDown concussion grenades

2 x P-90 Assault Rifles

2 x Stinger rocket launchers

I hope that this is in order.

Jonathan Mokoena:

Dear Mrs. Bristol,

Why not come down with the whole arsenal in the British Army armoury. That will be splendid.

Jonathan

Lady Agatha Bristol:

Dear Mr. Mokoena,

The correct form of address is Lady Agatha.

I would point out that the security of the Royal Family is of paramount importance. National Security issues can affect the whole world.

Princess Margaret:

My Dear Lady Agatha,

While I am pleased that you value Our security, this seems a little over the top. I feel we should discard the automatics and the rocket launcher, and retain the side arms as an absolute minimum.

I hate to think of Princes Darren and Wayne around anything more substantial, especially after the trouble with their catapault during the last speech by Her Majesty. Lord Marmite had a bruise the size of a walnut beneath his silks. Please downsize the arsenal, before you frighten our hosts off completely.

Sir Marmite Luny-Binns:

Your Royal Highness,

I am just back at my desk after my unfortunate accident, and am alarmed by news of the removal of some small arms by Lady Agatha from the Women's Institute Brigade offices here at the Palace. It is all getting terribly out of hand. What real evidence has Mokeona given us that the money exists, what guarantees does he offer for your safety? Your charging of expensive watches to the household accounts is also a matter for concern.

Please, listen to an old friend and reconsider the whole venture.

Marmite

PS Thank you for the flowers and chocolates, they were lovely but I prefer soft centres.

Jonathan Mokoena:

Dear Margaret,

The truth I have unveiled,and it's now your turn to make do your promise,and finalise this matter. The issue of your security is uppermost in my mind,and anything that affects you obviously affects me,since we are on this together.I am not immuned to problems too.

Your security in Ghana is guaranteed since this country is a tourist attraction and has a good number of foreigners. Over 15,000 nationals of Europe,Asia and American citizens sojourn here.This you can see on the beaches, roads, streets and even on the pool side of any good hotel. Nothing negative will befall you.

Princess Margaret:

Dear Jonathan,

Thank you for your kind assurances concerning Our security. You will understand our wariness as I once had my bottom pinched in Kampala, not a pleasant experience.

Do you have a list of recommended night clubs? I imagine We will want to get out a bit. Sir Marmite has heartily recommended that the Princes see the exotic dancers.

We look forward to seeing you on the 14th.

Jonathan Mokoena:

Dear Mragaret,

Do not bother I am not frightened by those ammunition,rather it makes a mockery of the whole thing,doesn't it?

Since you will be away for three days or so,I think you can do without fergie. I am still in the hotel waiting. What time is your flight? Like I said the hotel staff will pick you up at the airport. I am trying to be discreet as possible. My dress code will be casua,1 to avoid detection from any known diplomat in Ghana. Once you call I will run down to the hotel and meet you.

Princess Margaret:

Dear Jonathan,

I am loathe to travel without My dear Fergie, as she will inevitably pine without Me. I am sure you have a favoured elephant cub or perhaps a baby bullock to which you are attached?

I believe our flight will arrive at 5.30, but Lady Agatha can confirm all that sort of thing.

Is there any news about the X-Box? One can soon get right into the devilish things, and I find myself fairly addicted these days in between state engagements.

Lady Agatha Bristol:

Your Most Respected Royal Highness,

I have organised all the travel arrangements.

We have £100 notes available and they can be tightly packed in suitcases.

Jonathan Mokoena:

Her Royal Highness,

As per having some sight scene,this will not be a problem at all.There is no limit to joints that you can peruse in Ghana.There are also high calibre clubs foreigners like you normally visit. I hope we can have enough time to go round. I look forward to shaking your hands for the first time and hope to see you.

May the good Lord lighten our minds.

Jonathan Mokoena:

Dear Margaret,

I am still in the hotel,it is quite boring with just one or two persons to talk to in a day. I hopoe you can give me your final itinerary and also a phone call. My regards to Lady Agatha and I am happy she has succeded in scaling down her armoury.

Best Wishes, Jonathan

Jonathan Mokoena:

Dear Margaret,

It just occured to me that there is an info I have not given you. If you are calling me while in the hotel,then you will just call 024-7032xx, whereas if calling from London you include 233-24-7032xx.

The X-box I was told is one of the comnputer programmes that can be found on their system,so they told me.

Are you still coming on the 14th? Could you please contact the Security Company and inform them of our visit to their office come 16th Dec,2002. I am still waiting for your final contact.

Princess Margaret:

My Dear Jonathan

Be a good chap and attend to these details on My behalf. My party will be there on the 16th, they may wish to put out sandwiches and some cake for us (nothing too dry, and clean cutlery please). Lady Agatha will copy you in on the BA flight details.

Lady Agatha Bristol:

Mr. Mokoena,

We will be on flight BA160 to Cape Town, which I believe is the capital of Ghana.

Her Royal Highness may be addressed as Ma'am or Your Highness. Do not - ever - go to touch Her Majesty. Failure to comply could have dire circumstances and none of us want that. Do not offer your hand unless it is offered first by Her Highness. Do not speak unless spoken to, and bow when Her Highness comes into the room. I'm sure you can grasp these simple matters of etiquette.

Princess Margaret:

My Dear Lady Agatha

It is a good job that I appreciate your little jokes. Please put Jonathan out of his misery with the right information. Jonathan we will be flying out first thing tomorrow so please ensure all is in readiness. We do not wish to be embarrassed by any snarl ups.

Lady Agatha Bristol:

Your Most Gracious Royal Highness,

I would not joke in Your presence. I have booked the flights to Cape Town, which I believe is in your desired country of Sudan.

Jonathan Mokoena:

Dear Agatha,

You have to know I can easily read inbetween the line.This poses no problem at all.If you can hand down some points of etiquette with such dexterity,why then do you mix up simple matters like, destination etc.I do not expect an answer on this.

I wonder.

Lady Agatha Bristol:

Dear Mr. Mokoena,

I think that you are perfectly aware of my feelings—that you are a greedy, ghastly little man whose only interest is in lining his own pockets. I am, however, duty-bound to follow my orders.

Jonathan Mokoena:

Dear Margaret,

I know you have read Agatha's bombshell to me,it's copied to you. Well the question is where are you in all these and what will happen now? There has never been an admonition from you to her,on her utterances.

Princess Margaret:

My Dear Jonathan

I apologise for poor Lady Agatha's behaviour. I have been sympathetic to her lapses, as we were all under a strain which I felt it best to conceal. Lady Agatha has been very close to Sir Marmite (they fought in the Falkands together) and his illness has been distracting to her.

The worst has happened, My friend, and you should prepare yourself. At 12.08 last night, at his home at the Toxteth Palace, Marmite passed on. He had been at his desk, brave soul. But a relapse, brought on perhaps by his unwise exposure during the recent badger baiting tourneys, hastened his demise. I am distraught at such a loss for the Commonwealth, indeed the world. I ask that you bear with us. There will be a few days of national mourning, followed by the funeral at Westminster Abbey. Sir Marmite will be missed. I am sure that his warm nature and aristocratic charm warmed your heart, as it did all who knew this brave, one-armed bon-vivant. I cannot write anything else at the moment, as tears are making it hard to see the keyboard.

Princess Margaret:

My Dear Jonathan

Thank you for understanding about the delay which the sad loss of Sir Marmite has brought. Your silence as a matter of respect in our moment of grief is much appreciated.

I was wondering if we can arrange to see you in England during the ceremony. There is a spare seat at the Abbey with a view of the cortege, and within easy distance of the snack table. The following names are on the confirmed mourners list, and if there is anyone you recognise, please tell us so that we can seat you together:

Mr Zuma Mako, King Etete, Mr Barry Kelly, Pres Abacha, Jonas Savimbi, Pres Mobutu, Emir and Mrs Usman, Pres Mobutu II, Pres Kabila, Pres Abacha II, Engr Mack Davies, Mr Reginard Tuner, Mr and Mrs Fredrick Ndiaye, Pres Abacha III, Chief Michael Williams, Mr Bruce C Warren, Pres Mobutu III, Engr Allan P Seaman, Engr Creek Johnson, Mr Smith B Andraes, Engr John Creek, Dr Andrew Kamara, Mr Oyeyemi, Pres Robert Guei, Mr and Mrs Adamu, Dr Stephen Smith, Dr and Mrs Paul Williams, Pedro F Hasler, Mr Robert Eke, Dr and Master Butulazi Abinadar, Mr Nazral Allahi, Dr MUS Ibrahim, Dr and Mrs Abubakar, Sadiq Dan'azimi, Chief Mishack Noel, Chief Willson Kumallo, Mr Gerrand Schwartz, Mr Smith Sithole, Mr Emeka Obinna, Chief Vincent Kamara, Ilichy Miracsky, Captin Stabbin, Michael M Barrymore, and Lonslo Tossov.

Once formalities are concluded in the Abbey, we can discuss your interesting offer, perhaps over a scam sandwich, as you seem to swallow everything else...

Jonathan Mokoena:

DEAR MARGARET,

I WILL RATHER BE HERE SINCE I HAVE ALWAYS KNOWN THAT THE DEAD MARMITE IS ONLY YOUR CREATION AND A FIGMENT OF YOUR IMAGINATION

I HAVE ALWAYS KNOWN THIS IS A JOKE,SO DO NOT BOTHER ANYMORE.I WILL LOOK OUT FOR MORE SERIOUS PEOPLE. THANKS FOR YOUR TIME AND ENTERTAINMENT.

JONATHAN

Princess Margaret:

My Dear Jonathan

Do not thank me, as your own gullibility and greed have given much pleasure to many people (and will continue to do so, on the web). Of course, you may be speaking to me somewhere else, and not know it - this "goodbye" could be premature. Thanks for the photocopy of your passport. It will be a big help to the prosecuting authorities.

Jonathan Mokoena:

Please stop mailing me.

Lady Agatha Bristol:

You won't even know it's us. Looking forward to continuing our correspondence!

Yours ever,

Lady Agatha Bristol, CBE

A PARTY GAME

Here is a party game to help scam-proof your friends. It is adaptable as a drinking game if you are so minded.

- ❍   Choose two scam letters.
- ❍   Give one to a friend.
- ❍   Take turns reading alternate paragraphs.
- ❍   Be very serious.
- ❍   If any of the following words or phrases are spoken, the guests must shout the word or phrase and shake noise-making objects (or drink, or all of the above):

_ lawyer	_ modality
_ confidential or confidentiality	_ parenthesis (or end-parenthesis)
_ expenses	_ risk-free
_ ghastly	_ secret
_ God	_ trust fund
_ government	_ urgent
_ million	_ Western Union

Whoever laughs first loses, but it's not a bad way to lose.
Three pairs of letters are included below to start you off.

ROUND ONE

I AM DR. (MRS.) MARYAM ABACHA, WIFE OF LATE GENERALSANI ABACHA, EX-MILITARY HEAD OF STATE OF NIGERIA WHODIED ON THE 8TH OF JUNE 1998 OF HEART PROBLEMS. ICONTACTED YOU BECAUSE OF MY NEED TO DEAL WITH PERSONSWHOM MY FAMILY AND I

HAVE HAD NO PREVIOUS PERSONALRELATIONSHIPS.

SINCE THE DEATH OF MY HUSBAND, MYFAMILY HAS BEEN SUBJECTED TO ALL SORTS OF HARASSMENT AND INTIMIDATION WITH LOTS OF NEGATIVE REPORTS EMANATING FROM THE GOVERNMENT AND THE PRESS ABOUT MYHUSBAND. THE PRESENT GOVERNMENT HAS ALSO ENSURED THATOUR BANK ACCOUNTS ARE FROZEN AND ALL ASSETS SEIZED.

IT IS IN VIEW OF THIS, THAT I SEEK YOUR CO-OPERATIONAND ASSISTANCE IN THE TRANSFER OF THIS SUM OFUS$50,000,000 (FIFTY MILLION UNITED STATES DOLLARSONLY) BEING THE VERY LAST OF MY FAMILY FUND IN MYPOSSESSION AND CONTROL. THE FEDERAL GOVERNMENT SEIZED ALL OUR PROPERTIES AND FROZE ALL OUR ACCOUNTS BOTH LOCAL AND INTERNATIONAL.

AFTER THE DEATH OF MYHUSBAND, BUT MY ONLY HOPE NOW IS THIS AVAILABLE US$50MCASH WHICH MY HUSBAND CAREFULLY PACKAGED AND DEPOSITEDAS PHOTOGRAPHIC MATERIALS WITH A SECURITY COMPANYOUTSIDE NIGERIA.

WE THEREFORE NEED YOUR URGENT ASSISTANCE TO CLEAR THIS MONEY FROM THE SECURITY COMPANY AND MOVE IT TO YOUR COUNTRY OR ANY OTHER PLACE FOR INVESTMENT INTO A PROFITABLE BUSINESS.

IF YOU ARE WILLING TO ASSIST US IN CLEARING AND INVESTING THIS MONEY ON OUR BEHALF,PLEASE, CONTACT OUR LAWYER (LAWYER CHRISTAIN ADAMS OF INTEGRITY CHAMBER) IMMEDIATELY WITH THE FOLLOWING EMAIL ADDRESS:chrisada@justice.com. HE WILL GIVE YOU THE DETAILS AND NEGOTIATE YOUR REWARD WHICH I CAN ASSURE YOU WILL BE VERY SUBSTANTIAL.

I CANNOT DEAL DIRECTLY WITH YOU BECAUSE I AM BEING MONITORED BY GOVERNMENT AGENTS. PLEASE ENSURE TO KEEP THIS PROPOSAL VERY SECRET AND CONFIDENTIAL AND IF YOU HAVE ANYQUESTION PLEASE YOU ARE FREE TO ASK FOR ANWSERS..

SINCERELY, DR (MRS.) MARYAM ABACHA   I AM MRS. P. MOBUTU SESE-SEKO, WIDOW OF LATE PRESIDENT MOBUTU SESE-SEKO OF ZAIRE, NOW KNOWN AS DEMOCRATIC REPUBLIC DU CONGO (DRC). I AM MOVED TO WRITE YOUTHIS LETTER IN CONFIDENCE CONSIDERING MY PRESENT CIRCUMSTANCE AND SITUATION.

I ESCAPED TO COTE 'D' IVOIRE. MY HUSBAND LATER MOVED TO MOROCCO WHERE HE DIED OF CANCER DISEASE. THE NEW HEAD OF STATE OF (DRC) MR. LAURENT KABILA HAD MADE ARRANGEMENTS WITH THE SWISS GOVERNMENT TO FREEZE ALL MY LATE HUSBAND'S BILLIONS IN SWISS BANKS.

I AND MY CHILDREN DECIDED TO LIE LOW IN AFRICA TO STUDY THE SITUATION. ONE OF MY LATE HUSBAND'S CHETEAUX IN SOUTHERN FRANCE, ESTATES IN BELGIUM AND COFFEE PLANTATION IN BRAZIL HAS BEEN CONFISCATED BY THE RESPECTIVE GOVERNMENTS, AS

SUCH I HAD TO CHANGE MY IDENTITY TO A DIFFERENT ONE SO THAT MY INVESTMENT WILL NOT BE TRACED AND CONFISCATED.

I HAVE DEPOSITED THE SUM OF FOURTY-FOUR MILLION UNITED STATES DOLLARS ONLY (US$44M), MAINTAINED BY A SECURITY OUTFIT FOR SAFE KEEPING IN ONE OF THE AFRICAN COUNTRIES. THESE FUNDS ARE SECURITY CODED TO PREVENT THEM FROM FALLING INTO WRONG HANDS.

I WILLINTRODUCE YOU TO MY SON, MR. BAHIR MOBUTU SESE-SEKO, WHO IS PRESENTLY BASED IN THE COUNTRY WHERE THIS FUNDS, IS BEING KEPT.

I WANT YOU TO ASSIST IN INVESTING THIS MONEY, BUT I WILL NOT WANT MY IDENTITY REVEALED. I WILL ALSO WANT TO BUY STOCK IN MULTINATIONAL COMPANIES AND TO ENGAGE IN OTHER SAFE AND NON SPECULATIVE INVESTMENTS. MAY I EMPHASIZE THE CONFIDENTIALITY, WHICH THIS BUSINESS DEMANDS AND HOPE THAT YOU WILL NOT BETRAY THE TRUST WHICH I REPOSE IN YOU. IF YOU ARE READY TO ASSIST US, MY SON SHALL PUT YOU IN THE PICTURE OF THE BUSINESS.

YOUARE ADVISE TO CONTACT MY SON MR BAHIR THROUGH THE EMAIL: johnson_mobutu@africana.com TO DISCUSS THE MODALITIES INCLUDING REMUNERATION FOR YOUR SERVICES.

BEST REGARDS,MRS. P.M. SESE-SEKO

ROUND TWO
From : Johnson Edward
Abidjan, Ivory Coast West Africa.

Dearest ,
Pls do reply me with my private email above for the confidentiality of this transaction. I got your name from the Internet, I prayed over it and selected your name due to its esteeming nature and the recommendations given to me as trust worthy person that I can do business with and by the recommendation , I must not hesitate to confide in you for this simple and sincere business .

I am Johnson Edward the only son of late Mr. and Mrs.George Edward. My father was a very wealthy cocoa merchant in Abidjan , the economic capital of Ivory coast, my father was po isoned to dearth by his business associates on one of their outings on a business trip . My mother died when I was a baby and since then my father took me so special.

Before the death of my father in a private hospital here in Abidjan he secretly called me on his bed side and told me that he has the sum of ten million,five hundred thousand United State Dollars. USD ($ 10.500,000) left in fixed / suspense account in one of the prime bank here in Abidjan ,that he used my name as his only son for the next of Kin in depositing of the fund.

He explained to me that it was because of this wealth that he was poisoned by his business associates. That I should seek for a foreign partner in a country of my choice where i will transfer this money and use it for investment purpose such as real estate management or hotel management .

Sir, I am honourably seeking your assistance in the following ways: (1) To provide a bank account into which this money would be transferred to . (2) of serve as a guardian of this fund since I am only 22years. (3) To make arrangement for me to come over to your country to further my education and to secure a resident permit in your country.

Moreover, sir i am willing to offer you 15 percent as compensation after the transfer of this fund into your account overseas.

Furthermore, you indicate your options towards assisting me as I believe that this transaction would be concluded within fourteen (14) days you signify interest to assist me.

Thanks and God bless. Best regards,
Johnson EdwardFROM: Miss L. B. CHRISTOPHER
MISSIONARY QUARTERS A15
CHURCH ROAD ACCRA GHANA

Dear respectful one
I feel good contacting you today I have read from your add in Internet knowing quiet well that this contact will bring a lasting relationship.With regard to your reputation and co-worshipper of God who will not disappoint me nor deny me in faith, I am directing this letter of assistance to you.

I am Miss Louisa. Christopher the only daughter of Mr.Christopher from Republicof Zimbabwe. My father was a wealthy Gold/Cocoamerchant who has business in many countries in Europe, America and Asian countries.According to my father, my own mother Died when I was about six, which means that I did not even know my mother very well.

Thestory is that my father Mr. Christopher was Poisoned to death by his business associates.But when he was about to die, he called us beside his sick bed and told us that he deposited the sum of Two Million seven hundred thousand United StateDollars(US$2.7M) with a bank there in Accra, the economic and administrative capital of Republic of Ghana.

Right now I am a first year student of business management.My only problem now is that since my father has been poisoned to death by his business Associates, I don't even trust any other person here again including my father's brothers and sisters.

I wantyou to help us in the following ways:1)I want you to provide a personal / company's bank Account where this amount here (US$2.700,000.00) can be Transferred.2) You are going to be the manager of this fund and Also my personal guardian. 3)You are going to procure admissions for us to continue our studies in your country.

You are going to receive 15 percent of the total sum for providing a bank account for this transfer.

We hope to receive your response, as it will Encourage us, to stop establishing further contacts as It regards to this subject matters, so that we will furnish you With a number where you can reach us Direct, on receipt of your positive response.

Waiting to hear from you soon Pls
Miss L.B. Christopher
MAKE IT A GREAT DAY!

ROUND THREE
From: "wayne mike"

REQUEST FOR URGENT BUSINESS RELATIONSHIP

First I must solicit your confidence in this transaction, this is by virtue of it's being very confidential.

I am Mr Wayne Mike, a director with the Bond Bank of Nigeria Lagos. I came to know of you in my private search for a reliable and reputable person to handle this confidential transaction which involves the transfer of a huge sum of money to a foreign bank account requiring maximum confidence.

The proposition an American, late engineer Charles Fredrick, an oil merchant/contractor with the Federal Government of Nigeria, until his death three years ago in a ghastly motor accident, banked with us here at Bond Bank, Lagos, and had a closing balance of US$15,000,000,000:00 million (fifteen million united states dollars) which the bank now questionable expect to be claimed by next of kin or alternatively, be donated to a discredited trust fund for arms and ammuninations at a military war college here in Nigeria.

Fervent efforts being made by the Bond Bank to get in touch with any of the Charles's family has proved abortive. This is because of the perceived possibility of not being able to locate late. Engineer Charles's next of kin (he has no wife or children) that the management under the influence of our chairman and member of the board of directors, retired major-general Kalu Ike Kalu, that an arrangement be made for the funds to be declared unclaimed and subsequently, be donated to the trust fund for arms and ammunation to further enhance the cause of war in Africa and the world in general.

In other to avert this negative development, some of my trust colleagues and i now seek your permission to have you standing as next of kin to late. Engineer Charles's, so that the funds will be released and payed to your account as next of kin. All documents and proofs to enable you get the funds will be carefully worked out and moreso re-assuring you of a 100 percent risk free involvement.

You will get a negotiable percentage of this money for assisting. We shall also map out a percentage of this money to take care of inccidental expenses that may arise. 30 percent will be for you, percent10 will be for any expensence that when come on our way, than percent60 will be for me and my colluges.

If this proposal okay by you, and assure us that you will not take undue advantage of the trust we hope to bestowe on you and your company, kindly get to me immediately via, email. If not interested please keep it very confidential.

Yours sincerely,
Mr. Wayne Mike From: "Omar El-Dagash"

Subject: Confidential Investment Proposal

First, I must solicit your confidence in this transaction, this is by virtue of its nature as being utterly CONFIDENTIAL and TOP SECRET. Though I know that a transaction of this magnitude will make any one apprehensive and worried, but I am assuring you that all will be well at the end of the day.

Let me start by introdusing myself properly to you. I am Mr. Omar El-Dagash, a Manager at the Union Bank Nigeria PLC, Lagos. I came to know of you in my search for a reliable person to handle a confidential transaction which involves the transfer of a huge sum of money to a foreign account requiring maximum confidence. I am not too really sure if you are my long lost contact whom I am trying to reach, but in anyway, please do take this message with a good heart and report back to me if you are not the person I think you are. I would explain more latter.

THE PROPOSITION: A foreigner, late Engineer Johnson Creek, an Oil Merchant / contractor with the federal Govenment of Nigeria, until his death three years ago in a ghastly air crash, banked with us here at Union Bank PLC., Lagos, and had a closing balance of USD$38.M (Thirty Eight Million, Five Hundred Thousand United States Dollars) which the bank now unquestionably expects to be claimed by any of his available foreign next of kin or alternatively be donated to a discredited trust fund for alms and ammunition at a military war college here in Nigeria.

Fervent valuable efforts are being made by the Union Bank to get in touch with any of the Creek family or relatives but all have proved to
no avail. It is because of the perceived possibility of not going to be able to locate any of late Engr. Johnson Creek's next of kin (he had no known wife and children) that the management under the influence of our Chairman, board of directors, Retired Major General Kalu Uke Kalu, that an arrangement for the fund to be declared "UNCLAIMABLE" and then be subsequently donated to the Trust Fund for Alms and Ammunition which will further enhance the courses of war in Africa and the world in general.

In order to avert this negative development, myself and some of my trusted colleagues here at the bank now seek for your permission to have you stand as late Engr. Johnson Creek's next of kin so that the fund, USD$38.5M would be transferred and paid into your account as the beneficiary next of kin. All documents and proves to enable you get this fund have been carefully worked out and we are assuring you a 100 percent risk free involvement.

For your assistance, your commission would be 30 percent. 10 percent has been set aside for expenses while the rest would be for myself and my colleagues for investment purposes in your country.

If this proposal is OK. by you and you do not wish to take advantage of the trust we hope to bestow on you and your company, then kindly get to me immediately via my email.

Regards,
OMAR EL-DAGASH

CHAPTER 7

WHAT YOU
CAN DO

In which we finally discuss headers.

DELETE IT

The healthiest thing is to just erase the email. Spam laws won't help. The Lads are criminals and don't care. First, though, print the email and stick it on your parents' refrigerator with a big skull and crossbones.

FILTER IT

Many ISPs offer filters, which rank incoming emails, such as SpamAssassin:

> Content preview: DR DESMOND BRWON NIGERIAN NATIONAL PETROLEUM CORP LAGOS REQUEST FOR URGENT BUSINESS RELATIONSHIP ... TRANSFER OF US$30,000,000.00

> Content analysis details: (9.1 points, 5.0 required)

pts rule name	description
0.4 SUBJ_ALL_CAPS	Subject is all capitals
0.0 URG_BIZ	BODY: Contains urgent matter
0.2 RISK_FREE	BODY: Risk free. Suuurreeee....
0.4 US_DOLLARS_3	BODY: Mentions millions of $ ($NN,NNN,NNN.NN)
0.5 NIGERIAN_BODY2	Message body looks like a Nigerian spam message 2+ etc.

The best filter, though, is your brain. Subject lines provide a hint:

> Business Relationship
> Urgent Business Relationship
> Request for Urgent Business Relationship
> Strictly Confidential
> Strictly Confidential/Urgent
> Business Proposal Strictly Confidential
> Confidential Urgent Business Proposal

The pattern should be emerging.

> Attn: President/M.D./CEO/Dear no one in particular

is another dead giveaway, even if you are a president, doctor, CEO, or dear, or all of that. You may reject out of hand anything "from" the Abacha, Savimbi or Kabila families. They are not writing to you. Emails From: and To: the same person are suspect, unless these are party invitations from friends, or memos from the boss. Subject lines suggesting an opportunity to bilk a government agency or sports association should be considered satire (and an attempt to rob you):

> Nigerian National Petroleum Corporation
> Petroleum Trust Fund
> Capital Flight
> FIFA World Youth Championship

Unfortunately for the other, no doubt innocent people bearing these names, a large proportion of scam emails are from someone named Bello or Usman. "Dead bank customer" letters disproportionately mention members of the mysteriously unlucky Creek family, who were all engineers, all ran off the road or died in airplane crashes, and all left no family. The mere mention of the name Creek should make the scam-o-meter click loudly.

"SHIELD" YOUR EMAIL ADDRESS

AOL provides a mails control feature, blocking mails from addresses not on a user's approved list. Other ISPs are starting to add an option which sets incoming emails from unknowns aside and prompts their senders for a human response before delivering them. This is meant to defeat automated spam; it may discourage the lazier scammers.

An email address displayed on a web page is harder to harvest automatically if obfuscated:

> j_okafor_AT_mycompany_DOT_com
> k_obasekiNOSPAM-at-yahoo.com

or displayed as a graphic.

REPORT IT TO THE ISP(S)

The scammer may have several providers, for his internet connection (dial-up, DSL, cable, ethernet, wireless) and email account(s). An ISP will not respond to a complaint without a header from the offending email. A header is information attached to an email, which traces its journey across a network. It is needed to determine if the spam came from "inside the house." The following email header will be analyzed below:

Received: from web21309.mail.yahoo.com ([216.136.173.254]) by arts3.arts.state.tx.us
with SMTP (Microsoft Exchange Internet Mail Service Version 5.5.2650.21) id CRR9DYQV;
Wed, 6 Feb 2002 05:43:03 -0600
Received: from [193.110.2.40] by web21309.mail.yahoo.com via HTTP; Wed, 06 Feb 2002
03:43:03 PST
Message-ID: <20020206114303.57413.qmail@web21309.mail.yahoo.com>
Date: Wed, 6 Feb 2002 03:43:03 -0800 (PST)
From: ibunor onanefe <ona_ibunor@yahoo.com>
Subject: Urgent Secret Business Transaction
To: You!

The last four items are usually all anyone wants to see. (By the way, the name in the From: field, among other things, can be set to anything you like. Try sending yourself email from "James Bond," or "General Abacha.") The messier lines are tacked on by the successive computers (mail servers) through which the email passes on its journey. Headers are not shown by default, but you can easily uncover them by clicking a link or setting a menu option, depending on the email provider.

TRACING EMAILS

The example provided above is relatively simple. Headers may involve many more "hops." Not all emails can be traced, or not easily. Porn mails generally have forged headers, and are often sent via exploited email servers. So far, though, the 419ers aren't really hiding. To trace the above email, we start at the top and work down—back in time—to the earliest believable record, seeking the internet protocol (IP) address of the computer from which the message was *physically* sent. The numbers contained in square brackets are the interesting ones.

Received: from web21309.mail.yahoo.com ([216.136.173.254]) by arts3.arts.state.tx.us

The final stop on this email's journey was a university in Texas (US). The header claims that the university mail server received the email from a Yahoo mail server with the IP address 216.136.173.254. Is this believable? In other words, does the IP address "216.136.173.254" really belong to Yahoo?

The "host" command in Unix (or "nslookup" in Windows) shows:

percent host 216.136.173.254
254.173.136.216.in-addr.arpa domain name pointer web21309.mail.yahoo.com

Reverse lookup shows:

```
percent host web21309.mail.yahoo.com
web21309.mail.yahoo.com has address 216.136.173.254
```

This seems believable. Working backward:

```
Received: from [193.110.2.40] by web21309.mail.yahoo.com
```

Yahoo received the email from a computer with IP address 193.110.2.40. No domain name is associated with the address. Does the trail end there? Maybe not. IP addresses are listed in Regional Internet Registries:

RIPE—Europe and parts of Africa—www.ripe.net
AFRINIC—Began taking on parts of Africa in 2005—www.afrinic.net
ARIN—Canada, US, Caribbean and sub-Saharan Africa—www.arin.net
LACNIC—South and Central America—www.lacnic.net
APNIC—Asia—www.apnic.net

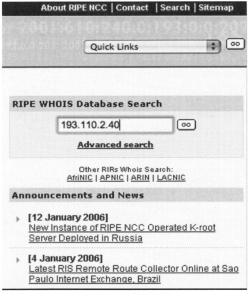

The Registries allocate blocks of IP addresses to ISPs, which dole out addresses to customers. They also provide a *whois* service which can be queried directly from the command line:

% whois 193.110.2.40

This will spit back information about the "ownership" of the IP address. For variety, however, let's visit one of their web sites. Along with information about Internet governance, these sites provide a graphical version of the "whois" service, which shows that this IP address is allocated to Prodigy, an ISP in West Africa.

```
inetnum:    193.110.2.0 - 193.110.3.255
netname:    PRODIGY-01
descr:      Prodigy International
descr:      Nigeria
notify:     lir@ipplanet.net
```

**Web site of Réseaux IP Européens
Network Coordination Centre.**
Courtesy: RIPE NCC

So the scammer's email provider is Yahoo and connectivity provider is Prodigy. (Prodigy is mentioned as an example, not because it's being singled out.) Reputable ISPs provide contacts, typically "abuse@someISP.com." A polite complaint might be phrased as follows:

"The following attempt at fraud seems to come from your facilities (see message with header below). Thanks for your appropriate action."

However, it may be a waste of time to contact the local ISP in West Africa. They usually get internet service from a satellite communications provider (here, IP Planet), which may be more helpful or better equipped to block the IP address.

Scammers also work out of more wired places. For example:

```
Received: by pop8.mx.voyager.net (mbox the_recipient@voyager.net)
    (with voyager.net's vgrpop Wed, 12 Mar 2003 04:41:03)
Received: from n2now2633.com (node-d-faa2.a2000.nl [62.195.250.162])
    by mx1.mx.voyager.net (8.12.8/8.10.2) with SMTP id h2C9crDR069472
    for <potential_victim@voyager.net>; Wed, 12 Mar 2003 04:38:54 -0500 (EST)
Message-Id: <200303120938.h2C9crDR069472@mx1.mx.voyager.net>
From: "Harry Frank" <harryfrank2003@rediffmail.com>
Reply-To: harryfrank75@netscape.net
To: potential_victim@voyager.net
Date: Wed, 12 Mar 2003 10:30:43 +0100
Subject: SEEK FOR ASSISTANCE.

Dear Sir/Madam,
I am Harry Frank the son of Dr.Tango Frank who was murdered in Zimbabwe.
{blah blah} I am seeking for asylum in The Netherlands. {blah blah blah} ... call
me on this number 0031-630-xxx-xxx.
```

RIPE shows that **[62.195.250.162]** is allocated to a Dutch ISP; the telephone number is Dutch. When "Harry Frank" says he is in the Netherlands, he probably is.

REPORT THE SPAMMER'S ISP TO A BLACKLIST

Responsible ISPs don't like their servers used for spam. Irresponsible ISPs may be reported to "real time black hole" services—privately-maintained registries of ISPs thought to be enabling spam on purpose, or who are unresponsive. Many ISPs will block wholesale any traffic from ISPs on such a list. There are a number of registries, some soliciting referrals, others relying on their own data collection.

REPORT THE SPAMMER TO THE INSTITUTION HE IS MIMICKING

Banks and payment services such as eBay and PayPal have fraud investigators who track fake bank web sites, but it's unusual to get personal feedback. (A "phishing" site may be hosted *within* a legitimate web site—the good guys may have been hacked, and should be notified. Nowadays many bad guys are less interested in defacing a server than in staking it out to store porn, run secret web sites or carry out denial-of-service attacks.)

REPORT IT TO THE COPS

While complaints are useful in linking incidents, police generally only investigate actual loss.

Interest may increase if a scammer is physically in your country, or pursuing related crimes such as identity theft, credit card fraud, wire fraud, counterfeiting, selling stolen property, and visa fraud, which may support prosecution even if there is no loss. If you are traveling abroad, you should contact your embassy.

RESPOND

Police and most anti-scam groups advise against this, and in the case of ordinary (porn, financial, hair loss) spam, it only brings more spam. Some people have responded to scammers with exceptionally vile language, and claim they stopped hearing back (from that particular scammer).

Others have responded more intimately:

Scammer:

> I am Lawyer Alistair Murdoch, an attorney at law. A deceased client of mine died as the result of a heart-related condition in November 2002....

Target:

> Lad, take my email address off your mugu list, and then enter "Mugu, please keep off" for your other GUYMEN.

Scammer:

> Dear xxx, Chop mOney, I dey hail ooooo!!!   bROS mAGA fINDER.

Target:

> Haba! LAD: Dem Guymen send you? No Dey go Corner-corner Wuru-wuru Mago Crape Money. Eh-yah Money yab man No be me and you. Rimuv address so Find my trouble and Make I see road. Na so I see am o! You sabi now?

SCAM-PROOF YOUR COMMUNITY

Tell your family and friends. Post scam-o-grams at work, the Laundromat, the library, the bowling alley, your place of worship. Businesses can play a role, especially banks and schools. Every interaction is an opportunity to scam-proof a customer. The fraud warnings, which are increasingly given to customers, should mention the 419 scam. Anyone who opens a bank or credit card account, applies for a loan, enters university, starts a job, goes on unemployment or disability, retires, signs up for email, buys a computer (or sells one—unwiped hard drives are a source of personal data for fraudsters), applies for a driver's license or passport, or joins a professional association is someone who can be educated. Some people respond more to humor than to fear. Perhaps a prize might be awarded for the funniest incoming scam letter. Spreading the word is the best defense.

COMEDY BREAK: WHEN GOOD SMURFS GO BAD, OR DEATH BY UMLAUT

Jörö Brummbär meets yet another "Mrs. Abacha."

It helps to know that the real Mariam Abacha is the widow of a former president of Nigeria, General Sani Abacha. It also helps to know that Jörö means "grumpy dwarf" in Finnish, and Schlümpfe means smurf and Brummbär "grumpy dwarf" in German.

In real life Jörö/Dorito and other alter egos is/are a lecturer in economic geography in Finland.

This is the most complicated scam-o-correspondence yet—can you keep track of the imaginary personalities? They are:

Scammer(s) pretending to be:
Mohammed Abacha
Mariam Abacha (mother of Mohammed)
Hamed Bala (their "lawyer")
Roger Stam (their "contact" in Holland)

Anti-scammer pretending to be:
Jörö Brummbär—Master Smurfherd
Otan Poskeen—His lawyer
Päl Gargamel—His dimwitted but loyal bodyguard

Mohammed Abacha:

Subject: SEEKING HONEST ASSOCIATE

Pardon me for contacting you without any prior introduction. I had to bribe the prison attendants to secretly allow me open an email address from the computer in their office. My name is Alhaji Mohammed Sani Abacha, son of the late Nigerian Head of State, General Sani Abacha. I am currently in detention at the Kirikiri Maximum Security Prisons, Lagos on what is to me, on political grounds.

You would have read the news of how the government claims that my father looted their treasury before he died. Since the assumption of power by the civilian government, my family has known no peace. The government has set out to persecute my father's family for both real and imagined sins of my late father. They have confiscated all the assets they could lay hands on, frozen the family's accounts and generally emasculate the members of my family.

All these victimization have left my mother in a difficult situation in the battle for survival. In view of this experience and to avoid further decimation of the family's fortunes, my mother and I have decided to entrust the family's hidden funds under the care of a trustworthy foreigner for safekeeping. Her problem is that she is virtually under house arrest and constantly monitored.

Let me therefore inform you that before the freezing of accounts in Nigeria, we were able to withdraw monies totaling US$45,000,000.00 (Forty Five Million US Dollars Only). It is my wish and my mother's that you assist us in the safekeeping of these monies. My mother will be able to discuss with you if arrangements are made through our lawyer, Messr abdulsan and abdulsan & Co. (Legal Practitioners & Notaries Public). Note that all correspondence shall be through the lawyer.

CHIEF hamed bala(SAN) bala & bala & CO. (Legal Practitioners & Notaries Public)
email:hamed_808_bala@yahoo.com
Tele phone; +234-80-332231xx.

I have arranged with my mother that 25 percent of the sum will be for you, while 5 percent of the total sum have been earmarked for expenses that might be incured.

Please keep me posted as I will be looking forward to your favorable response.

Regards,

ALHAJI MOHAMMED SANI ABACHA

Jörö Brummbär:

Dear Mr Abacha,

I read your email with GREAT interest and was appalled to read about the fate of your honourable family and their hard-earned cash that they've had to work for with blooded knuckles. Some people just cannot appreciate the hard-work and long days of despots.

But I'm confused how I could help you out, I'm a simple man of simple means, as I am a clergy at a local Schlümpfe shelter near Tromsö in Norway. We also breed schlümpfes and could have great use of this sum of money you mentioned, as we are renovating the houses of orphan schlümpfes that we've found in the woods near to my castle.

Please send further instructions and excuse my bad English...perhaps you or your lawyer speak Swedish, French or German?

Best regards, Jörö Brummbär, GM and Schlümpfe-extraordinaire

(*Enter the Scammer's "lawyer"!*)

Hamed Bala:

Dear Joro,

Thanks for your interest to assist my client. I am will be transacting this business on behalf of the abacha family as i have been given the mandate. The fact is that already the funds has been deposited with security company in Holland and you will be expected to travel to Holland to pick up the funds. i will advice that you forward you tel number so we can have one on one conversation.

Regards, Ahmed Bala

Jörö Brummbär:

Dear Mr Bala,

Thank you for your quick reply. First I feel the need to clarify my name, my first name given to me by God is Jörö and here in north Norway were people are humble servants of God, we must be addressed by the names given to us by God. If you cannot write 'ö' on your computer I would kindly ask you to spell it Joeroeoe, or address me by my last name Brummbär with appropriate titles. Are you a servant of the Lord, Mr Bala? I need to know before we can continue this transaction.

I'm not sure I understood; I should travel by aeromachine to this Holland to pick up the 45 000 000 Only? I'm not sure I could carry this much money, I'm quite old and my leg was severed by a rabid schlümpfe that me and my man servant, Päl Gargamel, tried to catch last fall.

I'm not sure what you know about north Norway Mr Bala, but phone lines are very rare here. I live alone in my castle, with my man servant, Päl Gargamel, and we have to walk into the local village for local people, Royston Vasey, to get access to this internet. The winters are very harsh and my castle do not have phone lines as they are unreliable and it is dangerous to fix them during the winters because of the wild schlümpfes roaming the woods.

I hate to ask this from a respectable attorney like yourself, Mr Bala, but how will the travel costs be covered?

Best regards,

Jörö Brummbär, GM

Servant of the One God and Schlümpfe-extraordinaire

Hamed Bala:

Dear mr Brummbar,

I quite understand your situation but there is no way this transaction can be completed without you travelling to pick up the funds. If that will be convinent, get back to me so i can give you the information of the company in Holland.

Regards, Hamed Bala

Jörö Brummbär:

Dear Mr Bala,

THANK YOU for the VERY SWIFT reply! I wish more attorneys could be as efficient as you! The local attorney, Azrael Pinkus (J.D), here in Royston Vasey is quite the little rascal, and it takes him AGES to reply to ANY letters. Your quick and eager attitude has convinced me that you are TRULY a servant of the LORD.

Now enough of the chit-chat and back to the issue at hand. My name, it is Mr

Brummbär, not Mr Brummbar. But PLEASE just call me Papa Joe, that's what my FRIENDS call me. And I think that to succeed we must TRUST eachother Ahmed, may I call you Ahmed?

I have spoken to my man servant, Päl Gargamel, he is trust worthy and strong (almost like an ox, I think he can carry ALL the 40 000 000 US$ only from this security firm), and he has agreed to travel by aeromachine to Holland to pick up this 40 000 000 US$ Only. I have agreed to give him 15 percent of my share. He is most eager, he has been longing for new clogs, but because he is only a mere man servant he has not had sufficient funds. Until now.

He said he would also be interested in some jiggy-jiggy in Holland, because we get it very rarely here in North Norway, with all the harsh winters etc., the schlümpfes can't provide us with everything a man needs, but neither of us knows this country, Holland, very well. I do not want to send Päl into the mouth of the lion, if you know what I mean. He is very dear to me, like a son to me, although he is a bit slow, and I do not want ANY HARM to come to him.

PLEASE REPLY ASAP WITH MORE DETAILS! We really, really, really need this MONEY ASAP! BEST regards, Yours,

Papa Joe

(Jörö Brummbär MD, Schlümpfe-extraordinaire)

(*Mrs Abacha herself steps in.*)

Mariam Abacha:

From: "Mrs mariam Abacha"

Dear Mr Brummbär,

I was informed by my Attorney (Hamed bala) about your desire to help me with my funds, the money is the last of my family thus am beliving in you that you will do your best to see that things work out perfectly as my Attorney has informed me that you are am honest man.

I have attached my picture for you to know whom you are dealing with, i urge you to send me yours so that i will get to know you in return, am beliving in God that things will work out smoothly.

blessings,

Dr mrs mariam Abacha.

(*There was a picture of Mrs Abacha and of the money [US$40,000,000 Only].*)

Hamed Bala:

To: "Jörö Brummbär"

Hello Papa Joe,

The content of your mail is well understood.If you are sending your man servant to pick up the consignment, provide his details such as 1.His full name 2.His address. This information will enable me prepare power of attorney giving him authourity to claim the funds. Moreso, You will give him money to clear the consignment. I advice that you call me on this number +234-8033223xxx.

Regards, Hamed Bala

Jörö Brummbär:

Dear Hamed,

I'm sorry for getting back so late. Sunday has been busy with laying out schlümpfe traps, as we are nearing the busiest season. It has been a harsh winter and until now we have not been able to catch as many as we would have liked to.

I tried to call you this morning when I was in town, but there must be something strange with your phonelines in Nigeria because I did not get trough, it didn't even give a signal.

Thank Mrs Abacha for her KIND letter, and compliment her on her photo, she looks like a true servant of the LORD! Maybe when this is all over she will be able to vist my humble castle personally, we have great praying facilities here.

My man servant, Gargamel, sends his regards, he is very eager to go to Holland, I must say, he is hardly working, eating or praying any more just talking about the money and Holland.

As requested I have added photos of me and my man servant, Päl Gargamel.

I have to go now, there are other local folks who want to use the local computer (I have to use a local computer in the local shop, and the owners, Tubbs and Edward are very strict how long one can use the computer). God Bless You!

sincerely, Papa Joe

(I attached a picture of Papa Joe [a picture of Finland's foreign minister] and one of Gargamel [a picture of the world strongest man].)

Hamed Bala:

Hello Papa Joe, Thanks for your mail and pictures.I have that rest of mind that you are genuine and glad to complete this transaction with you. I have forwarded your picture and that of your man servant to mrs Mariam Abacha and she was pleased.

i want you to inform me when you will be available to pick up the funds in Holland.

Regards, Hamed Bala

(Why should scammers have all the multiple personalities? Jörö has his own imaginary lawyer.)

Otan Poskeen:

Dear Mr Bala,

I was asked by Jörö Brummbär to contact you. I am the master of hunt for Dr Brummbär. Dr Brummbär had a nasty accident yesterday hunting a dangerous schlümpfe, which had escaped. Dr Brummbär fell down a shaft in an old mine and was injured severely, although he will, if it is God's will, survive this terrible ordeal. However, he will be confined to hospital and asked me to finish this transaction with you. If this is acceptable, I will travel to Holland with Dr Brummbär's man servant, Päl Gargamel to pick up the money.

Otan Poskeen

Forester and master of schümpfe hunt

(Jörö's manservant steps forward!)

Päl Gargamel:

BALA,

IT IS ME GARGAMEL, MAN SERVANT IN DR BRUMMBÄR. TERRIBLE THING HAPPEN: DR BRUMMBÄR FALL DOWN HOLE YESTERDAY HUNT FOR EVIL SCHLÜMPFE. DR BRUMMBÄR TO HOSPITAL. HE TELL FRIEND, OTAN, TO HELP YOU ME BRING MONEY FROM HOLLAND. OTAN IS FRIEND TO DR BRUMMBÄR, YOU WRITE HIM!! WE MUST HAVE MONEY, DR BRUMMBÄR MAY NEED OPERATION.

Hamed Bala:

Dear Otan Poskeen,

I was very suprise when I got your mail since this business suppose to be a confidential one which no other person sholud know. But When I got your mail from Brummbär's man servant,I dicided to contact you. I am very sorry about Doctor's condition, I hope he will recover soon. However, we should hasten everything up so that we can conclude the transiction and send money for his operation. The ball is now on your side. Please as soon as you are ready to travel to Holland, you should inform me so that I should give you further directives on what is required.

Otan Poskeen:

I understand you were surprised, it is not everyday that a schlümpfe hunter with dr brummbär's experience would wander into an abandoned mine in the night, in order to catch one of his escaped schlümpfes, and instead he slips down a hole, breaking both legs and most of his ribs and spleen. I don't know what you know about North Norway but it does happen from time to time.

Doctor yesterday put Dr Brummbär in supervised coma; it might take up to half a year. you could send him some flowers. i'm sure he'd appreciate it once he's woken up from the induced coma.

Because the schlümpfe hunt must go on, I have moved into the castle with gargamel and we are running the business together. I assure you that you can TRUST meI one of dr brummbärs closest friends, we served in the war together, I owe him my life. I have attached an old picture of myself so you can see who you are dealing with. We can travel to Holland soon, like next week, but won't we need any papers or modalities or similar?

(Attached was a picture of John Gotti, notorious mafia boss in the US in the 70s and 80s.)

Hamed Bala:

Dear Otan Poskeen,

I am happy with details of your mail. I can now give you the details of the transaction.

You are required to contact the company where the trunk is deposited in Holland. The company will required : 1.your international passport. 2.The consignment code: C/E/01900-NG 3.Proof of diposit code: BALA/00000-C/E

Please you should contact Roger stam in Holland on telephone 31-613788xxx he will advice you on further requirements.

Thanks and God bless

Otan Poskeen:

Bala,

1. I can fly down to Holland on Thursday if required.

2. I'm a man of action, I don't really care if the connection is bad in Holland or here; the main point is that I could not reach this mr Stam, okay? I'm not content of sitting on my hands and waiting for the phone lines to repair themselves or whatever when I could fly down and sort everything out in person, okay?

If you want to stop dancing around the Christmas tree, spending your and my valuable time and money, please contact Mr Stam and tell him I'm flying into Holland on Thursday and he should meet me. I'm not the sort of guy who sits on my ass and wait for my nuts to get busted, okay?

P.S Dr Brummbär is still in an induced coma.

Hamed Bala:

Otan Poskeen

Thank for your efforts. I can take you for your words. I am able to speak to Mr. Roger and he said he will like to brief you on requirements in holland. So since you cannot reach him on phone I will advice you to contact him on his email address "rogerb14@hotmail.com." We let him know that you are our partner. Moreover the documentions has been change to your name. This is good to avoid mistake of any kind. Do not forget the code as it is the only way to make the claim.

(The anti-scammer's imaginary lawyer emails the scammer's contact in the Netherlands.)

Otan Poskeen:

Subject: Regarding the consignment in your possession of deposed Nigerian ruler X

TO THE ATTENTION OF ROGER STAMM;

I was asked to contact you regarding my trip to Holland to pick up a consignment that your security company is overseeing. The codes for the consignment are as follows:

The consignment code: C/E/O1900-NG

Proof of diposit code: BALA/00000-C/E

The guy who I've been dealing with is one Hamed BALA, I take it you know what it's about? Good, because I intend to finish this transaction ASAP. I have other business afterwards, okay? So in brief I have arranged to fly into Holland this Thursday. I expect you to meet me because I know jacksh*t about Amsterdam, and don't speak the language of Dutch, okay? I have told Bala that I prefer to do this transaction face-to-face, I don't have time to try to reach you by phone, I'm a man of action. I take it we can sort out the modalities when we meet.

Roger Stam:

Dear Mr Otan Posteen,

Your consignment is here an safe, The informations your provided has been conpared and found correct. What you will need to do is to fly to Amsterdam and i will arrange for you to be picked up. You will have to come with five thousand euros(5,000.00) been for the handling charges and stamp duty. Looking forward to seeing you

Otan Poskeen:

Everything is arranged. I will fly into Amsterdam on Thursday, with the 5000 euros. I will fly from Norway, Oslo via Helsinki and my flight number is AY 841, and I will arrive in Amsterdam 09:50 AM, okay? You need to send someone to meet me and he must carry a sign with my name in capital letters. I do not want to encounter some impostor. I require that we also use a simple code phrase, okay?

So, he should say to me: "Give the password."

to which I will reply "Say the magic word."

to which he should reply "SAGAPO"

I will NOT approach or deal with ANYONE who does not carry a sign with my name OR know the code phrases, and I will CERTAINLY NOT hand over money to anyone who does not follow these instruction.

(For those not inaugurated into the fine kitch-trash sung at the Eurovision song contest in 2002, the code phrases are taken from the lyrics of Greece's unforgettably kitsch entry; S.A.G.A.P.O.)

Roger Stam:

Dear Mr Otan Poskeen,

Your email was well understood and all instructions layed out will be followed for security reasons. Write me before you depart. Looking forward to meeting you.

(At this point I might point out that "otan poskeen" means "I'll blow you" in Finnish. Mr Roger is after all, meeting the plane and passengers coming from Finland.)

Roger Stam:

Dear Mr Poskeen,

You're nowhere to be found, if you are in Amsterdam, call me on 0613788xxx.

(But Jörö is not in a coma after all!)

Jörö Brummbär:

URGENT: PLEASE READ IMMEDIATELY

DEAR HAMED,

This is Papa Joe writing you, you are in GREAT DANGER. The man who contacted you, Otan Poskeen, is a dangerous conman. His real name is NOT Otan Poskeen, but Dorito "The Black Spider" Bambini, a leading member of one of the most renowned gangster families in Scandinavia. Bambini came to my castle, with violence he forced me to tell him everything about the 40 000 000 dollars. He killed most of the schlümpfes in order to get the info from me!

He has now travelled to Holland to steal the Abachas money. He would probably not have made contact with your man at the airport but rather have followed him around Amsterdam, tracking his every move and waiting to overtake you and steal ALL the money. He is a PROFESSIONAL conman, and has conned many GOOD, HONEST, LAW ABIDING, GOD-SERVING and NICE African businessmen in the past. God knows what he has done with dishonest ones who have lied to him or tried to scam money from him and others...

Please be careful. Mr Bambini is not one of the good guys. To make this ordeal worse, I was informed one hour ago that he has disposed of Päl Gargamel in a most brutal manner. He was found on a toilet in the Oslo airport, head down a pissoir; a Bambini trademarked execution method. You should warn your collegues in Holland to contact the police before it's too late! Bambini will stop for NOTHING!! Hence his name, the BLACK SPIDER!

I pray for the safety of your collegues.

CHAPTER 8

A (SHORT) BIT ABOUT TELECOMMUNICATIONS

Considering the obstacles, there is an impressive level of internet activity in Nigeria. Africa has low fiber optic coverage—almost all international bandwidth is provided by satellite—and the lowest telephone and internet density, under one percent. The latest cable system for carrying international internet and voice traffic, SAT3, runs from Portugal around Africa with "drop" points" that include Lagos, finishing up in Malaysia. However, internal landlocked areas must still connect to it through landlines, satellite terminals or wireless radio, so there is not yet widespread access.

This is slowly changing as governments privatize telecommunications companies and grant licenses to secondary carriers. During military rule, Nigeria's national telephone company, NiTel, was neglected. As recently as 2001, there were fewer than one million landlines for 120 million people, with long wait times for new installations, and shaky connections. There is pent-up demand and plenty of ambition to fill it. The mobile phone business is booming, far outpacing the growth in landlines, and the capital city, Abuja, is slated for city-wide wi-fi service in the next few years.

Meanwhile, many businesses and ISPs still rely on VSAT (very small aperture terminal) satellite services, a popular way to provide internet access in unwired areas. In the email header example of Chapter 7, the ISP of origin was obvious. Quite often, though, the trail stops at a VSAT provider. VSAT is provided by specialty firms in countries such as Denmark, Israel, the UK, and USA. They serve the larger ISPs in West Africa, which in turn serve businesses, smaller ISPs and cybercafés.

Dial-up internet service is still very expensive—about $45/month, against average income of $400/year(!). Of course many people make more than this. Still, most internet users go to the cybercafés. These range from well-provisioned facilities with support staff and their own generators (pretty much a necessity for a stable business, and must be kept fueled), or small operations running on dicey power, or kiosks inside other businesses. These face many challenges. Some are generic locations, competition, staffing. Others are specific—quality of service, unreliable power, maintaining computers. The same trends, which increase telecommunications markets—deregulation, increased bandwidth, more peering arrangements, trade liberalization which makes equipment cheaper—also increase competition. Alternatives to cybercafés are appearing, with cell phones which can handle email and web pages. Top scammers have access to dedicated connections in separate businesses, or go elsewhere—Johannesburg, Amsterdam, London, Madrid, Houston. Still, cybercafés provide the best anonymity for a scammer. Many cafes are actually thought to be in the business, opening up at night to a different sort of clientele. It must be tempting to look the other way in a competitive, low-margin business.

What can cybercafé owners do about fraud on the premises? They often put up warning signs ("no email extractors! no scam emails!") but it must be daunting to face down scammers. Continually sniffing network traffic in real-time would be impractical and probably bad for business. Most people use free webmail accounts and monitoring outgoing web traffic would be a challenge, especially if it's encrypted! Customers with laptops would be upset if SMTP traffic were blocked. Many smaller operators are not equipped to proxy email and web traffic. This level of surveillance is not something cybercafés in more developed countries routinely practice, unless they feel they have a problem.

The Dublin arrest described in Chapter 3 illustrates the point. A system administrator found out his café had been blacklisted. The header of the offending 419 mail pointed to the range of temporary ("DHCP") addresses assigned to laptops brought in by customers. The logs showed a matching address with a timestamp and the MAC address of the laptop (information about the make of its network card). An African visitor had come in with a laptop during the time in question. The next time the visitor returned, the sys admin started watching his traffic in real-time. (Tech summary: promiscuous mode, tcpdump and ethereal, i.e., snooping.) There was a lot of outgoing mail traffic, with the same content as in the original 419 email. By the time over one thousand had gone out, the police were on the scene. This was when the customer tried to eat the USB memory stick. A more detailed version was posted on a Linux users' web site, then pulled off pending the trial. It's a nice lesson in real-time forensics.

Most system administrators won't have time for this, or feel it's their responsibility apart from responding to complaints after the fact. A corporation has the right to filter outgoing email to protect internal information, and to catch outgoing spam, which might subject it to liability, but customers are not employees. On the other hand, a cybercafé is a business and can't afford to be blacklisted. Meanwhile the average Nigerian police station doesn't have enough furniture, let alone computer expertise. In fact, police have been accused of extorting money from café owners to ignore scam activity, or, conversely, rushing into cybercafés in a show of force and causing indiscriminate damage. The industry is not highly regulated as regards data retention or domain name registration. (For that matter, long-term data retention is not mandated in the industrialized countries.) At one point Nigeria even had issues over control of its national domain (.ng).

The Nigerian government has expressed interest in filtering *outgoing* spam, possibly via future Internet Exchange Points—multi-ISP hubs. Currently, VSAT providers are responsive to complaints. An engineer at one VSAT company told me that blocking IP addresses had become so laborious that his company was looking into automatic filtering. He was manually blocking hundreds of IP addresses, only unblocking them after some suitable response from the ISP in question. One "yahoo yahoo" boy or girl, paying roughly $1/hour for access to a PC in a cybercafe, can send out thousands of spams in an hour.

There is an entire industry devoted to catching spam, but the algorithms aren't the problem here, and the technology is not difficult. The more challenging questions are—who can do it? who should pay? is it ethical?

Filtering outgoing mail looked nifty to me at first, strictly from a technical point of view, but false positives aside, I would resent *my* outgoing emails being examined at the frontier—as do no doubt Chinese citizens. Nigerian ISPs may ask (and do) why the burden of filtering should be on them rather than free webmail providers such as Yahoo. Perhaps filtering could be based on volume. ISPs in other countries routinely limit the number of outgoing emails, to throttle spam.

In any case, filtering will not stop 419, though it will probably force small-timers out of the business. More business will simply be conducted from abroad, or routed through exploitable open relays. Filtering won't catch follow-up letters, which are slightly less boilerplate. It won't stop check fraud. It won't stop scammers from harvesting addresses, or posting in chat rooms. Filtering won't stop scams, any more than it has stopped spam. The last defense, then, is educating potential victims.

Some overseas callers have had their Plain Old Telephone calls to Nigeria diverted to scammers, which suggests infiltration or bribery. A Ghanaian businessman shared his experience:

My Dear Nigerian friend X had met with me in Europe. He was in fine form and the discussions were full of warmth and joy. After he returned home to Nigeria I called him in his office from Europe to talk with him. X was in high public office so I was not surprised when a voice other than his answered the phone. I was told X was seriously ill and had been rushed to hospital that morning. I was asked the nature of our relationship; on saying I was a good friend I was given the phone number of the hospital and the name of the doctor to call.

When I called the hospital and asked for the doctor he came on the line and said X was in critical shape and they were waiting for money about a $1000 to buy the drugs they needed for a life saving operation. I asked where his wife was and was told by the doctor that despite informing her she had not shown up. The doctor suggested that if I really cared about my friend's life I should try and send some money by Western Union. I then tried to call X's wife and home but could not get through to the numbers. I wondered how a high-ranking public official could be in a position like this. So I called the doctor again. He said that X's wife was probably upset with him because he may have had a mistress but more importantly X had only 2 hours for the operation to be performed and went on to describe some medical condition I did not understand.

I told him that I was going to send the money by Western Union as he requested. After cashing the money to send, I decided to get a friend in Nigeria to go to the hospital and check to see if X was there and also meet this doctor. I did not have X's home address and it was by now evening when his office was closed. After an hour my friend called me from Nigeria. There was no hospital by that name, there was no doctor, it was one big 419 scam which I almost fell for.

Would we all react so calmly in a similar situation?

Scammers have in fact set up mini-telephone companies. The Nigerian national carrier, NiTel, issued a warning:

> For the benefit of the public, we like to advise telephone caller and called parties as follows: To alert their relatives and other (international) callers to always carefully ensure foolproof identification of the call-receiving party before they discuss any money transfer (or other confidential) issues over the telephone.
>
> To caution such relatives to beware of the many cheap call cards manufactured and sold by some companies in a number of foreign countries and which are used for Africa-bound calls. We observe that while some of these cards actually carry calls to Nigeria, such calls appear doomed to terminate on illegal V-SAT equipment set up by the foreign-based card companies and their local accomplices disguised as telecommunications companies in Nigeria. These local agents use their equipment to eavesdrop on callers' conversation, impersonate the bona fide telephone owner and dupe the two parties of money by hi-jacking funds transfer details or soliciting fund transfer from them under various guises. Proceeds from this criminal act of fraud (usually in foreign currency) are believed to be shared periodically between the local fraudsters and their overseas accomplices.
>
> To be vigilant over calls received on their telephone lines and to urgently alert the nearest NITEL or police formations about any suspicious ones so that these can be traced.

Scammer "specialists" can make a Nigerian telephone number appear to be located abroad. However, the increasing availability of VoIP in cybercafés—voice calls routed over the internet from start to finish—makes it easier for a scammer to disguise his origin. The services of telephone spoofers may become obsolete.

COMEDY BREAK: BEAUJOLAIS NOUVEAU

The founder of a mad sect (Scammomama à l'Epée Flamboyante) poses as the proprietor of a Beaujolais vineyard to waste a Lad's time. Will the Lads endow a Nostradamus Study Center?

Mr. Ayo Patrick Mbagi:

> Dear Sir,
>
> You may be surprised to receive this letter. I am Mr. Ayo Patrick Mbagi, the son of Dr. Matelo Mbagi, a wealthy farmer/politician in Zimbabwe who was murdered in the land dispute in my country.
>
> Before the death of my late father, he had taken me to Johannesburg to deposit US$20.5 million (Twenty million, Five Hundred thousand United States dollars), in one of the security companies, as he foresaw the looming danger in Zimbabwe. This

money was deposited in two boxes as Family Treasures to avoid much demurrage from the security company.

As the eldest son, I am saddled with the responsibility of seeking a genuine partner that could assist us without the knowledge of my government who are bent on taking everything we have got, and the South African government seems to be playing along with them. To this end, we need your assistance to stand as the Beneficiary of the Consignments in Europe. I have a sufficient CONTACT person in South Africa who can help us move this money under DIPLOMATIC COVER to another Security Company in Europe. This is 100 percent legal and will not pass through normal Customs/Airport Screening.

Thus, if you are willing to assist us, you can contact me through my email addresses, with your telephone, fax number and personal information to enable us discuss further details.

Yours Faithfully

Enter JUSTIN PTIDERPOURLAROUTE (Phonetics: "Just a last one before we hit the road.") Justin is a Nostradamus enthusiast and I am sure he will find some fit quatrain or sexain fit for every occasion...

Justin Ptiderpourlaroute:

Dear Mr. Ayo Patrick Mbagi,

I was just rereading our great French prophet, Nostradamus, when I got your message.

(Michel Nostradamus was a 16th century French astrologer and physician. His Centuries, *an assortment of brief rhymed prophecies called quatrains and sexains, have been interpreted as predictions of the French Revolution, the Second World War, and many other events ranging over half a millennium. Nostradamus is perhaps the most respected occult prophet of all time.)*

I always do everything important by Nostradamus prophecies.

The sexain I had just read before having your mail is the following:

Que d'or d'argent fera despendre,

Quand fermier voudra Ville prendre,

Tant de mille & mille soldats,

Tuez, noyez, sans y rien faire,

Dans plus forte mettra pied terre,

Cognon ayde des Pensuarts.

which fits perfectly with your message, the sad story of your country and of your late father. I therefore consider this to be of good omen. Please let me know what I should do to enter business with you.

Yours

Justin Ptiderpourlaroute

Co. Beaujolais Justin

333, rue des embrumés

95300 - Pontoise

0892 68 45 35

Nostradamus can't be wrong, so let's bait our prospective mugu again... I even opened a new account called "nostradam" to look credible...

Justin Ptiderpourlaroute:

Dear Mr. Ayo Patrick Mbagi,

I was very interested by your offer, the prospect seems good as the quatrain I pinned today:

Celuy qui a, les hazards surmonté,

Qui fer, feu, eauë, n'a jamais redouté,

Et du pays bien proche du Basacle,

D'vn coup de fer tout le monde estouné,

Par Crocodil estrangement donné,

Peuple raui de veoir vn tel spectacle.

says our business can only be fruitful !!! I am surprised I got no answer from you, who contacted me in the first place when I asked nothing.

Let me introduce myself, I am an old learned gentleman from an old famous French family, with enough money to live more than cosily. The money you kindly offered me would enable me to set up a study center where Nostradamus predictions could be studied seriously and translated in order to be applied with rigeur to present and future situations. Of course, upon my death, I would bequeath to this Nostradamus Center my complete library with all my rare books, my hotel particulier in Paris, my painting collection (I have some very rare old paintings) and my famous Beaujolais vineyards (Beaujolpif Justin—Mal aux tifs le matin...).

If you are interested by Nostradamus, I could even make you the director of this center as I will need somebody honest I can put my trust in. (tu parles !!!)

Hoping to hear from you, as it seems to be Nostradamus' wishes.

Justin Ptiderpourlaroute

The fish is baited. He sent me this same message twice!!!

Mr. Ayo Patrick Mbagi:

DEAR SIR,

FIRST OF ALL, ON BEHALF OF ME AND MY FAMILY HERE, I WOULD WANT TO SAY THANK YOU. FIRST FOR TAKING YOUR LIMITED TIME OUT TO ASK FOR MORE DETAILS. ALSO FOR YOUR INTEREST TO ASSIST US IN OUR BID TO CONCLUDE THIS RANSACTION. THE FUNDS ARE PRESENTLY UNDER THE CUSTODY OF A SECURITY FIRM IN EUROPE. THE SECURITY FIRM DO NOT KNOW THE CONTENTS OF THE CONTAINERS. WE CANNOT PRESENT OUR SELVES AS THE BENEFICIARY BECAUSE OF OUR POSITIONS HERE AND WE ARE UNDER TRAVEL WATCH.

I WOULD HENCE REQUIRE YOUR:

1.FULL NAMES AND ADDRESS (CORRESPONDING WITH YOUR PASSPORT) OR THE FULL NAMES AND ADDRESS OF YOUR COMPANY.

2.YOUR I.D NOS.

3.ANY OTHER PERSONAL DETAILS OR REMARKS.

PLEASE FEEL FREE WITH ALL THESE DETAILS BECAUSE WE ONLY NEED THEM TO ARRANGE FOR THE AIR WAY BILL DOCUMENTS AS WELL AS FILLING YOUR DETAILS AS THE RECEIVER OF THE CONSIGNMENTS. THESE ARE VERY LEGAL PROCEDURES AND DOES NOT GO CONTRARY TO ANY INTERNATIONAL LAW.

AS SOON AS WE HAVE CONCLUDED THE COURIER OF THESE CONSIGNMENTS, I WILL START MAKING ARRANGEMENTS FOR MY FIRST SON, (LANGA) 31YEAR OFAGE, TO MEET YOU IN EUROPE. OUR CONTACT AT THE SECURITY COMPANY IN EUROPE WILL MAKE NECESSARY RRANGEMENT WITH YOU FOR AN ACCOUNT WHERE THE FUNDS WILL BE DEPOSITED IN ANY PART OF THE WORLD.

BUT WE DO URGE YOU TO KEEP THIS TRANSACTION CONFIDENTIAL. ALSO WE WOULD BE WILLING TO GIVE YOU 15 PERCENT OF THE AMOUNT AFTER THE CONCLUSION OF THIS DEAL AS WE ALSO HOPE FOR YOUR NDERSTANDING. LET IT BE KNOWN TO YOU THAT WE ARE A LITTLE BIT WEARY, BUT WE HAVE THE UNDERSTANDING THAT FRIENDS ARE DISCOVERED AND FRIENDS ARE MADE. LET TRUST AND HONESTY BE OUR WATCHWORD THROUGHOUT THIS TRANSACTION.

N/B. THERE IS TELECOMMUNICATION BREAKDOWN IN MY VILLAGE, IN THAT CASE
I WILL BE CALLING YOU FROM THE PUBLIC PHONES UNTIL OUR PRIVATE LINES
STARTS WORKING

(Justin is so pleased Nostradamus was right!!! Morever, this year's wine will be outstanding, so he decided to have his portrait on the bottles—a nice Victor Hugo picture. Who could be a better choice for an "old learned gentleman"?)

Justin Ptiderpourlaroute:

Thanks for your message, I will be delighted to help you as it will help make my dream come true: a Nostradamus International Study Center. I already have a castle for this in my Beaujolais vineyards, but it is so expensive to fit it properly for my high goal: a scientific approach of Nostradamus Centuries (his prophecies).

I found today another sextain which augures well from our cooperation:

Tost l'Elephant de toutes parts verra

Quand pouruoyeur au Griffon se ioindra,

Sa ruine proche, & Mars qui tousiours gronde:

Fera grands faits aupres de terre saincte,

Grands estendars sur la terre & sur l'onde,

Si la nef a esté de deux freres enceinte.

Which means we will have no confidentiality problem the both of us being truly and thoroughly honest. I am still offering you or your son Langa the management of this International Nostradamus Study Center, as I want it to be in the hand of a really trustworthy being (and I know I will have no problem since Nostradamus seems to recommend you!!!).

The heat we had this year was wonderful for the grapes and we are going to have a real outstanding wine with this year's crop. I will call it "Cuvée Les Centuries." I had a Beaujolais label made with my portrait on it. I'm rather proud of it. What do you think about it?

Now my dear, just tell me what you need.

When I cannot sleep, I am up to mischief... Cave Beaujolaise does really exist, but in Saint-Julien, and the fax and telephone numbers are correct, te he te he!!!

Justin Ptiderpourlaroute:

Sujet : I am a forgetful old man !

I was a bit tired with overreading Nostradamus without my glasses as I seem to have lost them yesterday, and I forgot to give you the details you asked. Here is what I found:

Aupres du jeune le vieux ange baiser,

Et le viendra surmonter a la fin:

Dix ans esgaux aux plus vieux rabaisser,

De trois deux l'un l'huitiesme seraphin.

I analysed this one thoroughly, and it means ours will be a speedy and sure business. Haut les coeurs!!! Now, here are my business particulars:

Justin Ptiderpourlaroute, Propriétaire

Cave Beaujolaise de Saint Justin

69640 SAINT JUSTIN

Tél : 04 74 67 57 xx

Fax : 04 74 67 51 xx

Banque : Crédit National Pinardier - St Justin

As you may guess, my dear parents called me Justin to match the name of our beautiful village, so it went with me wherever I was (great patriots, my parents, they called my sisters France, Marianne and Clairette).

Now, as I am deaf since the war, when I was still a kid (a bomb exploded near the keg inside which I was hiding in and I got wood splinters and beaujolais into my ears, which split and drowned my eardrums, which is why I turned for solace to Nostradamus to find the cause for such an unjust fate as I had a highly musical ear and wanted to become a lyre concert player), it would be better to keep to emails. If you still want to talk to me, which I can understand, please SCREAM into the telephone as I will not hear one sound otherwise. Please do not hesitate and choose what suit you better. Now, my dear, things are in your hands.

(I am really warming to eccentric old Justin and his Nostradamus Center, so I insist on doing business!)

Justin Ptiderpourlaroute:

Dear Mr. Ayo Patrick Mbagi,

How is the family? Did you think about my management offer for our International Nostradamus Study Center?

It is with great enthousiasm that I read the quatrain I pinned today (I always use a long hat pin topped with a black pearl...). it does speak of a great sumn of money hidden in a trunc coming accross to a vineyard. Our business deal was really written in God's book! See for yourself:

Le camp du vemple de la tierge vestale,

Non esloigné d'Ethne & monts Pyrenées:

Le grand conduict est caché dans la male,

North getes fluues & vignes mastinées.

Please let's go on with our project, I can hardly wait to see it completed.

Mr. Ayo Patrick Mbagi:

Justin

Can you give me a number i can call you on?

(Can't these guys read? I told him I was deaf since childhood!)

Justin Ptiderpourlaroute:

Dear Mr Mgabi (or can I call you Ayo ?),

Remember I have split and drowned eardrums since I was a kid, so please SCREAM into the phone to be heard. (te he te he)

Here is my own personal number: (33) 04 74 67 57 xx and please be careful with the time difference since I am an old man and need rest !!!

The sexain I picked today does not seem very favorable, may be I should change my hat pin?

Vin à foison, tres bon pour les gendarmes,

Pleurs & souspirs, plainctes cris & alarme

Le Ciel fera ses tonnerres pleuuoir

Feu, eau & sang, le tout meslé ensemble,

Le Ciel de sol, en fremit & en tremble,

Viuant n'a veu ce qu'il pourra bien veoir.

(Justin spawns another incarnation of himself:)

Mme. Herma Phrodite:

Dear Sir,

You don't know me, my name is Mme Herma Phrodite. I don't know how to break the news to you, but there has never been any Justin Ptiderpourlaroute (this is a French joke meaning just a last one before we take the road).

My son Ceta Phrodite, 15, has been pulling one on you on his father's computer. The photo he sent you is one of our greatest poet Victor Hugo, but I suppose you never heard about him in Nigeria. The only positive side is that he did some research on Nostradamus on the internet.

I just don't know what to do with this kid, he has been getting out of hand since his father, a lawer, left the house to go and live with a blonde large-boobied road-pizza waitress with the IQ of an ungifted mussel ... He is so furious with him that when somebody ask him what his father does, he answers he is a nude dancer in a gay club!

My Ceta told me, too, that you were not quite honest either and that your letter was intended too get money out of insuspecting idots (Advance Fee Fraud, he called it). He called you a "mougou or moogoo or mugu" whatever this is. If this is the case, may God's eye fall on you and reduce you to ashes !!!

Herma Phrodite

(And then suddenly out of the blue—or did it take this long to sink in???)

Mr. Ayo Patrick Mbagi:

YOU MOTHEFUCKER YOU GO TO HELL. NO TIME LOOSE WITH YOUR KIND MOTHERFUCKER. FUCK YOU FUCK YOU FUCK YOU NO GOOD MOTHERFUCKER

(Here is the end of a beautiful story. Justin will never get his Nostradamus International Study Center. Sniff...)

CHAPTER 9

ANTI-SCAMMING FOR BEGINNERS

Mr. "X," may we ask you a question?
It's amazing is it not?
That the city pays you slightly less than fifty bucks a week
Yet you've purchased a private yacht!
I am positive your Honor must be joking
Any working man can do what I have done
For a month or two I simply gave up smoking
And I put my extra pennies one by one
Into a little tin box...
– *Fiorello*, the musical

People around the world have found, in corresponding with the Lads, an outlet for their literary leanings. The results can be funny, or mean-spirited, or illuminating and unexpectedly frank. A few notes for prospective anti-scammers:

This is not the world's healthiest hobby. Get some fresh air!

If you take precautions, you are unlikely to come to harm, but 419ers are not nice people.

If you are suggestible, don't start! Beware the impulse to turn a scammer to the path of light, it *won't* happen. The scammer may have interesting things to say about how corruption and joblessness have driven him to this scamming life. This is not the start of his rehabilitation, only of your being duped. If you can't remain detached, this is not the hobby for you.

Scam-baiting is collaborative fiction, and as such may not be your cup of tea. It requires a certain talent for manipulation, a sensitivity to your scammer's moods, and patience.

If you are undeterred, the pointers below will be useful.

GET A LIFE

A scam-baiter needs a persona. Some of the best have been created from thin air; others were borrowed from history, cartoons, or movies. Captain Picard, the Kray brothers, and Cthulhu have all met the Lads.

GET YOUR LIFE AN EMAIL ACCOUNT

Your persona needs a separate free webmail account. Making up the biographical details when you sign up will be good practice for corresponding with your scammer. Pick a good password (*not* the same as for any other email account) and change it at random intervals. Don't make the password hint too simple or reflexively make the answer a true one. Consider anonymizing your email. This means disguising its physical source.

FIND YOUR CADRE

Joining forums such as 419eater (www.419eater.com) is a good way to learn techniques, such as anonymizing yourself as suggested above. Some other forums are listed in the appendix.

ADOPT A SCAMMER

If you've never received a scam-o-gram, pick one and answer it anyway. "Spare" scammers are shared around on anti-scammer bulletin boards. Many anti-scammers are generous with advice. The 419 Eater board has a forum topic devoted to "surplus mugu" mail. Search the web, using keywords "guymen" or "mugu." Scammers use those terms to stake out bulletin boards and warn off other scammers. Post there, if only to say, "nice site," and you'll probably hear back from a scammer. Answer in character, expressing mystified or skeptical or enthusiastic interest in the proposal. Relax—the scammer will take it from there.

RE-INVENT YOURSELF

Your Lad has constructed a story—you can too. Do not use your real name, address, phone number, or bank details. You are not obliged to give any information, but if you do, be creative.

Telephone: Some scam-baiters provide the number of a "psychic" hotline, or a law-enforcement agency, or the payphone behind a gas station. The operators at Buckingham Palace, the CIA, and McDonald's headquarters are probably all-too-familiar with the Lads. One scam-baiter provides the number of a towing company in Moscow (Russia, not Idaho). (Remember, this is not funny for the person receiving the call.) Web services such as k7.net can be used to receive phone calls and faxes as electronic files. You can also give one scammer the phone number of another scammer, though this will probably bring the correspondence to a screeching halt.

Passport/driver's license: Some anti-scammers refuse to limit themselves to nations or real timelines. Reality is just a crutch for people without Photoshop. What would two famous faces look like, morphed together? And why confine yourself to the non-animated world?

Frederick J. Flintstone license
Courtesy: "Frederick J. Flintsone"

Lee Harvey Oswald license
Courtesy: Adam de la Torre

Adam requested and received an interesting photo in return (below)..

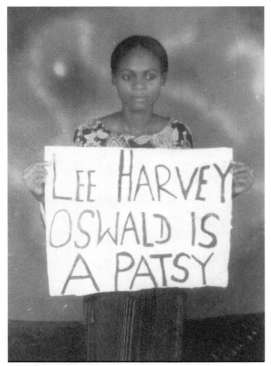

Scammer Rejects Lone Gunman story
Courtesy: Adam de la Torre

Address: While it might be safer not to accept mail from the Lads, some scam-baiters rent post office boxes for the purpose.

Bank account: Ever heard of Bonkers Bank, PLC? Or Kreplach Brothers Merchant Bank (payment arm for the Foreign Office)?

Meeting scammers: Don't. Not unless the police are coming along.

KEEP IT GOING

This is *your* imaginary life. Invent some perverse family or business situation. Be elsewhere—in jail, or at the South Pole hunting the aquatic Bigfoot, or sequestered on a dramatic jury trial. Pretend to be gullible. Get drunk and type poorly. Misspell your scammer's name, differently each time. Switch languages if you have a few. Try machine translation and then reverse machine translation.

The Lads like to pose as Christian or Muslim converts, as necessary. Test their knowledge of scripture. Drift off topic. Talk politics. Ask about your scammer's personal life. Suggest romantic interest. Take offense for no reason. Insist on being addressed properly. Insist that you didn't receive an attachment, or that it contained a virus, which needs removal (helpful hints may involve re-formatting the hard drive). Insist you can never get through on the phone. Suggest your scammer's

Personal Detail Questionnaire

Please complete and answer the following questions to the best of your ability.

Your name? **SHARON STONE**

When and where were you born? **1928 / ABIDJAN**

Are you in robust health? **NO**

Have you ever had genital warts? **NO**

Have you ever had hives? **NO**

Have you ever had siblings? **NO**

How would you describe your body? **AVERGe high**

Have you ever been in police custody? **NO**

Are you now or have you ever been a member of the Osmond Family? **NO**

Do you intend to overthrow the United States Government? **NO**

Do you take drugs such as Rogaine, Viagra or Preparation H? **NO**

What is your favourite colour? **BALACK**

What is your favourite food? **Foutou**

What is your least favourite star sign? **LOVE**

Are you familiar with the teachings of Ivana Trump? **NO**

Would you be prepared to adopt a colony of orphan bees? **NO**

What was your favourite school subject? **ENGIiSH**

Raindrops keep falling on my head. What would you do? **I will move it On my head**

What would you be doing if you weren't completing this form? **I will not like it**

Church of the Blessed Beehive Questionnaire Courtesy: Rev. Bob

phone is being tapped. The typical 419 scam begins with a man pretending to be a woman, and then referring you to his "lawyer" or "son." They don't like to go on being women. Insist on dealing with the woman. Get your Lad's email account cancelled—he'll be back, on another account. (If he flies away, he was never yours to begin with.) Send two scammers' mails to each other. Ask each to meet you at the same time and place.

Impose arcane rules for secure communication. Insist on challenge phrases. Invent a secret code. You can always fall back on an oldie such as *rot13*, which simply replaces each letter in the alphabet with another letter thirteen places forward or back in the English alphabet. For example:

"hello mugu" = "uryyb zhth"

There are web sites which will do this for you. Even if your Lad uses such a tool to decode the result, it's extra work for him.

Demand a photo of your scammer holding a sign with your "name." The following was extracted from a Lad with dreams of playing pro football (soccer) by a mischievous soul who posed as a scout for Manchester United:

The bunch at 419 Eater (www.419eater.com) have raised this to a high art in the Hall of Shame for doctored IDs, recorded phone messages, and a gallery of Lads willing to pose with strange objects on their heads. 419 Eater also pursue more hard-core activities described in Chapter 10.

The Lads like to make their victims fill out forms. Make up your own and ask your scammer to fill it out. Criticize his spelling and make him fill it out again.

Reverend Bob of the Church of the Blessed Beehive came up with these important questions (see above):

Danny the Footballer
Courtesy: 'Juan Kerr'

Jack de Grandeur (in real life a geography professor in New York) invited the Lads to join the (US) Republican Party (left):

Suggest that your scammer's lawyer is either an idiot or treacherous. (Since the "lawyer" is either the scammer himself or someone he works for, this is guaranteed to annoy.) The Foreign Office specialize in extracting loyalty oaths (opposite, left):

Lance DuLac required his Lad to swear allegiance to the US National Security Agency (opposite, right):

Grand Old party Application

Courtesy: 'Jack de Grandeur'

A loyal scammer
Courtesy: 'The Foreign Office'

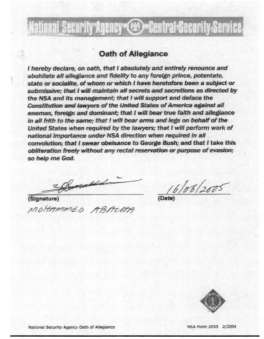

Oath of Allegiance to the NSA
Courtesy: 'Lance DuLac'

Invent your own treacherous friends, who try to cut separate deals. If multiple personalities prove a strain, enlist real friends. Encourage them to display their own time-wasting quirks. If you work in teams, consider using PGP to encrypt and authenticate your emails. If you share different languages, consider using them. Tell your scammer someone else made you a better offer. Negotiate percentages of the imaginary money. Insist you *did* send the money order; see how many trips he will make to different branches of Western Union.

Make imaginary reservations on real flights to wherever he is planning to meet and kidnap you. Promise presents. Linger over the details. Discuss preferred brands of laptop computer, watch, or suit (what are your scammer's bodily measurements and are they inadequate in any way?). Insist on being met at the airport with an interesting slogan in your favorite language. Lady Agatha Bristol of The Foreign Office insists on fresh flowers in her hotel suite. Brad Christensen, known for the anti-scam website quatloos.com, demanded to be taken on safari to see live pterosaurs.

Miss the flight because customs officials interrogated you, and seemed to know your scammer's whereabouts. Or email to say you've arrived, and then ask your Lad to come to the most expensive hotel in town and inquire after you by an alias, which sounds humorous when spoken aloud. Or say you've arrived, thank him for sending (pick another scammer's name) to meet you and say the deal is about to go forward.

Get sick, lose your memory and make your scammer explain everything again. Die, and have your wealthy brother take over the correspondence. Construct obituaries. The death may have been caused by unusual events (the truth is out there!) (see next page):

Arrest Made in Desert Penguin Attacks

Local ranch owner held pending investigation into origin of large penguin attacks near Zzyzx Springs

columnist's name & photo removed

Recent problems in the area surrounding Zzyzx Springs, have disturbed many in the surrounding areas. Reports included missing scouts, campers and damage to structures.

While the situation is far from being resolved, progress appears to have been made with the arrest today of Charles Addams, a farmer who took over the old Zzyzx Ski resort.

Mr. Addams has converted the old ski resort in to a penguin farm. Many mocked his efforts, saying the desert was hardly the place for a penguin farm.

Now it appears that the operations at this farm have somehow bred penguins up to 7 feet in height, larger than the farm was capable of holding. Many appear to have gotten loose, and the only conclusion is that these penguins are responsible for the recent outbreak of violence in the area.

Stories of huge penguins with flaming eyes are hardly to be believed, but the truth behind the horrible mutations may be more frightening. It appears that up to 20 penguins, all larger than the average man, are now roaming the desert.

Don't Go Here: *the road to Zzyzx Springs*

Calls for the National Guard are largely going ignored, as the current emergency is small compared with the devastation in New Orleans.

Scientists from UCLA are said to be on their way, but some Baker residents are calling for more vehement action.

A vigilante effort to get at Mr. Addams, and then perhaps the remaining pen-
Continued A7

Arrest made in desert penguin attacks

Courtesy: Lance DuLac

Undergo a crisis of conscience and insist that the imaginary money go to the poor. (You do realize it's imaginary money, don't you? If not, then start again at page one of this book, and copy it in longhand on a grain of rice.)

Some Lads will stick with it as long as money's in the wind. When should you stop? Whenever you like. Drop it in midstream for any reason. Stop if bored. Stop if it feels unsafe. If you decide not to start, that's good too. I humbly suggest that the best scam-baits resist the big put-down. Instead they disengage, leaving the Lad never knowing it was all a waste of time. A real sting preserves your Lad for future generations of anti-scammers.

COMEDY BREAK:
LOVE BLOOMS FOR ARNOLD FANNERMAN

Arnold Fannerman is a shy, single fly-fishing magnate (in real life, an American classical pianist/former radio DJ). Arnold hears from "Hilary Alfred," a refugee with a marriageable sister!

Hilary the Scammer:

DEAR SIR,

MY NAME IS HILARY ALFRED SON OF LATE DR.ALFRED PAUL FORMER MINISTER OF MINES AND POWER OF SIERRA LEONE IN WEST AFRICA.

MY FATHER AND MOTHER LOST THEIR LIVES IN THE HANDS OF THE REBEL SOLDIERS LED BY MAJOR JOHNNY KOROMAH.AS THE WAR PRESSED HARDER,I OPENED THE UNDERGROUND SAVE OF THE FAMILY VILLA IN READINESS TO MOVE OUT FROM THE COUNTRY,I FOUND DOCUMENTS CONCERNING ONE TRUNK BOX CONTAINING EIGHTEEN MILLION FIVE HUNDRED THOUSAND DOLLARS (US$18,500,000) MY FATHER DEPOSITED WITH A SECURITY COMPANY IN COTE D'IVOIRES.

WE ARE CONTACTING YOU TO ASSIST US IN THE FOLLOWING WAYS.
1. HELP US TO RETRIEVE THE CONSIGNMENT.
2. TRANSFER THE FUNDS INTO YOUR ACCOUNT OVERSEAS.
3. HELP US TO CROSS OVER TO YOUR COUNTRY.
4. GET A REPUTABLE SCHOOL FOR JOSEPHINE TO CONTINUE HER STUDIES.
5. RECOMMEND PROJECTS TO INVEST THE FUNDS.

WE WILL OFFER YOU 10 PERCENT OF THE TOTAL SUM AS YOUR COMMISSION.
YOURS SINCERELY,
HILARY ALFRED

Arnold:

Dear Hilary:

Such a terrible time for Sierra Leone! I have seen on the news the terrible crimes committed by the rebels there. I will be happy to assist you in any way I can.

I am the owner/operator of a large fishing business. Perhaps we can utilize the business to receive the funds? Also, may I ask the age of Josephine? I have long considered helping a distressed person in Sierra Leone, or other troubled African country. I am unmarried, and would inquire about asking for her hand in marriage. I mention this in all seriousness. Is it possible for you to send a photo of your sister, with other biographical details?

Best

Arnold D. D. Fannerman

Hilary the Scammer:

DEAR A. D. D. FANNERMAN,

SIR,

I AND MY SISTER JOSEPHINE IS HAPPY TO HEAR FROM YOU HAVING CONTACTED YOU FOR HELP. MY SISTER JOSEPHINE IS NINTEEN YEARS OLD(19YEARS), WHILE I AM TWENTY TWO YEARS OLD(22YEARS). I AND MY SISTER IS IN THE CAMP HERE IN ABIDJAN HOPING TO GET OUT OF THIS SUFFERING SITUATION ONE DAY.

OUR FATHER'S CONSIGNMENT IS LYING THERE ACCUMULATING DUMORRAGE, THE SECURITY COMPANY DO NOT KNOW THAT THE CONTENT IS MONEY(eighteen million five hundred thousand).I WOULD LIKE YOU TO COME TO ABIDJAN TO CLEAR THIS CONSIGNMENT.

LASTLY,CALL MY SISTER JOSEPHINE. DO NOT BE ANNOYED FOR NOT SENDING HER PICTURE TO YOU,IT IS BECAUSE WE DO NOT HAVE MONEY TO SCAN IT TO YOU.

HOPING TO HEARING FROM YOU SOONEST.

Arnold:

Dear Hilary:

Thank you for your speedy reply! I am very excited about our transaction. Could you advise me about the best way to travel from Miami Florida US to Abidjan? Please advise me as to how much the demurrage will cost. I am sure I will be able to cover it, but I must know how much cash to bring.

I would like to hear from your sister directly, so I will have a sense of what kind of person she is.

I am 5'9", weigh 165 pounds, and am in top physical condition, as you will see when I arrive. I am 34 years old. I have 2 homes, one in Miami, and the other in New York City, from where I transact much business.

Perhaps we can arrange a transfer of beneficiary on the security deposit. Please send a facsimile of the certificate of deposit, and I will communicate directly with the company.

Have no fears, I will help you recover from your awful circumstances, as it is the Lord's work to help those in need.

Arnold Duwa Diddy Fannerman

Josephine, the Scammer's "Sister":

MY DEAREST FANNERMAN,

I AM IMPRESSED WITH YOUR MAIL.I DO WISH THAT WE HAVE SEEN FACE TO FACE,ALL THE SAME,I AM VERY GLAD AND DO HAVE INTEREST IN YOU AS TO

MAKE A FULL TIME HOUSE WIFE WITH YOU.

I AM 4.5ftTALL,BLACK IN COMPLEXION,WITH BROWN EYES. MY AMBITION IN LIFE IS TO BECOME A NURSE AS TO TAKE CARE OF OUR CHILDREN. I AM NINTEEN YEARS OLD(19),GOD FEARING PERSON,BORN IN A CHRISTIAN FAMILY. I LOST MY PARENTS DURING THE WAR.I AM ONLY LEFT WITH MY SENIOR BROTHER HILARY.

YOUR ANSWER TO US IS FROM GOD,AS WE ARE OPHANS,I WOULD LOVE YOU TO CALL ME ON THIS NUMBER;225-077xxxxx, NINE O'CLOCK ABIDJAN TIME SO AS TO HEAR YOUR VOICE AND DISCUSS MORE.WE ARE IN THE REFUGEE CAMP .
THANKING YOU FOR YOUR CARING DEAR. I LOVE YOU.

YOURS DARLING,
JOSEPHINE ALFRED.

Hilary the Scammer:

DEAR UNCLE A.D.D. FANNERMAN,
SIR, I AM QUITE IMPRESSED WITH YOUR WILLINGNESS TO HELP US,TO CROWN IT ALL,YOUR CONCERN TOWARDS US.

FIRSTLY,YOU CAN FLY WITH EGYPT AIRLINE AS IT COMES TO ABIDJAN OFTEN.

SECONDLY I CONTACTED THE SECURITY COMPANY,THE DIRECTOR DR WEST UZONDU IS NOT ARROUND,HIS SECRETARY GAVE ME HIS EMAIL ADDRESS (first_se2000@yahoo.com) SAYING WE SHOULD ASK YOU TO CONTACT HIM AS THE BENEFICIARY.

UNCLE,DO GIVE US YOUR NUMBERS WHERE WE CAN FAX TO YOU THE CERTIFICATE. EMAIL TO US THE DATE OF YOUR ARRIEVAL AND DO CALL THE SECURITY COMPANY.

HOPING TO HEARING FROM YOU AND GOD BLESS.

(*I checked out the address "first_se2000@yahoo.com" at yahoo profiles and found, to my shock and dismay, that the account had only been opened THAT VERY DAY!! Can one not even trust his own nephew and future brother-in-law in this hopeless world??*)

Arnold Dutifully Contacts the "Security Company":

Dear Dr. Uzondu:

My name is Arnold Duwa Diddy Fannerman. I am interested in a transferal, to myself, of a box deposited in the name of Dr. Alfred Paul. The box contains "family treasures." This is in compliance with the wishes of the family. In fact, there is a possibility that I will be joining this family through marriage. Please inform me of what is expected of me to complete this process.

Arnold:

My Dear Nephew Hillie, Dear Boy,

First drive all your worries out of your mind. I am aware of the terrible situation you are in, together with your delightful sister. But whenever your burdens seem unbearable, whenever all you can see is darkness, though it may be under the glare of the noonday sun, just remember your Uncle is here! He will wash away your troubles as easily as you lick away the last few grains of rice from your hands after a meager meal. I have sent an email to the security company.

At present, I am caring for my elderly mother. My father passed away, and my mother's health has been declining. She is residing with me, and is always concerned about my welfare, and is nosey besides. If she suspects that I am having dealings with strangers in Africa, she will tell every relative who has ears to hear! I do not wish to endanger our transaction. As I can no longer adequately care for her, she will be moving to a nursing home. Yes, my dear Hillie, it is also a sad time for us here, so we have a bond of tribulation among us ... you, I, and the charming Josephine. Once the move is accomplished, we may have telephone contact. Until then, email the security document(s), or anything else you feel will help us to bring the transaction to a 100 percent (ONE HUNDRED PERCENT) hitch-free conclusion.

How many days do you think our business will take? I have settled on the Ivoire Inter-Continental Abidjan Hotel, on Boulevard Hassan II. Do you know it? I am unfamiliar with hotel standards in your country, and would hate to arrive there only to find vermin infesting the room.

Now let me apprise you of a new development. I have received a letter from your sister Josephine. I think she likes me! If you could only see her letter—it was so sweet and loving. I want you to know, dear nephew, that I am an honourable man. It would be unthinkable for me to carry on any communication with your sister without your permission. I fervently hope that we have your blessing. It may sound strange, but I sense real love and caring in her words. Your revered late father must have raised his children right, with a truly Godly modality.

Well, that is it for now, my poor troubled nephew Hillie. Have courage! Try not to think of the past, but look ahead to the day when you and Josephine (such a pretty name!) will be with me in my country, far from the filthy and degrading refugee camp wherein you now find your most precious selves.

With familial love, I remain,

A. D. Diddy Fannerman

Arnold:

My Darling Josephine,

How wonderful it was to receive your letter! Your words were as a sweet bouquet to my eyes. No one has ever called me "darling" before, and I must tell you, my sweetest girl, it was thrilling to hear it. I feel as if I have known you my whole life.

You see, Josephine, I have been so lonely. I have spent my whole life only thinking of money... how to get it, and then how to get more. I never even had any real friends, because I was always too busy cooking up new business schemes, investing my earnings, always counting, counting, counting... Please try not to think badly of me because of this. However, the result of all my labours has been a full bank account, and an empty heart... full moon and empty arms.

Last year I celebrated my arrival at a certain financial milestone by purchasing a 36 (THIRTY SIX) foot Chris Craft cabin cruiser boat, which I keep docked at the Miami Seaquarium. (Please don't think I am bragging! I know, sweet Josephine, that you would never determine a person's value by the possessions he may have, or the size of his bank account.)

I thought this vessel would bring me happiness, but do you want to know something, my dearest Josephine? It has only brought me emptiness! Where is the joy when there is no one to share one's good fortune?! Sometimes I feel like the poorest beggar, when I see an ordinary family walking in the street enjoying each other's company, even if they are dressed in rags! I would give up my homes and everything else to the meek and destitute, if only I could find happiness like that.

Is this making sense? I hope you do not mind that I pour my deepest, most heartfelt feelings out to you. I only wish we could be together, with your head resting next to my heart, gazing up at me with your beautiful brown eyes. Oh my dearest Josephine, forgive me for speaking to you like this. We do not know each other, and perhaps you think me too forward. All I know of you is that you are the sister of a stranger in distress who reached out to me across the ocean, in pathetic desperation, for a way out of his trials. Yet we three have already forged a bond, a bond that, God-willing, will continue and grow ever stronger with the passing years.

So you want to be a nurse? How very like you...always thinking of the other person before yourself...that's my Josephine! You mentioned that you want children? How many would you like? I would like 3 (THREE). Two (2) boys and a girl. I would name the boys Cyril and Waldo. The girl might be named Yetta.

You know, Josephine, with all this talk about children, I must confess, I have never been with a woman, you know what I mean? I have seen pictures, and even saw a part of a film once, until I realized what was happening and I ran out! It all seemed so strange to me. Many of my countrymen do not think twice about performing these wicked acts. I do not know why God thought it necessary to force his creatures to behave so unnaturally so they may have children. But we will deal with these things in their own time, my dearest Josephine.

I have spoken too much already. PLEASE write back as soon as possible.

Love,

Your Arnold D. Diddy

Josephine:

MY DEAREST DIDDY,

I READ YOUR MAIL WITH INTEREST,I DREAMT OF YOU LAST NIGHT,SEEING BOTH OF US IN THE CHURCH DOING WEDDING;I WISH MY DREAM COMES TRUE.I DO UNDERSTAND THE SITUATION OF THINGS,AS I WAITED FOR YOUR CALL LAST SATURDAY-NO PROBLEM.I MISSED YOU.

HOW ARE YOU DEAR?HOPE YOU ARE FINE. IF YOU SUGGEST THAT WE HAVE ONLY THREE CHILDREN, YOU ARE THE MAN OF THE HOUSE,THE BIBLE SAYS THAT WE SHOULD RESPECT OUR HUSBAND AND BE SUBMISIVE TO THEM.

MY ELDER BROTHER HILARY HAS BEEN SO HAPPY TO HAVE YOU AS HIS INLAW AND HE TOLD ME HE IS GIVING US HIS BLESSING.IN OUR TRADITION,ONCE OUR ELDERLY ONE GIVES HIS BLESSINGS,THINGS WORKS WELL.

DEARLING I AM YOURS,BE ASSURED OF ME AS I AM STILL A VIGIN.OUR FIRST CHILD WILL BE A GIRL AS I LIKE GIRL TO HELP ME IN MY DOMESTIC WORK.DO EMAIL ME TO LET ME KNOW WHEN YOU ARE COMING.

WITH LOVE FROM

JOSEPHINE FANNERMAN

Hilary:

DEAR UNCLE,

I DO APPRECIATE YOUR EFFORT TO SEE THAT WE COME OVER TO UNITED STATE OF AMERICA. I WILL SCAN THE CERTIFICATE OF THE CONSIGNMENT. I WILL ON MY OWN FIND TO YOU THE BEST HOTEL IN ABIDJAN. CONCERNING YOUR FAMILY,I DO PITY THAT WE HAVE THE SAME NOTION,ONLY THAT YOUR MOTHER IS STILL ALIVE-GOD KEEP HER FOR US TO SEE HER AS OUR OWN MOTHER.

LOOK UNTO GOD FOR MORE BLESSING,DO NOT THINK TOO MUCH WE WILL BE WITH YOU TO ENJOY THE GOOD THINGS YOU HAVE FOR US.PLEASE DO NOT LET THE SECURITY COMPANY KNOW WHAT IS IN THE CONSIGNMENT,IT IS A SECRET.WE WILL INVEST THE MONEY IN YOUR BUSINESS. BE REST ASSURED THAT I AM IN SUPPORT OF YOU MARRING MY SISTER.I BELIEVE YOU WILL TAKE CARE OF HER,SHE IS ALWAYS TALKING ABOUT YOU.

GOD BE WITH YOU,MY REGARDS TO YOUR MOTHER.

Dr. Uzondu, at the Scammer's "Security Company":

FROM THE DESK OF CHIEF SECURITY OFFICER;DR WEST UZONDU.

TO:MR A.D.D. FANNERMAN,

WE REQUEST YOU TO FORWARD YOUR OFFICIAL LETTER HEADED PAPER REQUESTING YOUR WILLINGNESS OF TAKING THIS CONSIGNMENT AS THE BENEFICIARY IN HELPING THE OPHANS TO FORWARD THEIR EDUCATION.THIS SHOULD BE SCANED AND FORWARDED BY EMAIL FOR SECURITY REASONS. YOU SHOULD SEND A FEE OF FIVE THOUSAND FIVE HUNDRED AND FIFTY DOLLARS(5,550US$)IN FAVOUR OF MR NELSON N .EGBUTA . BEAR IN MIND THIS CONSIGNMENT HAS BEEN YIELDING DEMMURAGE, YOU WILL BE INFORMED THE AMOUNT AFTER THE APPROVAL FEE OF THE ABOVE SAID AMOUNT. WE WILL WANT YOU TO COME AND CLAIM THIS CONSIGNMENT. WE ARE LOOKING FORWARD TO RECEIVING THE APPROVAL FEE THROUGH WESTERN UNION.

REGARDS

DR WEST UZONDU.

Arnold:

Dear Dr. Uzondo:

The approval fee of US$5,550 will be no problem. My only problem is this: while funds taken from my company "BLUE CRESCENT EAT-M-UP WIGGLE BABY PLASTIC WORMS INC." (well known in the sporting world) are under my control, my accountants demand documentation. Can you email to me some sort of document, which notes that the money is targeted towards redeeming the box in question? As soon as I receive this, I will send the money.

Arnold:

Dearest Josephine,

It was thrilling to receive your letter, and to see you sign it "Josephine Diddy." I hope all this comes to pass. But we will know more when we meet in Abidjan. After all, we do not really know each other yet. Maybe you will not like me when you see me. But I can assure you that I am a good-looking healthy man.

I want you to know that I will be leaving on the 15th of April. I will arrive there in the evening of that date. I am buying an "open return" ticket. This way, if we really think we are meant for each other, we can spend extra time together. This is an advantage to owning a company...there is no boss I must answer to, and my time is my own.

Now I must tell you something, which I hope will not cause you to have second thoughts about marriage. I know that you are Christian, and I have great respect for the Christian religion. But, my dearest Josephine, I am Jewish.

My ancestors come from Bialystock, Poland. My grandfather was named Itzik Diddowitzsteinkovsky, a very common name, but not appealing to Americans. Upon arrival in the US, he shortened the name to Diddy, to suit American life and tastes. I want you to know everything about my family, and when we see each other, I will tell you more about our history.

In order for us to be married, you must convert to Judaism, the Israelite-Hebrew religion. As you know, Jesus Christ was Jewish. If He were alive today, He would give us His blessing. Remember, Jesus Christ did not know about "Christianity," as it did not yet exist. He was a yeshiva bocher. Let me tell you what this means for us, stating only the most important particulars, which you must know beforehand:

We will keep a "kosher" household. We will eat no pork, nor fish without scales (sharks, eels, etc). We will not eat any food which contains oats, barley, malt, spelt, or milt. Any water we drink must be heated to 42 (FORTY TWO) degrees Celsius. We may eat foods of any colours except yellow (no bananas). We will not eat any dairy products with meat at the same meal. Any animal we eat must not be slaughtered in a cruel fashion, but must die painlessly by lethal injection. You can read all these injunctions in the bible, for example, concerning the meat and dairy: "Thou shalt not boil a kid in its mother's milk."

We will go to the "synagogue," the House of Worship, 3 times each day. You will look down from behind a screen in the women's gallery, where you will get to know the other wives of the congregation.

Whenever you have your monthly menstruation, you will remain apart from me at a distance of at least 60 (SIXTY) cubits, and be careful not to touch me. When your menstruation is complete, you will go to the "mikveh," the ritual bathhouse, and clean yourself. Then you can come home to me and we will have intimate relations.

As far as these intimate relations are concerned, it is forbidden for us to gaze upon the naked body of the other. Therefore, when we do have intimate relations, you will cover yourself with a sheet which has a circular hole cut in it at the appropriate place. In this way, we will be able to have children without degrading ourselves by close physical contact. While having these relations, we will think only of holy things, and not behave lustfully or in a jocular fashion. Do not be offended, my dearest girl. One must speak directly about such things, so there will be no misunderstandings later.

You must, the day we are married, remove all hair from your head and body. In place of your natural hair, you will wear a wig. This is so no other man may look with a lustful heart upon your own hair. You will dress so that your body is covered to your ankles, and so that your arms and ears are covered as well. You will learn to prepare suitable dishes for our family to eat. This includes, but is not limited to: Gefilte fish with sliced carrots and horse radish, stuffed kishke, tzimmes, borscht with sour cream, brisket, boiled chicken, hamentashen, challah (braided for shabbos), kugel, noodle pudding (mmm!), and honey cake.

Please do not be alarmed. You will be relieved to know that my mother's 3 sisters will oversee your every move.

Please understand, dearest Josephine, the importance attached to these matters. I would encourage you to pick up a copy of the "Kitzur Shulchan Aruch" by Rabbi Solomon Ganzfried at your local bookstore in Abidjan. In it you will find all the instructions for maintaining a kosher household, and for leading a "frum" (holy) life. I would not want to spring these matters on you by surprise, so it is best that you prepare. If there is true love, everything else will follow.

Please inform Hillie that I am in touch with the security company, and we are making arrangements for the transfer of the approval fee. I have withdrawn it from the company treasury, but cannot send it there until I have the paperwork. This may sound complicated, dearest Josephine, but it is a simple matter, and is done every day.

My company is a well-known manufacturer of fishing equipment and artificial baits. All the money from the security box will go into its bank account, after, of course, we take a small advance for expenses ...only a few hundred thousand dollars... :). Don't worry, my sweet girl, I am basically an honest man, who has achieved a high station in life through hard work.

Dearest Josephine, tell me whether you feel you can comply with my wishes, so I will feel free to complete this transaction with a heart full of gladness at the anticipated outcome.

Your Diddy

Josephine:

MY DEAREST DIDDY,

I RECEIVED YOUR MAIL WITH ULTIMATE HAPPINESS.IT DOES NOT MATTER THE RELIGION YOU ARE BUT WHAT MATTERS IS THE LOVE WE HAVE FOR EACH OTHER.WHAT I NEED IS YOUR CARING WHICH I KNOW YOU CARES. LOVE IS BLIND,IT DOES NOT MATTER HOW YOU LOOK PHYSICALLY, SPIRITUALLY AND OTHERWISE BUT RATHER THE LOVE OF GOD WHICH MY PARENTS TAUGHT ME BEFORE THEIR UNTIMELY DEATH.BE REST ASSURED THAT I LOVE YOU FROM THE DIPPEST OF MY HEART NO MATTER HOW YOU LOOK LIKE.

I HAVE BEEN HAVING SLEEPLESS NIGHT,GIVE ME YOUR FLIGHT SCHEDULE FOR ME TO GET PREPARED AND WAIT FOR YOU AT THE AIRPORT. PLEASE,I WILL LIKE YOU TO SEND ME MONEY FOR ME TO USE TO BUY THE BOOK YOU ASKED ME TO BUY SO AS TO START STUDING IT.I WILL BE GREATFUL TO RECEIVE THE MONEY.

ON THE SIDE OF THE SECURITY COMPANY, THEY DO NOT KNOW WHAT MY FATHER DEPOSITED, DO NOT TELL THEM(IT IS MONEY) ANYTHING THEY ASK YOU TO DO,DO IT. I WILL INFORM HILARY TO EMAIL YOU THE DOCUMENTS. I WILL LIKE TO REMIND YOU THAT AFTER OUR MARRIAGE,I WILL TAKE THE POSSITION OF THE

DEPUTY DIRECTOR IN ASSISTING YOU IN THE COMPANY.

YOUR LOVE,

JOSEPHINE DIDDY.

Arnold:

My Dearest Josephine,
I am so happy that you will agree to join my religion to be my wife. Thank you!

You mention that you will be "Deputy Director" of Wiggle Baby after our marriage. I would like nothing better. It is difficult to run a large company alone. But you should undergo training in business before you can do what is expected of the director of a company, and especially a company as large as Blue Crescent Wiggle Baby! I will be happy to send you to business school.

Let me inform you of developments. When I presented the Approval Agreement to our treasurer, he advised me to travel there and meet the people involved before sending money via Western Union. So I shall do this. Have no fear, I will bring the cash! I calculate the demurrage due to be about 108,000 dollars US. As your first job as Deputy Director, I would like you to inform Dr. Uzondo of this plan.

I cannot wait to meet you. I also had a dream about you, 2 nights ago. I was walking through a swampy bottomland on a dark and misty night. Crocodiles were snapping at my legs as I walked, when from out of the mouth of one crocodile came...you! You walked...no, floated...towards me and gave me a wide smile, opening your arms wide as if to embrace me. Blood was dripping from your teeth. Then I woke up, sweating profusely. They say bad dreams bring good luck!

I have purchased a copy of the Kitzur Shulchan Aruch for you, my dearest. By the way, I hope you will be at the airport to greet me. I will be very disappointed if you are not there. I think I would just turn around and go back home! so be sure to come to the airport on the 15th.

All my love, Zei Gezund!

Josephine:

DEAREST DEARLING DIDDY,

I DID AS YOU SAID BY GOING TO MEET DR UZONDU,HE DID TOLD ME THAT HE HAS SENT TO YOU A LETTER OF AGREEMENT AND THAT THEY ARE WAITING FOR THE APPROVAL FEE WHICH IS BEEN DEMANDED FROM YOU.

HE SAID THAT WITHOUT FIRST PAYING FOR THIS APPROVAL FEE,THERE IS NO WAY THE CONSIGNMENT WILL BE HANDED OVER. THE DEMURAGE MONEY CAN COME WITH YOU WHEN YOU ARRIVE. PLEASE DEARLING,PAY THEM SO AS TO AVIOD

SUSPECT FROM THEM.

I WILL BE AT THE AIRPORT TO WELCOME YOU WITH MY WARMEST ARM. DR WEST PROMISED TODAY TO GET US OUT OF THE CAMP.

I DREAMT OF YOU LAST NIGHT,I KNOW GOOD THINGS IS COMING ON OUR WAY. HAVE A GOOD NIGHT.

YOUR LOVE

JOSEPHINE ZEI GEZUND.

Arnold:

Dearest Dearling Josephine, Dear Girl:

I received your letter with gladness. Do not worry, sweet girl. I assure you the security company will get the money. 5550 dollars is a small amount. But with a view to the final amount, which is not so small, I must be able to say to the treasurer, "Yes I have met everyone, and they are all decent people."

You mentioned that Dr. Ozondu wants to take you out of the camp. I hope there is nothing more than a business relationship between you, though I am happy that he has been kind to you. I do get a bit jealous.

Please, Josephine, tell me what size dress you wear, so I can stop off at a store called "Victoria's Secret" and buy presents for you. Do you like jewelry? In America it is the custom for a man to buy his woman gifts of gold and diamonds. Please go to a jewelry store and look at some things. If you see something you like, I will bring something of the same type and quality. Do not worry about the price.

Dearest Josephine, please describe conditions at the camp. If things are really bad there, perhaps I should help you before I get there. Please describe every little thing to me, so I can have an idea of exactly how you are living. Describe your house, your neighbors, your street, the food you eat, the water, everything.

I will be arriving April 16th at 6:05 PM. The flight is Air France #702. I can't wait to see you.

Josephine:

Subject: DIDDY I LOVE YOU WITH ALL MY HEART.

I WAS SO EXCITED WHEN I READ YOUR MAIL.YOUR PLANS IS O.K BY ME.

DR UZONDU IS A NICE MAN, HE KNOWS YOU ARE MY HUSBAND,HE IS HAPPILY MARRIED WITH CHILDREN.TODAY,THEY TOOK US OUT OF THE CAMP TO A GOOD PLACE.CAMP LIFE IS A HORRIBLE PLACE,THE FOOD THEY COOK THERE IS NOTHING TO TALK HOME ABOUT-THANK GOD YOU ARE ON MY SIDE.

DEARLING,YOU NEED NOT TO EXPERIENCE SUCH LIFE.

I COULDN'T HOLD MY SELF ON THE GIFT YOU ARE BRINGING TO ME.I LIKE GOLD JEWELRIES,BOTH WATCHES AND BANGLES.MY DRESS IS 42,I LIKE IT DIFFERENT COLOURS I WILL BE HAPPY TO RECEIVE THEM.WHAT ARE YOU GOING TO BRING FOR MY SENIOR BROTHER HILARY?I THINK HE WILL LIKE SHOES,WATCHES AND SUITE,HIS SIZE IS 42 FOR SHOES AND FOR SUITE IS 45.

I CAN NOT SLEEP BUT TO WAIT TO THE D-DAY.I LOVE YOU SO MUCH.TELL ME SWEET WORDS TO MOVE ON WITH TODAY.

YOUR LOVELY DEARLING,

JOSEPHINE DIDDY

KISS ME.

Arnold:

Dr Uzondu:

I am afraid my hands are tied with respect to the approval fee. You have your rules and I have my company procedures. If it is impossible for you to receive the $5550 upon my arrival, tell me so I can cancel my reservation on Air France flight 702, due to arrive in Abidjan at 6:05 pm on April 16th. But, it is impossible to believe that you must refuse the fee if offered upon my arrival. I beg you to consider this option, as the items in the trunk are the last links to the orphans' father and mother, and are of great sentimental value.

You have not responded to my request to confirm the demurrage fee, about 108,000 US dollars. It will be a simple matter to forward to you this fee also upon my arrival in Abidjan.

Uzondu:

Sir,

A board meeting was held concerning your request to come to Abidjan with the Approval fee, a motion was raised concerning not treating your matter as a constitutional procedure of handling matters, oppositions from here and there was laid against me maybe, my interest on your matter.Firstly,you never told us that you will be coming with the Approval fee. Sir, I believe with all fairness,you are welcome.

Your calculation seems to be alright.You are suppose to come with one hundred and eight thousand dollars (us$108.000.00) to payoff the demurrage. I assure you maximum security right from the airport to your lodgement and reiterate absolute treatment to you on your claim to the deposited box. We work 24hours everyday,you are free to call me any time.

Josephine:

MY DEAREST DEARLING DIDDY,

ARE YOU O.K?.I KNOW YOU ARE PREPERING FOR YOUR COMING TO ABIDJAN.I HAD A DREAM LAST NIGHT SEEING YOU HOLDING ME TIGHT,POURING KISSES ALL OVER ME,I JUST WISHED YOU ARE HERE WITH ME LAST NIGHT.

LIKE I SAID,WE HAVE BEEN TAKEN OUT OF THE CAMP TO A RESIDENTIAL BUILDING OWNED BY THE SECURITY ORGANISATION,I'M SO HAPPY TO MYSELF EAT GOOD FOOD SINCE EVER OUR PARIENTS DIED.

I WILL BE HAPPY TO ASK YOU THE DRESS YOU WILL PUT ON FOR ME TO IDENTIFY YOU AT THE AIRPORT.AS FOR ME,I WILL PUT ON A RED BODY HUCK WITH WHITE STRIP AND A JEAN TROUSER-HOPE IT IS O.K BY YOU.

WITH LOVE FROM JOSEPHINE DIDDY(MRS)

Arnold:

Dearest Josephine,

I was overjoyed to hear from you! I have much business to finish before leaving. Wiggle Baby is a very big company.

I bought you and Hillie each 2 (two) watches, for a total of 4 (four). One is called "Rolex." It is very elegant. I also bought a "Piaget" watch for you. It looks more like jewelry than a watch! It is made of white gold with small diamonds and rubies. I can't wait to see your face when you see it! Believe me, your life will be changing. Soon you will forget that you were in a camp.

I told my Rabbi about you. He is happy for us. I, along with several other families, provided the funds to build the Temple of Solomon here in Miami. You cannot imagine the pride I feel when I attend the daily sacrifices. It is a beautiful ceremony, especially when the Levites begin to sing. As the Diddy family goes back to the Kohanim (priests) of Jerusalem, we are entitled to a share in the Terumah (priest's share). After our marriage, we will go to the Temple and offer a bullock for sacrifice. We will join hands and sprinkle blood upon the altar, then go home and feast on the Terumah. You will love it, I am sure.

Dr. Uzondu says it will be ok for me to pay the approval fee when I arrive. This is a sure sign that everything will work out as planned.

All my love

Hilary:

DEAR UNCLE,

MY SISTER JOSEPHINE TOLD ME OF YOUR ARRIEVAL TO ABIDJAN ON THE 16th, I

AM HAPPY TO RECIEVING YOU AS MY INLAW.I ASSURE YOU MAXIMUM WELCOME TO ABIDJAN. THE WAY MY SISTER TALKS ABOUT YOU SHOWS ME THAT SHE IS REALLY IN LOVE WITH YOU.

Josephine:

MY DEAREST DEARLING DIDDY,

I COULDN'T HOLD MYSELF WHEN I READ YOUR MAIL.TELL ME WHAT KIND OF FOOD YOU WOULD WANT ME TO PREPARE.I KNOW YOU WILL BE HUNGRY WHEN YOU ARRIEVE.I WILL PREFER TO COOK RICE WITH BEEF FOR THE EVENING SO AS TO KNOW HOW I WILL COOK FOR YOU WHEN WE GOT MARRIED. I WISHED MY FATHER IS ALIVE TO WITNESS OUR MARRIAGE, BECAUSE YOU WILL MAKE IT A ROYAL WEDDING.I KNOW CNN WILL CARRY IT ALL OVER THE WORLD.

ALL THE ARRANGEMENT HAS BEEN MADE TO SECURE YOUR SECURITY BY THE SECURITY ORGANISATION. DO NOT ALLOW THEM TO OPEN THE BOX,PAY OFF THEIR DEMURRAGES AND REQUEST THEM TO HANDOVER THE BOX TO YOU.I DON'T WANT THEM TO KNOW THE CONTENT (THE BOX CONTAINS MONEY,us$18.5m.BUT IT IS LABELLED FAMILY TREASURE).

DEARLING, TELL ME SWEET WORDS FOR I AM DYING TO SEEING YOU WITH MY WARMEST ARM AT THE AIRPORT. I LOVE YOU,HAVE A SWEET NIGHT,DON'T FORGET TO DREAM OF ME AS I WILL DO THE SAME. I KISS YOU.

Arnold:

My Dearest Josephine,

Your letter was wonderful, as all your letters are. I have just been to the barber shop to get a nice haircut so I will look my best when we meet. I have even oiled my payes (earlocks), and bought a new tzitzit and a nice blue knitted yamulkeh just for you. I am shaking all over with excitement...

Do not worry, I will not mention anything about the money to Dr. Uzondu. I always had a good business sense. Many times, business deals are presented to me, which are not really suitable, and I have a 6th (SIXTH) sense about such things. For example, I know that you and Hillie are 100 percent (ONE HUNDRED PERCENT) solid people, reliable and trustworthy. Some people might have difficulty ascertaining such things, but I have a gift for spotting sincere individuals. If a person is unreliable, or even dishonest, I can tell right away, even before I meet them! When you say that you are on my side, I know deep in my heart that nothing bad could ever happen to me.

You mentioned that you will be cooking beef and rice for us. That is my favorite dish, after chicken grieven with oyster sauce! I am sure it will be delicious!

I have one small request... you know, I travel frequently on business. But I am never met at the airport by a lovely woman! In fact, I usually arrive alone. When I see other people met by their loved ones, and presented with flowers, I always wish that it could be me! So, if you only could, will you meet me with flowers? I do not mean a few little blossoms, but a big, colourful bouquet containing dozens of bright, fresh flowers. If you could do this, I would see that your love is truly deep. I am just so excited, my dearest girl. Nothing like this has ever happened to me, and I know I will remember the date April 16, 2002 for the rest of my life. I know that you will, too!

I am impressed that Dr. Uzondu managed to relocate you to a better domicile. Please let me know how much he has spent, so I can give him the money, without having to ask him how much he paid. It is a question of honour.

I am a little concerned about going through customs with the watches, jewelry, and cash. Do you suggest that I declare it all, or should I conceal at least the watches and jewelry?

I see that you have a sense of humour! You say CNN will carry our wedding all over the world. Hahaha! That is very funny, Josephine dearest! I am very happy to see such a quality in you.

By the way, it would be wonderful if Hillie could join us in the Jewish religion. Can you tell me please if Hillie has been circumcised? If he has not been circumcised, do not worry. As a member of a Priestly family, I have performed many circumcisions for the children of my congregation. I would be honoured to perform this sacred duty for Hillie. Tell him not to worry, as I have very steady hands, if I have not been drinking too much schnapps.

Josephine:

MY DEAREST DEARLING,
I WENT TO THE SALON TO DO MY HAIR;JUST TO LOOK NICE FOR YOUR LIKING. HOW DID YOU KNOW THAT I AM COMING TO MEET YOU WITH SOME FLOWERS, FLOWERS SIGNIFIES LOVE.MY MOTHER TAUGHT ME THIS BEFORE HER DEATH.

THERE IS NO POINT DECLAERING WHAT YOU HAVE AT THE AIRPORT. YOU MAY HIDE THE MONEY IN A CIGARATE PACK, JUST TAKE ONE OF THE PACKET IN A ROLL, EMPTY THE CIGARATE AND INCERT THE MONEY IN ALL THE PACKET PUT IT BACK AT THE ROLL.IN OTHER WAY,YOU CAN HIDE THE MONEY IN YOUR SUIT AND MY PRIVATE PART(paint)FOR THEY DO NOT SEARCH FORIEGNERS ESPECIALLY THE AMERICANS. I WILL BE AT THE GATE WITH MY FLOWERS.

DEARLING,I AM SO EXCITED TO SEEING YOU AT THE D DAY. HILARY IS CIRCUMCISED BY OUR LATE FATHER BUT NOT IN OUR OWN RELIGION(hindus)BUT YOU CAN CIRCUMCISED HIM FOR OUR OWN BETTERMENT.DO REMEMBER THAT I AM ON YOUR SIDE.

Arnold:

Dearest Josephine,

Yes it is amazing about the flowers! This proves we are meant for each other. About hiding the money...I don't think you have any idea how bulky all that cash is! On your advice I will not declare it. If you are sure I won't be searched, I will put it in my suitcase.

I will be bringing my circumcision knife. I will examine Hilly and confirm that he has been properly circumcised. If not, it will be a small matter to finish the job. Please tell him not to worry. It is sometimes an almost painless operation. He should be walking again after only a few days. You also mentioned that Hillie was not circumcised according to the Hindu religion, and that your own religion is Hindu. But I thought you are Christians. Or did I misunderstand something?

I cannot believe that we will be meeting each other in just a couple of days!

Josephine:

I READ YOUR MAIL WITH ULTIMATE INTEREST AND HAPPINESS. I HAVE BEEN RUNING ARROUND TO SEEING THAT ALL ARRANGEMENT IS BEEN MADE TO YOUR ARRIEVAL. YOU ARE MY BLOOD,NOTHING WILL SEPARATE YOU FROM ME;I MEAN,NO MAN BORN OF A WOMAN CAN DO THAT,MY LOVE FOR YOU HAS GONE TO A GREAT EXTEEM,I AM YOUR FLESH,GOD KNOWS THAT(SORRY TO USE THIS WORD,I 'M USED TO IT).

AT THE CUSTOM GATE,DO NOT TELL THEM YOUR MISSION OF COMING ONLY TELL THEM YOU HAVE COME TO SEE YOUR WIFE JOSEPHINE AND YOUR INLAWS.

ON THE SIDE OF HILLY'S CIRCUMSCISION, HE WAS CIRCUMSCISED BY OUR LATE FATHER,IT IS BASED ON THE CHRISTAIN RELIGION NOT HINDUS.I AM ONLY SAYING THAT HE CAN BE RE-CIRCUMSCISED ON OUR OWN RELIGION(hindus). MY FAMILY IS A CHRISTAIN FAMILY, OUR LATE PARENTS WORSHIPPED IN A PROTESTANT CHURCH. I WAS BORN WITH A SILVER SPOON, MY FATHER WAS A MINISTER OF MINES AND POWER BEFORE HIS UNTIMELY DEATH BY THE REBELS THAT KILLED HIM.THE KILLING OF MY PARENTS SCARTTERED MY DREAMS OF BECOMING WHAT I WANT TO BE,BUT I WILL GAIN ALL I HAVE LOST.WITH YOU,MY DREAMS COMES TRUE. TILL WE MEET TOMORROW.

Josephine:

I FELT HUMULIATED HAVING WAITED FOR YOU AT THE AIRPORT,I WAS FULL WITH SHAME,I CANNOT FACE THE WORLD ANYLONGER WITH FLOWERS AT MY ARMS AND MY BELOVED ONE NOT ON THE FLIGHT,I KEPT GUESSING LIKE A WIDOW WHILE THE PASSANGERS DESEMBARKED FROM THE PLANE,AIR FRANCE BOEING

702 FROM PARIS BY 18.50pm,WHAT A DISGRACE,AN AGORNEY,A SHOCK.

I NEVER KNEW WHAT IS CALLED DISAPPOINTMENT IN LIFE UNTILL YOU GAVE ME ONE.WHAT REALLY HAPPENED?WAS THERE ANY PROBLEM?OR SHOULD I SAY WHAT YOU HAVE BEEN TELLING ME IS ALL FALACY?WHAT COULD BE THE CAUSE OF ALL THESE?I SWEAR PROSTERITY WILL NOT FORGIVE YOU;YOU SAID YOU LOVED ME, IS THIS HOW YOU WILL KEEP ME AS A WIFE? MY DREAMS SCHATTERED,WHEN I TAUGHT I HAVE YOU AS MY LAST HOPE. EXPAIN TO ME FOR I WILL DIE NOT TO SEE YOU NO MORE

Arnold to Hilary, Josephine, and Uzondu:

Sorry I missed you at the airport.

Do you know how many letters from 419 guys I get? I think at least 20 in the last 3 months...

Best of luck, and ZEI GEZUND!

Waldo Fleckenhurst (my real name)

(I don't think I'll be hearing from Hilary/Josephine again. I wonder if they found a girl to bring to the airport? Maybe she would have been a suitable wife. I guess I'll never know!)

CHAPTER 10

EXTREME ANTI-SCAMMING

419 no be thief, it's just a game
Everybody dey play em
if anybody fall mugu,
ha! my brother I go chop em
— Nkem Owoh

Extreme Anti-Scammers have more serious ways to cause mischief. A few points:

• This chapter describes their techniques in general terms only. A technical primer might be taken as encouragement to try the same things at home and I don't provide legal advice.

• I admire the efforts of anti-scammers to save others from being scammed, so nothing's mentioned here which hasn't been openly discussed on web sites for some years. People wishing to join the ranks of the Extreme will have to earn trust over time in appropriate forums. If you're sincere, you'll find your cadre.

• This is not necessarily an "anti-establishment" activity. Many anti-scammers are happy to help law enforcement and some have contributed information leading to arrests.

COMPLAINING, ON STEROIDS

Some anti-scammers stick to contacting ISPs and black hole registries, but they do it aggressively. This is something the reader can do without special training. Over time, it has had an effect. Anti-scammers have begun to complain of shortages of scammers to bait—by the time they respond to Urgent Proposals, the scammer's account has been cancelled. Others prefer to leave a scammer's email account in place and sign it up for "ordinary" spam (Viagra, penny stocks), or use his name to post in porn chat groups.

JOKEWARE

A South African anti-scammer worked up an email attachment, which did nothing, but, when opened, contained this notice:

By opening this attachment, you have installed SkamTrak™ on your system. SkamTrak™ is sanctioned for use by Interpol and the FBI, and is used to trace email suspected of being used in fraudulent operations. By arrangement with major anti-virus and anti-spyware vendors (Norton, McAfee, XBlock and others) their products will not alert users to the presence of SkamTrak™ on a computer.

Evidence obtained by SkamTrak™ is admissible in court. Because you have been informed of its installation, your use of the system is deemed to constitute consent thereto. Under the law, we must also inform you of the procedures necessary to remove SkamTrak™.

1: Make a backup of the address book of your email client.

2: Delete the contents of your address book.

3: Using a printout from your backup, manually re-enter the addresses you wish to retain in your address book. NB: It is insufficient to simply restore the contents of your backup to the address book. The code for SkamTrak™ is written into the buffer zones of the technical headings of the addresses and will reactivate if a restore operation is performed.

Whilst every effort has been made to ensure that SkamTrak™ is compatible with all software platforms, loss of data may occur. If you feel SkamTrak™ has damaged your system, you may qualify for compensation. Any claims should be lodged with the U.S. Federal Bureau of Investigation.

SkamTrak™ - Skimming the Scam Scum for Safer Surfing

— Created by "Blunderov" (Saviour of the Universe Vapourware Ventures (Pty) Ltd.)

SkamTrak™ inspired another anti-scammer, "Fred Flintstone," to create a website with a Flash animation, to which scammers were lured via email. The animation popped up a "progress bar" stating that SkamTrak was indeed being installed, and popped up the message "You are a 419 scammer." The thoughtfully included "uninstall" button crashed Internet Explorer.

EMAIL RECONNAISSANCE AND INFO-WARFARE

The next step up in Extreme Anti-Scamming is to break into scammers' email accounts. This is often easy to do for reasons, which the intelligent reader will guess, or which will be obvious on re-reading chapter 9. If more effort is required, a keystroke logging program "keylogger"—can be deployed in the form of a "trojan," to get the scammer's password. A keystroke logging trojan records every key pressed and sends this data back to its' 'master,' typically using the IRC chat protocol.

A trojan is a program with a secret function which appears to, or may even do something useful as a decoy. It might come packaged as a picture or game, or in a file downloaded from a file-sharing service. Unlike a virus, Trojan cannot install and run itself, although once installed it may mail off copies of itself—or spread viruses. While a user may install it voluntarily, the user is not always needed to start up a trojan. Web browsers and mail readers can start programs too. A vulnerable web browser may invoke helper programs such as ActiveX objects, which will run a trojan from a malicious web site; a vulnerable mail-reader may run the attachment when the email is opened.

One way to deploy a keylogger is to send the scammer an email with the trojan as an attachment. Alternatively, the email might contain an invitation to visit a website, which will try to download the logger to the scammer's PC. (This may sound a lot like "phishing," and it is.)

Once inside a scammer's email account, the anti-scammer may simply lurk in order to learn whom the scammer is targeting and who his partners are. Some anti-scammers attach a "sig" to the scammer's email account. A "sig" (signature) is boilerplate text, which can be automatically added to all outgoing emails—a feature normally used for job titles, or favorite quotes. "I am a con artist" would be a self-defeating sig. An anti-scammer may send confusing messages to the scammer's colleagues from the scammer's own account. The most common action is to warn off the potential victims in the inbox, but some people are hard to "save." No one likes to feel a fool.

Sometimes scammers make things easy. Here is an email sent by a scammer to his intended victim, which mistakenly included a message meant for the scammer's cronies. Note where he closes his letter to the victim, and starts writing to his "Bros."

FROM THE DESK OF,
MR ISAAC JOHN,
PHONE: 00234 8052465xxx
EMAIL: isaacjohn@terra.com.mx

HELLO MY GOOD FRIEND,

FIRST,I MUST SOLICIT YOUR CONFIDENCE IN THIS TRANSACTION, I KNOW THIS WILL COME TO YOU AS A SURPRISE BECAUSE YOU DO NOT KNOW ME. I AM MR ISAAC JOHN,I WORK WITH CENTRAL BANK OF NIGERIA, PACKAGING AND COURIER DEPARTMENT.

I GOT YOUR CONTACT THROUGH MY OWN PRIVATE SEARCH FOR SOME ONE I CAN CONFIDENTLY TRUST AND GOD FEARING PERSON. I WANT YOU TO HELP ME CLEAR THE TWO CONSIGNMENT, ONE IS IN HOLLAND AND THE ORDER ONE IS IN AMERICA, WHICH I SHIPPED THROUGH OUR NIGERIAN ACCREDITED COURIER AGENT, BUT THE CONTENT OF THE PACKAGE IS US$9,000.000.00 EACH, ALL IN US$100 BILLS, BUT THE COURIER COMPANY DOES NOT KNOW THAT, IT IS MONEY THAT I HAVE IN THE PACKAGE.

ALL I WANT YOU TO DO FOR ME NOW IS THIS, GIVE ME-
YOUR MAILING ADDRESS ,YOUR PRIVATE PHONE AND FAX

AND I WILL GIVE YOU THE DETAILS OF SECURITY COMPANY.AND I HOPE THAT AT THE END OF THE DAY , YOU WILL HAVE 30% AND 60% WILL BE FOR ME, AND 10% WILL BE FOR ANY MONEY YOU PUT INPROCESS OF CLEARING THE PACKAGE.

MY IDENTITY MUST NOT BE REVEALED TO ANYBODY, OTHER MODALITIES WILL BE DISCUSSED AS SOON AS YOU GET BACK TO ME INCLUDING SENDING OF THE KEYS TO THE BOXES TO YOU .

YOURS FAITHFULLY ,
MR ISAAC JOHN

Bros,

Like i was explaining on phone. What i want us to do now is this, We already work the man from here as the catch and the courier firm which is (Global Diplomatic Services)

The man has already paid $15000 to us which we collect by frist was delivery cost and the second time is customs fee when they came to our office to carry all over stayed consignment in our office that he pay $9500 to settle in other to get it back which we have done and now we are to deliver to him on monday as discussed. The manager name is James Connery and the secertrys name is Mary Allen this are the two people that has talk with him over here and he has also called us too in new york.

What we want to do now is to move with the consignment from new york to another state which will now be sized by the customs on your way to deliver for lack of documents which are Anti-terorist, Drug and mondy lundraying certificate which will cost about $ 23,500, but now he will be calling you from another state where it was size with you at the airport, untill we provide those documents, I know you will know how to play this part and i believe he will pay we have no problem with that.

Bros, you will have to call him from New York as the diplomat letting him know that your boss Mr. james Connery ask you to call him, that you are the one coming with his consignment to pennslyvania with other people you will have to deliver consignment too, and another call will be out of new york, which is where you were arrested with the consignment after delivery of other ones and want to come over to his place. you can choose any state you will be with the phone number of that place. and you will tell him when you call him from new york that you will be coming from that place ok.

Bros i leave the rest for you i know you know best and know what to say i am only letting you know how far i have gone and what has already been done.

After you go through this email please give me a call so that i will let you have the information of the mugu for next action.

Your Good Brother,
Nnamdi.

Predictably, the above email did not have the desired effect on the victim.

ACTIONS AGAINST FRAUDULENT WEB SITES

Scammers set up web sites to support their scams—copies of the web sites of real banks, or lotteries, or other, legitimate businesses. At first clumsy, these imitations have become more sophisticated, even providing ways to "log in" to an imaginary account.

This is similar to, but not the same as "phishing." A typical phishing attack begins with an email stating that a bank or credit card account may have been compromised. The victim is asked to visit a web site and provide account information, which can then be used to drain the account or commit fraud. The site may also download spyware to the victim's computer. So far this seems to be the specialty of Eastern Europeans, as are denial-of-service attacks (DDOS). In a DDOS attack, large numbers of computers are attacked and secretly taken over. Rather than being harmed in any obvious way, these zombified PCs are used to carry out coordinated attacks, typically being made to visit targeted websites all at once and repeatedly. The goal is blackmail or revenge, and such zombie crews can even be rented. A 419er web site seems to be meant only to support an illusion, although any personal information gleaned from a victim could be exploited or sold to others.

Both 419 scammers and (with more sophistication) phishers use fake security certificates. The real certificates, "seals" sold by companies such as Verisign and Thawte, are intended to guarantee the security and legitimacy of an electronic transaction. The clumsiest fake seal is a copied logo, which links to nothing. More sophisticated spoofs use programming to insert fake data in a browser's address bar or overlay the screen with graphical elements, which mimic a secure connection, e.g., the picture of a lock in a browser window. Some fraudsters have even managed to buy true seals. The best protection against fraud is common sense. An email from a bank asking for your password is suspect. A bank without a confirmed physical address is suspect. A business entity unknown to the relevant regulatory agency is suspect. Most of all, if a proposal is suspect, the source doesn't matter.

DEFACEMENT

Web sites can be taken over by exploiting weaknesses in the web server software and the underlying operating system, or by socially engineering (that is, fooling) the scammer's domain name registrar. The Lad Wrecking Crew take over bogus web sites and deface them, leaving behind brilliant visual calling cards. One features a collage of photos from the Japanese movie *Rashomon*, with dialogue spattered across the screen: "Do you remember a bank? There was never a bank here. It was a fantasy... in the mind of an internet scammer." Another is a lush and grotesque depiction of the horror movie character Freddy under the banner "Fake Banks Worst Nightmare." Around the border of the screen run the names of various anti-scam web sites.

DENIAL OF SERVICE

Another approach is to "DDOS" the criminals themselves—to exhaust the bandwidth of scammer web sites by tying them up with continual requests—except that the army is made up not of exploited PCs but enthusiastic participants. Artists Against 419 (www.aa419.org) began by using direct links in their own web pages to images on scammers' web sites. They progressed to organizing "flash mobs" in which people worldwide visited scammers' web sites all at once and repeatedly (thus providing an easy way for amateurs to join in). Flash mobs are drastic as they shut off access to every website sharing the scammer's internet service provider (a common arrangement—most public-facing web sites do not have dedicated computers). AA419 say they carry out DDOS attacks only on unresponsive ISPs. AA419 claim to have shut down over 130 fake banks, both through DDOS and, more diplomatically, by working with ISPs.

LEGALITIES

Evidence obtained in legally questionable ways can't be used in court, but anti-scammers are not entirely unappreciated by law enforcement. Sheriff Karl Dailey of Nebraska (USA) has worked with Artists Against 419, and uses a local radio show to warn people about fraud. The web site 419 Legal (www.419legal.org) was set up by Rian Visser of the South African police to coordinate efforts with anti-scammers. The moderators are anti-scammers screened by the police. Their efforts have led to arrests in South Africa and the Netherlands, including the closure of a fake South African embassy in Amsterdam.

PHYSICAL ACTION

Some anti-scammers descend into the physical plane. One team photographed scammers cooling their heels in a Dubai airport and got ("Solomon Mupesa," who was probably neither Solomon nor from Zimbabwe, as he claimed) to take a photo of *them* (displayed at www.africanscam.co.uk). Another anti-scammer mailed the Lads boxes of unpleasant-smelling stuff—a risky move as it works both ways and pressing "delete" doesn't make a crate of dog poo go away.

One extremely Extreme anti-scammer claims to have taken his martial-arts buddies to Amsterdam for a show-down with the Lads (www.scamorama.com/flyinglad.html). He assured me that no one was eliminated in the espionage sense of the word. I do *not* suggest anyone try this!

NETWORKS VS. NETWORKS

A Rand Corporation study of information warfare and terrorism proposes that it takes one networked group to compete with another. Its description of such groups fits both scammers and anti-scammers.1 At the core of scammer networks are the masters who head international teams, based on ties which are often ethnic but flexible, working from anywhere, using private lingo. At the edges of the network are "gatekeepers"—people in legitimate businesses who can launder money and provide facilities.

The Extreme are even more decentralized: leaderless, technically sophisticated, unencumbered by the need to meet a payroll, launder money, or handle logistics. Their "adoption" of scammers—described as "swarming" in the Rand model—acts as a sort of virus, wasting a scammer's time with false leads. It's not uncommon for an unlucky scammer to be "owned" by several anti-scammers, who bump into each other in the Inbox like burglars prowling the same house. United across ethnic and national lines, the Extreme Anti-Scammers are networked civilian crime-fighters.

COMEDY BREAK: FROM POLAND WITH LOVE

Dominatrix D breaks the heart of a scammer. In real life, D is a Polish translator. She was leading him on shamefully, as she had a perfectly good, non-imaginary boyfriend from Ghana.

Raymond the Scammer:

Dear SIR

I am a Branch Manager with STANDARD TRUST BANK(STB),My name is Mr Raymond Kuti a Banker. I am the Account Manager to ENGINEER A Dykes , who used to work with shell Development company in Nigeria. Here in after shall be referred to as my client

On April 21, 1999, my client, his wife, and their three children were involved in a car accident along Sagamu express way. All occupants lost their lives. I have made several inquiries to locate my clients extended Relatives. After these attempts, I decided to trace his last name over the Internet, hence I contacted you.

I have contacted you to assist in repatriating the money left behind by my client before they Get confiscated by the bank where this huge deposits were lodged, the STANDARD TRUST BANK PLC. Where the deceased had an account Valued at about ($6 million u s dollars) has Issued me a notice to provide the next of kin. Or have the account confiscated within the next ten official working days.

Since I have been unsuccessful in locating the relatives, I seek your consent to present you as the next of kin so that you and me Can share the money.60 percent to me and 40 percent to you An attorney will be contracted to help revalidated all the legal documents to back up any claim we may make. All I require is your honest cooperation to enable us see this deal through.

I guarantee that this will be executed under a legitimate arrangement that will protect you. from any breach of the law.

Best regards, Raymond

Dominatrix D:

Dear Sir,

I read your letter with great interest. I am just curious where you found my email address. If your proposition is still valid, please send me more information on what I should do.

I remain with hope,

Dori Kuklinski, Poland

Raymond:

Dear Dori,

Frankly,I got your address by trying to march the name of the deceased customer of my bank with yours and got your address revealed,hence,I decided to mail you.This is in the view of finding the relatives of the deceased whom bear the same name as you. We shall proceed by hiring an attorney who will obtain the documents which would present you as the next of kin.I shall also,give you the personal information of the customer so you can be well informed about him.

Once the attorney obtains the documents,like Federal High Court Of Nigeria sworn affidavit of Claim and Death Of the fund,we shall have your application processed and within 5working days your account shall be credited.I shall give you 50 percent of the total sum while my own part shall be transfered to a location which I will disclose to you as we move on.Please,be very committed and reply my mails swiftly.

You can call me on 234-8033462xxx anytime anyday.

I will entertain more questions from you in order to clarify you the more.

Thanks for your concern.

Raymond.

Dominatrix D:

Dear Mr. Raymond,

I am very happy you wrote me back! I was awake last night thinking what I could do when this transaction is over.

Most likely I will quit my job as accountant (Life Insurance and Securities Brokers in Wroclaw city in Poland) and set off for Australia or New Zealand where I will settle down.

I am a bit confused about this lawyer bit in your letter. How can I hire a lawyer in Nigeria? Do I have to go there? I have never been abroad and going on such a long trip makes me nervous.

Could you kindly write me few things about yourself? Are you going to help me in Nigeria? Is Nigeria a safe country? Do I need a visa if I have to travel there? Oh boy, it all seems so complicated!

I am impatiently awaiting your next letter.

God bless you, Dori K.

Raymond:

Dear Dori,

You are a very kind personality.I will wish to see you and have to discuss matters concerning business with you.I am 45 years old, married to Rosemary and blessed with three lovely daughters.I became a manager in 1999 and has worked diligently for this bank for close to 10years.

On the transaction,I had a deliberation with the attorney. His name is Philip aseke of El-Zabiri Chambers.Email:philipaseke@lawyer.com

Mr. Philip agreed to work for us on a service chatge of USD6,000 (six thousand United States Dollars).He stated that with that he will work to the Federal Ministry of Justice where Death certificate for the deceased Engr. Dyke will be released in your favour as next of kin.Also,an affidavit of Claim will also be issued to guarantee the transfer of the fund to your account.On the release of these documents,he will send copies to you and apply to our bank for the transfer of the fund to you.Please,write him and forward your account to him.I will come in when your application gets to the bank as I will use my discretion to get you settled.I hope you will not betray me when the money gets to your account.I will give you an account where my part will be transfered to when this is done. Thanks as I await your mail.

Raymond.

Raymond:

Dear Dori,

I have talked to the attorney who said you are yet to contact him at philipaseke@lawyer.com   .According to him everything is fine and he has said that the high court demanded USD4,000 to have the death and claim certficates released in your favour.He said once he gets this he shall forward an application for the transfer of the fund to you.I have given him apart of his service charge. I am working hard to raise the money but will like to that here that I might need a little assistance from you to be able to get this done.This will be the only place where we will be required to spend some money as I will work everything out when the appliction gets to the bank where I am the manager.

Please,let me know how much you can send so the attorney can have these certificates issued and sent to your mailbox. Please,stop keeping mute to me,try reply my mails.

Thanks and God bless.

Kuti.

Dominatrix D:

Dear Raymond,

I am very disappointed you're married. I was hoping that I might find a right man for me during this process. Are you sure you're happy with your wife? I guess she's getting older and after giving birth to three kids her body is disgusting. So what do you think about dumping her and marrying me instead? I am eagerly waiting for your response to this.

I am ready to go to Nigeria, but only on condition I will get married there.

Please advice,

Yours, Dori Kuklinski

Raymond:

Dear Dori,

I never knew you are a lady. I thought I was dealing with a fellow man. All the same I appreciate doing business with the opposite sex as they are very truthful and trust worthy. I will be very glad if you can make it to Nigeria, but this be after the completion of this transaction, with the money transferred to your account in Poland. I can marry you because I have not had the chance to hold and caress a white lady in my life.

On the transaction, please let me know how much you will be able to send to the attorney to enable him obtain the affidavits in your favour. The fees for the whole document is USD4,000 and I cannot get all that money. Let me know how much you can assist with.

Thanks and God bless.

Raymond.

Dominatrix D:

dear Raymond:

You wouldn't believe how happy you made me today with your kind letter to me. I am wondering, though, if your wife is comfortable with our getting married. Is it OK in Nigeria to have more than one wife? Are you a Muslim? I don't know anything about your country and I am curious I must say. Or maybe you're planning to divorce Rosemary and I will be a stepmother to your three lovely daughters? Also, my dear Raymondie you should send me your picture. It's only fair I know my future husband.

I am also thinking that if your plans towards me are sincere, you should send me an engagement ring. I'd prefer diamonds, but emeralds or saphires will do. My address is Kuklinski, 66-666 Wroclaw, Ul. Pocalujmniewdupe 23, Poland. My mother is keen on meeting you too. Will you come to Poland to meet her? Is it true that black men are wonderful and passionate lovers? I need to know before committing myself to you.

I will in due time contribute a part of lawyer's fee as you requested. I think the percentage should be same as with the funds—you should cover 60 percent and I will cover 40 percent. If you give me your account number I will wire the money next week. In the meantime please whisper sweet nothings to my ear.

Your future wife, Dori Kuklinski

Raymond:

Dear Dori,

How wonderful it is to read your mail. I am wondering if you are serious about getting married to me.I do not have any other option than to have you all to myself.I told you it is my dreams to get to hold and touch you.I will be sending my picture to you. On blackmen style of love, I believe God made blac men very strong sexually.I think we hold this against our other folks.

On the close of this transaction,I will travel to meet you in poland.I suggest you use part of the money when transfered to get a very good apartment in poland where we can stay.I am deeply concerned about you and will do everything to stay with you.I suggest I come to Poland with the engagement ring.This will be made with ivory with diamond stones.This stuff is obtainable here in africa.

I suggest you write to the attorney to let him know who he is working for.He will give you an account for the payment of your own poart.I suggest you make the payment with western union. You should know africa's poor banking system. Write the lawyer at: philipaseke@lawyer.com

Please Dori,tell me more about yourself.How old are you?Have you married before?What actually is your attraction to me when you are yet to see my face.I will like to see your mum.It is a great pleasure meeting you and believe Lord Jesus will keep us together.

Love,

Raymond.

Dominatrix D:

Dearest Raymond,

You have such a beautiful name. I am 34 years old, and since my biological clock is ticking I feel I am ready for marriage. It took me years to achieve the professional position and I neglected all options of marriage. I also need a husband who is older than I, and can take care of me and a baby. I want to have kids with you. Beautiful creatures running around and filling the house with joy. What a bliss! I think that you fulfill my dreams about a respectable and well-off gentelman I can trust and rely on. I promise I will be a good wife to you. One thing worries me, though, that is Rosemary. What will you tell her? Or maybe you're going to cheat on her and make her miserable? I wouldn't allow that. Maybe there's a way you can make her disappear? Think about it, Raymondie.

I am exhausted after a long day at work, so I will write mr. Aseke tomorrow. One more thing, about the ring. I think it would be better if you sent the ring directly to me. It will make my mother believe you're serious about me. It will also make me trust you more.

I love you my darling,

Your love, Dori

Raymond:

Dearest Dori,

I cannot explain with words how you make me feel.At times,I do not believe a lady like you in poland can cherish me based on only my couple of mails to you.I am very educated in the line of business.I studied accountancy in a famous nigerian university where I obtained my BSC.I went ahead and furthered my education with degrees in masters and PHD in business management in University of Ibadan Nigeria. Presently,I occupy the position of the managing director,hesd office of Standard Trust Bank with office at Marina,a very lovely location.I have been in banking for close to fifteen or sixteen years.I had worked as bankers to numerous well known africans and business director to many corporations in africa.

Seriously speaking,the problem on our path this day is how to get Rosemary out of the way.Though,she has been nice,I do no think there is any other thing I can do rather than start a good life with you.I suggest we can achieve this by me getting to Poland to have you all to myself.I cann take care of their affairs from there,because of my daughters.With time,I can really get so used to you that my only priority will be to serve my daughters because I would not want to have a little creature from god suffer. I hope I make a point to you and believe this is okay with you.

I suggest we get Philip,the attorney started with this transaction as this will fascilitate my transit to meet you in Poland.Write him and let him know when you will have your own part of the money sent.Please,inform me if you have located the westernunion office in your area.This will be the best way to have the money sent.

I really trust you so much and will love to meet your mother.I have the feeling you love her so much.Extend me warmest greetings to her.Tell her I will send african textile outfits for her.It is called tire abd dye.It is lovely.On the ring,I have ordered that it will crafted for me. I will definitely scan and send my picture to you on the weekend.

Thanks and God bless.

Raymond.

I love it when you call me Raymondie.

My direct mobile number is 234-1-775xxxx.Call me anytime anyday.

Dominatrix D:

Darling Raymondie,

I had a hectic day in the office and wasn't able to write to Mr. Lawyer. But will do it tomorrow. I am so happy receiving your loving letters. I am waiting for your lovely picture. I think what really counts in a relationship is a sense of value and inner beauty. The phisical beauty is just skin deep, and is not for real. I love you for the warm heart and the sense of trust and sincerity I feel from your letters. I know you love your daughters, but maybe they will be too much a burden to us. Why don't you think of something to get them out of our way along with Rosemary? We can always have more children and I am sure you'll love them very much too. This is just a food for thoughts for the weekend.

I love you anyway.

I will write soon, your wife Dori

Raymond:

Dearest Dori,

Sparing me time to just say I love you and delighted by the you have affected my life this few days.I will cherish your mails and relationship.I need to see you physically and get things started with you.Be fit for me.

Dominatrix D:

Dearest Raymondie,

I am sitting in front of my computer, trying to write a comprehensible letter to Mr. Aseke. WHAT should I tell him?? I love you and I need you and I miss you already. Maybe you can make a draft of this letter for me? I know I can trust you with my life... I cannot concentrate on anything else, I am thinking about you. I am reading your letters over and over again. I can feel a masculine beauty and strength emanating from them. Oh, how I wish you were here and held me in your strong arms. I cannot believe you made me feel this way my dearest darling Raymondie. I was afraid I would end up an old maid, but you made me feel like a young girl again. Thank you and bless you for that! Tell me what will you do to me when we finally meet. I want to crawl into my bed and pretend you're with me my dearest lover.

With warmest kisses, Dori

Raymond:

Wifey,

I just got back from work and decided to mail you. I am seriously thinking about leaving the kids. I know kids from you will be very wonderfull and I will cherish them so much. I will like to take you to my village to meet with my relatives. Please, try and write Philip tomorrow. He has already started making efforts to get the affidavits of claim to enable my bank work on the remittance or wire of the money to your account. Also, I need you to forward the account where the money will be directed to. This is very imperative. If we conclude this transaction next week, I will be coming to Poland to meet you. I really need to see your face. What are the kinds of things you like doing? How is your love life? What kind of work do you do? Please, tell me more about yourself.

Finally, did you find the western union office in your location. Philip suggested that that will be the best way to get your own part of the fees.

I urge you not to indulge in hectic duties. Get your nerves relaxed and think more about meeting me. I love you and can't wait to touch and feel you in my arms.

Always,

Raymond.

Dominatrix D:

Darling,

This is unbelievable! I got your letter just when I was sending mine. So we are already tuned into each other. It must be a sign from God that we are made for each other, a heavenly match! Of course I will go to Nigeria with you. You know the Ancient Romans wedding vows: Ubi te Gaius, ego Gaia—where you are a master there I am a mistress. I will follow you everywhere! You asked me about my love life, well I've been so busy pursuing my career that I haven't had a decent boyfriend or a lover yet. I am pure, Raymond, and nobody has made me a real woman yet. I was saving myself for that one and only, and finally I found you. So you must be gentle with me. I was imagining my first time many times, and now I am ready for you.

About the other things you asked about: I am not very much into physical activities. I read, I cook (I am an excellent cook), and I love to watch movies on TV and video. I don't have many friends, but I love animals and I have 7 cats and a little fluffy dog called Willis. Do you like animals? Do you have any pets? I also love classical music and I play a trombone. Do you play any instrument? Do you like music?

I cannot wait till your next letter.

I love you, your wife Dori

Raymond:

Darling,

How delighted I am to write you. I have been busy in the office trying to sort a transaction. How are you today? I am getting closer to you by the day.

On your questions,I love Rythm and blues.I use this to relax my nerves after a hard day at the office.Recently,I am beginning to relax with these songs thinking about you.You have brought joy into my life. Im play what we call the talking drum, though I am not too perfect in it.

On the transaction, just write Philip Aseke.Tell him the amount you will be able to raise and let him direct you on the means to get this sent to him. I paid him part of his service charge before he could start on this.

Honey I intend to be all over you the first day we meet.We will have alot to talk about and at the end of that show some good love.I wish I can stretch my hands and hold you.I am already thinking about that day because it is going to be my first time holding a white lady.I will make that moment worth-while.I love dogs but only scared that they might hurt me because I had stay at home.I have birds (parots) and enjoy their talks.

I will wait for your more passionate mails to me.Thanks and God bless.

Dearest Raymond.

Dominatrix D:

Sweet, dear Raymond,

Yes I miss you and yes, I'm thinking about you all the time. I pray to God we meet as soon as humanly possible. I am still waiting for your picture. Please, dear, don't make me wait too long.

Now I will tell you what my usual day looks like: I wake up about 7 am, have quick shower, get dressed, have a bite and drive to work. I work as a chief accountant at Life Securites and stockbrokers in Wroclaw, about 30 km drive from my little town. I finish work around 5 pm although sometimes I have to stay in the office up to 7 or 8 pm, depending on the amount of work. When I get home I walk Willis for about 30 minutes, then I feed my cats and I talk for an hour or so with my Mother. Sometimes on the way home I pick a movie from a video rental shop, and then I watch TV or video till I fall asleep.

My life is not very exciting as you see and what was missing in it was a MAN, a masculine beast to spend hot nights with. Now I have someone to think about and dream about. As I told you before I love to cook. I love Italian and Mexican food, and would love to try some African dishes. Darling, I was thinking I'd love to have you here before the weather gets cold. How soon can you make it to Poland? Or maybe I should go to Nigeria, and get married there? If I come to Nigeria, I could bring all money we need and sign the documents there. I can take a couple of weeks off and I could be there in about 10 days. I only hope you'll solve the Rosemary problem by the time I get there.

When will the ring be ready? I can't wait to see it. I have a problem with ivory, as I think killing elephants for ivory is cruel and unethical, and besides importing ivory to Poland is prohibited. Make the ring gold or platinum instead.

Let me know what you think about me coming to marry you in Nigeria.

I love you with all my heart

Raymond:

Dori,

I am sorry I could not write you ealier than now.Toay I went to church and there are very few Internet cafés that open around here on this religious day.I was able to drive out far to get a place to write to you ,my love. I miss you dearly and read your mails with passion.How sweet it is to get your inspirational mails.

About myself,I am 6"6 inches and chocolate in complexion.I am biult and muscular and will very much love to hold you in my tight firm of love and warmth.It has been too long that I got this feelings that presently occupy my thoughts.You are indeed, someone to be with. If you really want to be here just work on it.Nigerian consulate will freely give you an entry visa.If your mum feels reluctant, you can make her speak with me on phone.I can assure her of the genuity of my love to you.I really love your with the write ups I get from you.i can't wait for take full charge of you in bed during the cold weather.Just work on this and my life will forever be fulfilled.

Back to the business.Just write Philip and tell him that he should work things out to have the money transferred as soon as possible,probably next week.Let hi know how much you are sending and tell him I will get the remaining. I still suggest darling that you look up for a western union office. Jus do your best.I commend the efforts you are putting in this and I promise to be the best to you as long as you guarantee me of your transparency.I love.

Just do what I have told you and see what we will be able to achieve this week.

Thanks,

raymond.

Dominatrix D:

Dearest Raymondie,

Why didn't you send me your picture? Also I need to know what you did about Rosemary. Is she still around? I am determined to come to Nigeria and give myself to you but only when you permanently solve the problem with your present wife and the children. All my further steps depend on what you do about freeing yourself for me.

I talked with my Mother and calling you is out of the question—we don't have a phone at home. Another thing is my Mom cannot speak English. So send the ring and get rid of your family. Then I will write to Mr. Aseke and send the money to him and come to Nigeria to marry you with the rest of cash. I am sorry to give you these strict conditions but I have to make sure you're sincere and devoted to me.

I am sending you my picture. Please, my dearest RayOfLight send me yours, I can't wait to see your masculinity in full glory.

I love you with all my heart,

Dori Kuti

Raymond:

Dear Dori,

Why is my proceedings with you on the transaction viewed at the Internet?I just opened a website as informed by my friend and found every things I have said to you on view.I am not happy one bit and needs explanations.

Thanks,

Raymond.

Moreover,I could not open whatever you sent to me in the meaning of your picyure.

Dominatrix D:

Dear "Raymond,"

If you saw the web site you probably know that a lot of people made a fool of you. You are a fool and mugu. You are also a scammer, a thief, and you give your country a bad name.

My name is not Dori, I don't live in Wroclaw. I will not marry you. My juju is protecting me from assholes like you. I hope you'll get caught and rot in jail.

From Poland with love

"Dori"

(Another romance over...)

THE END

ALMOST

You are now a graduate of the Scamorama Scam-Proofing Course.

This book dealt with the Lads from Lagos, because so many have engaged them on the field of comedy. What does the future hold? Probably more of the same. As the world becomes more networked, it will become easier to carry out electronic crime from any location.

Scammers will send their daughters to prep school. Their sons will become lawyers. Look for the TV mini-series. Somewhere, the Nigerian Mario Puzo is doodling in a notebook.

But 419 is only one type of fraud, the 419ers a dot on a vast canvas, and they won't hold center stage forever... the Russians are coming!

Scam-baiter Anakin Skywalker met his comedic match in a practitioner of the classic Russian Bride Scam. In this thriving scam, men seeking brides are approached online by beautiful, compliant women from poor countries. They need nice men to take them away from all that. Expenses arise. You know the drill. Anakin's "love" (who may or may not have been a woman but was probably Russian to judge by the style), demonstrated real comedic chops, offering to join Anakin on the Dark Side, and expressing her wish for a son named Luke.

In a celebrated scam-bait, Jeff Harris (www.p-p-p-powerbook.com) tried to sell a computer through eBay. When he got a scamalicious offer, Harris created a mockup of a laptop (computer keys pasted to a notebook), mailed it to the scammer's mail drop (a London beauty salon) and sent his online buddies to observe. They reported back that the scammer, who paid hefty customs fees for the package, was no Lad from Lagos but had an Eastern European accent. (He responded with a DDOS attack on Harris's website.)

The impulse to con apparently knows no frontiers. The same principles hold true whatever the scam or the nationality of the person badgering you:

- if it sounds too good to be true, it is
- you can't win a lottery you didn't enter
- a dubious proposition is dubious, no matter whose stationery it's written on
- you are not obliged to answer!

The next time someone asks you to launder $50 million, you know what to do.

Scamalicious wishes and stay safe out there!

COMEDY FINALE: HOW CAN I HELP YOU?

The Unkindly Contributor, a scam-baiter who has tied the Lads up for more than a year at a time, makes it short and sweet for Jean-Claud Briggs, currently working out of the Yamussoukro Refugee Camp Cybercafé.

Jean Claud:

Subject: URGENT ASSISTANCE AND CONFIDENTIAL

Dear Respectful One,

I know you might be surprised on recieving this mail due to we have not met before. By brief introduction , I am Jean claud Briggs a citizen of Cote D'Ivoire and the senior Son of late Mr. and Mrs. David Briggs. My late parents was killed by the rebels in my home town Bouake the second Economic Capital of Cote D'Ivoire during the recent political Crisis. My parents was a wealthy Cocoa Merchant before they met their suden death .

Before their death in a hospital , my father disclosed to me of the sum of US$9.5 million dollars he deposited in one of the well known bank in Abidjan-Cote d Ivoire.

Dear, I am honourably seeking your assistance to stand as our Next of Kin and to act as guardian of the money for the transfer of the sum US$9.5 million dollars. We have choosen you to assist us invest the money in oil business where ever you felt will be the best place. I will also like you to make arrangement for me and my sister to further our Education in your country. We have decided to offer you 10 percent as compensation. Please get back to us with your bank account detail informations.

Finally ,we are lying helplessly in the refugee camp Yamussoukro-Cote D'Ivoire. We need your urgent attention to transfer this money to your account and our coming to your country for stay.

Expecting to hear from you.

Unkindly Contributor:

Thanks for your email. How can I help you?

Jean Claud:

Dear,

Thank you for your mail and sincere willing to help us, like I told you, we need your help to act as our late father's foreign partner, hence we have been directed by the bank according to my late father desire to transfer the money to his foreign investor before his untimely death. I will suggest to give you the bank contacts to enable you verify and get back to us for us to discuse on how we want the money invest in your country.

Bank contacts: telephone:+22503073xxx

Mr Irrone George (Corporate Affairs Director)

I hope to hear from you and also thank you for your effort in this matter.

Best Regards, Jean.

Unkindly Contributor:

Thanks for your email. How can I help you?

Jean Claud:

Please be more realistic, so that we can achieve this objective, consider our situation here and kindly contact the bank and arrange for the transfer of the money to your bank account.

I will like you to kindly send me your residential address immediately including your private telephone and fax numbers. I am waiting to hear from you immediately.

Unkindly Contributor:

Thanks for your email. How can I help you?

Jean Claud:

Subject: VERY URGENT

DEAR. Please stop fucking me up ok.

Unkindly Contributor:

Thanks for your email. How can I help you?

ACKNOWLEDGMENTS

Thanks to many fine people working in government, law enforcement, banking and computer security in a number of countries, for advice.

Thanks to Kenn, for the first logo.

Thanks to the many contributors to the ScamBase!

Thanks to Joe Wein for putting out important information about scams.

Laughs to J. Cosmo Newbury, Trevor Dykes, Diamond David Lee Roth, and a host of wits.

Respect to the Chaos Project, the guys at Comrade Kerensky's online taverna, Artists Against 419 and others who have saved people from being robbed.

The web site, which led to this book, Scamorama (www.scamorama.com), is a gallery of emails between scammers and their mischievous "victims" from Argentina to Turkey. Scam-o-salutes to Les Adorateurs de Scammomama la Superbe, Astro Jetson, Rev. Bob at the Church of the Blessed Beehive, Lizzie Borden, Jack Breda, Australia's Center for Research Into Advanced Pharmaceuticals, Mik Cisco, Jed Clampett, Beldar Conehead, Oliver Cromwell, Dominatrix D, Edmund Dantes, Jaja ibn Deek, Rev. Dredlock, Arnold Fannerman, Guy Fawkes, Oliver Flanagan, the Fred Flintstones (both of you), Allbee Franks, Jack Le Grandeur, Stu deBaker Hawke, Headshrinker, Will Hoseya, Lad Hunter, Lord Imhotep, Ishmael, Wally Jersey-Heifer (New Zealand's international man of mystery), Jörö the Smurfherd, Juan Kerr, Kris Kringle, Lance ±DuLac, Lord Frubert Latulant, Louise Lutefisk, Xavier Mouton, Lewis D. Noogie, Dr. Lizardo, Comrade Lykaon, Dr. E. Koli, Liza Krottenbacher-Schmerbauch, Mandy, Prof. Mallory of Miskatonic University, Pedro Martinez, Adrian Monk, Der Oberbootsmanfuhrer, Dr. Pakmesakkie, Monsieur Lepage, Phil Munglers, Seamus O'Paddy, Cem Pazarci, Cesar "Three Bucks" Pedraza, Juan Perez pere et fils, Captain Christopher Pike, Raynaz, the Last of the Romanovs, Bart Simpson de Québec, Señorita Natalia Sturgeon, Sven, Christopher Tennant, Sir Mark Time, the Unkindly Contributor, Harald Vombau, Xavier Xalisio, and many others.

Most especially, thanks to the Foreign Office for unflagging encouragement.

APPENDIX

WHO'S WHO, AND WHO ISN'T

The Lads like to pose as the sons and widows of politicians. They may cite news items about their real counterparts, to seem more convincing. The names of some frequently impersonated real people follow. The Lads do not confine themselves to tragic stories of Nigerian origin. If you receive a letter from someone not on this list, it does *not* mean the offer is legitimate. If you're still unclear on this concept, go back to the beginning of this book and read it out loud, while kicking yourself.

SENATORS AND REPRESENTATIVES IN THE NIGERIAN NATIONAL ASSEMBLY:

Members past and present fraudulently impersonated in scam-o-grams include **CHRIS ADIGHEJE**, **KASSIM OFOYO**, and **UBA UGOCHUKWU**. **Rep. MAURICE IBEKWE** was arrested on fraud charges and died in 2004 while in detention. **Senator CHUBA OKADIGBO** was impeached on corruption charges and died in 2003, a few days after being teargassed at a rally. See who really *is* who on their web site: www.nigeriacongress.org

MARIAM ABACHA Widow of the late former Nigerian President General Sani Abacha, a most scary dictator. Other impersonated widows: Filipino former first ladies ESTRADA and MARCOS (she of the shoes), Mrs. ARAFAT, Mrs. HARIRI (widow of the murdered Lebanese politician), Mrs. KABILA, and Mrs. SAVIMBI.

DIEPREYE ALAMIEYESEIGHA Former Governor of Bayelsa State in Nigeria. In 2005, he was arrested in London on charges of money laundering. Out on bail, he fled to Nigeria, where he was impeached. It was claimed he worked his escape in women's clothing, but no one's produced the photo.

ALHAJI BAYERO Emir of Kano State in Nigeria. An Emir is a Muslim dignitary. Alhaji is an honorific, meaning he has made a pilgrimage to Saudi Arabia. The Lads like to call themselves Alhaji. It doesn't mean they've made a hajj, or are even Muslim. It just sounds important—like chief, prince, engineer, and doctor.

HASSANAL BOLKIAH The Sultan of Brunei (nowhere near Nigeria). The Lads sometimes claim to have found your email address in his diary.

THEOPHILUS DANJUMA Former Nigerian Minister of Defense, current head of South Atlantic Petroleum.

ROBERT GUEI In 1999, led a coup against President HENRI KONAN BEDIE to become Ivory Coast's first military ruler. A year later he ran as a civilian candidate, lost, and died in the ensuing rebellion.

BOLA IGE Nigerian Minister of Justice and Attorney General. Assassinated in 2001.

AHMED TEJAN KABBAH President of Sierra Leone several times, interrupted by a coup (see SANKOH and KOROMAH).

LAURENT KABILA A president of the Democratic Republic of Congo. Assassinated by a bodyguard. Succeeded in office by son Joseph.

MIKHAIL KHODORKOVSKY Russian oil magnate who ran afoul of the Russian government and was sent to Siberia. His many "secretaries" do not seem to read or write Russian.

JOHNNY KOROMA An army officer in Sierra Leone who headed the Armed Forces Revolutionary Council following a military coup. He eventually became head of state. Eventually driven out, he was indicted for war crimes by a UN special court, fled, and later died.

NGOZI OKONJO-IWEALA Nigeria's finance minister.

BARACK OBAMA Junior United States Senator from the State of Illinois. Impersonated by scammers who describe themselves as "the Senator from Kenya" (Obama's father was Kenyan).

FODAY SANKOH Late leader of the Revolutionary United Front (RUF) in Sierra Leone. In 2000 he was indicted for war crimes by a UN court, and died awaiting trial.

MOBUTU SESE SEKO Late President of Zaire.

CHARLES SOLUDO Head of the Central Bank of Nigeria.

ROBERT MUGABE President of Zimbabwe, for as long as he wants to be. 419ers often claim to be Zimbabweans who have fled to South Africa to escape him.

STELLA OBASANJO Late wife of the President of Nigeria, Olusegun Obasanjo. Scammers are popping out of the woodwork offering to share her treasure.

NUHU RIBADU Head of the Nigerian Economic and Financial Crimes Commission.

JONAS SAVIMBI Late leader of Angolan guerrilla movement.

SUSN SHABANGU A Deputy Minister in the South African government.

CHARLES SOLUDO Head of the Central Bank Of Nigeria.

CHARLES TAYLOR Ex-president of Liberia. Currently exiled to Nigeria.

THOMAS UKOT Executive Director of the Niger Delta Development Commission (NDDC).

KEN SARO WIWA Political activist of the minority Ogoni people in Nigeria. In 1995, he and eight others were hanged by the government, after what was widely described as a show trial. His son, Ken Wiwa, has written about him.

WEB SITES

Government and Law Enforcement

Nigerian Federal Government: www.nigeria.gov.ng

Nigerian Congress: www.nigeriacongress.org

Nigerian Economic & Financial Crimes Commission: www.efccnigeria.org

Central Bank of Nigeria: www.cenbank.org

Ghana Police: www.ghanapolice.org

419 Legal (South African police): www.419legal.org

UK Metropolitan Police: www.met.police.uk/fraudalert

UK National Criminal Intelligence Service: www.ncis.co.uk

Canada (RCMP): www.phonebusters.com

US Internet Crime Complaint Center: www.ic3.gov

US Secret Service Financial Crimes Division: www.secretservice.gov/alert419.shtml

US Treasury Department 419 Page: www.ustreas.gov/usss/index.htm?alert419.htm&1

Anti-Phishing Working Group (International): www.antiphishing.org

Business and Travel Information

Nigeria Business Info: www.nigeriabusinessinfo.com/archive/419.htm

Canadian Consular Affairs Travel Report: www.voyage.gc.ca/dest/report-en.asp?country=218000

US Department of State Nigeria Page: www.travel.state.gov/nigeria.html

Tips for Business Travelers to Nigeria:
www.travel.state.gov/travel/tips/brochures/brochures_2113.html

Western Union Fraud Awareness: www.westernunion.com/info/faqSecurity.asp

Newsfeeds

AllAfrica (News Clearinghouse): www.allafrica.com

APC Africa ICT Policy Monitor: africa.rights.apc.org

BBC Africa News: news.bbc.co.uk/hi/english/world/africa

Nigerian Newspapers Online

Nigeria Daily (News): www.nigeriadaily.com

The Guardian (News): www.ngrguardiannews.com

Punch: www.punchng.com

Daily Sun: www.sunnewsonline.com

This Day Online: www.thisdayonline.com

Vanguard: www.vanguardngr.com

NigeriaWeb: odili.net/culture.html

Nigerian Cultural/Political/Humor Web Sites

(The selection is only a starting point and does not reflect a particular bias.)

Foolscap: www.foolscap-media.com

Free Africa Foundation: www.freeafrica.org

Motherland Nigeria: www.motherlandnigeria.com

Nairaland: www.nairaland.com

Nigerian Blog Aggregator: www.nigerianbloggers.com

Nigeria Village Square: www.nigeriavillagesquare.com

Private Groups Fighting 419 Fraud

Project 419 Coalition: home.rica.net/alphae/419coal

Artists Against 419: www.aa419.org

419 Eater: www.419eater.com

Private Support Groups and Websites for Victims

www.scamvictimsunited.com

www.scampatrol.org

www.fraudaid.com

Spam Blacklists

(A partial list—there are many)

Spamcop: www.spamcop.net

Open Relay Database: www.ordb.org

Spam Domain Blacklist (jwSpamSpy): www.joewein.de/sw/bl-log.htm

Spamhaus: www.spamhaus.org

WHY NOT TELL US WHAT YOU REALLY THINK

Sometimes a thwarted scammer cracks. The following bits of geopolitical discourse were sent to scam-baiters.

YOU ARE COMPLETE MUGU, AND YOU WILL FALL IN ONE WAY OR THE OTHER, YOU FEEL YOU ARE WISE THIS WAY, I WILL USE ANOTHER WAY TO GET YOU. YOU PEOPLE HAVE NOT FINISHED PAYING FOR WHAT YOU DID TO OUR FOUR FATHERS, YOU WILL SURELY PAY YOUR OWN ONE DAY. I PROMISE YOU. FOOL AND MUGU IS WHAT YOU ARE.

***

MY FRIEND,
I DONT THINK YOU HAVE WORK TO DO . ME MY WORK IS TO STAY IN THE COMPUTER AND FRAUD WHAT ABOUT YOU . USELESS ELEMENT.

***

you are a dead man already. Y ou know ho we are cos we are coming straight at you. I will shoot you through the nose.
Beleive me.
You can call the cops now, bitch-ass

***

Bastard,
You will never fine your asshole, i told you not to ever write me again, i am a don in Lagos, here is my home mother fucker, we are the lords in Lagos okay, you are just fooling your self, i told you i fuck your mama and your papa, i will make sure all your kids dont grow, and i will wipe your family out of existence if you fuck with me , you dont know me, dont ever thing of coming to lagos because that will be the end of your life mother fucker, i told you that you are like a small rat, in a tiny hole, all i need to do is to cover the fucking hole and let you die, dont play with me or else i will travel down to the state and look for you, listen you dont know anything about business,

before you were born i have been doing business all over the world, okay, you are too small for me, i have kill more than 3 people this year so if you fuck with me you are going to be the forth so dont mess mother fucker

...you are a mugu only defrent is you dont have money if you have you get to paid twomuch of money just look act time you are use to write all this shit ,come to me so that i will make you rich i have a lot of money last week i came there in canada i look for your offices onfortunate the transaction that bring me was over i can buy you thank you .

come let me make you a rich man in life my education stander is two much i loke to write you in this way if you can understan it ,i dont care who you are fuck you1000*end for remend fool for ever ,

every thing in this world come from africa but africa are sorfrin reason you white come to africa and still every thing dont worry we know how to bring them back to africa, keep usen the stupid ones but as for me i am two much ..since GOD CRETED WHITE AND BRACK YOU PEOPLE KEEP CHITING BRACK BUT IS ALL OVER WE BLACK GOT OUR ONW SENCE FUCK YOU FOREVER THIS NOT THE WAY GOD ALLMIGHTY WANT US TO DO BUT YOU REMAIN POOR THIS IS HOW CAIN AND EBEL DID YOU PEOPLE WANT TO DO THIS WAY TO ME IS IN POSOBLE TO HELL WITH YOU AND YOU FAMILY FOREVER IN THIS WORLD FUCK YOU YOU YOU YOU YOU YOU YOU YOUY YOU YOU AND YOUR FAMILY YOU CAN DO ANY THING TO ME TELL WERE ALL YOU IN CANADA I WILL COME THERE 2PAC SAID IF YOU HAVE MONEY THE WORLD IS FOR YOU SO THIS WORLD IS FOR ME I HAVE 20 ARTHORNEY WHICH I AM PAIDYING TELL WERE YOU ARE STA IN CANADA I WILL COME THERE MY FAMILY ARE LAVEN IN CANADA TOROTO FUCK I CAN FIRNISH YOU ANY THINGS THAT YOU NEED TO LOOK FOR ME

***

Listing let me tell you i have a companey in London and all so in Canada US and all so in my contry .iam a rich man i am not a woman ,any things you need to look for me let me know i will fornish you all reason 2pacK said that if you have money you have the world ,i will not tell you any thing,this work have defrent way to do it i like to write IN THIS WAY sombody who dont know any thing so that you people we fall in to it thank you dont reply me again because i am not goin to use this box agian if you need me just give you adress i we send my boys in canada there to see you thank you good bye .

***

SAY YOUR LAST PRAYER.YOU HAVE 250 HOURS TO BECOME A DEAD MAN.
I WILL TELL YOU THAT YOU DONT INSULT ANYBODY YOU SEE.
MY FAMILY WILL TAKE YOU SOON. THEY ARE IN YOUR COUNTRY.
THIS A MAFIA ASSYMENT.
SEE YOU IN HELL.
NB: I KNOW YOU,INFACT ALL YOUR INFORMATION.

CHECK IF YOU OFFENDEN ANYBODY CLOSE TO YOU.

REGARDS

ED.CAPO.SOCIETY

YOU ARE A POST DATED IDIOT OF THE YEAR 2003 YOU ARE AN ENEMY TO GOOD NEWS LOOK MY FREIND YOU ARE TOO POOR TO DO THIS CAN OF BUSINESS SEAT DOWN THERE GOOD THING OF LIFE WILL PAST YOU IF YOU DID NOT TAKE YOU TIME I WILL SEND GOD OF IRON TO FIRE YOU TO DEATH

***

... YOU SEE MY GOOD FRIEND xxxx, THIS BUSINESS IS LIKE A MAFIA GAME AND YOU CANNOT JUST STOP THE MAFIA FROM GETTING WHAT THEY WANT. THE US GOVERNMENT HAVE TRIED ALL THEY COULD AND NOTHING CAME OUT AND EVEN OUR GOVERNMENT TOO BUT YOU SEE THIS BUSINESS IS FOR REAL AND IT IS RATHER APPALLING TO KNOW THAT YOU ARE JUST TRYING TO FIND A TINY CRYSTAL GRAIN OF SAND FROM THE BEACH, HELL NO YOU JUST CANNOT DO THAT MY FRIEND.

YOU SEE MY FRINED, I WOULD RATHER ADVISE YOU TO PLEASE FIND SOME GOOD TO DO FOR YOURSELF RATHER THAN BOTHERING YOURSELF ABOUT ME CUZ YOU WILL NEVER BE ABLE TO MATCH ME IN ANY WAY. I LIVE LARGE IN MY COUNTRY AS I DRIVE " COME ON WHY DO I WANT TO JOIN ISSUES WITH YOU, YOU AIN'T WORTH IT". ALL I WANT TO SAY IS THAT I COULD OFFER U A DEAL WHERE WE COULD BE BUDDIES, IF YOU UNDERSTAND WHAT I AM TRYING TO TELL YOU AND YOU MUST BE WILLING AND READY TO WORK WITH ME.

NB: I WANT YOU TO BE THAT FOOLISH AND STUPID ENOUGH TO SEND THIS CORRESPONDENCE AROUND TO PEOPLE CUZ THAT IS MY AIM TO KNOW HOW SMART YOU ARE CUZ YOU GUYS ARE REALLY DUMB. ASTALAVISTA MY FRIEND AND CIAO!!!

***

dear fool,

infact you are greatest fool ive ever come across.you are going to be killed by crocodile. your ancestors are fools.and fools shall your generaion be. infact,the cia are already after you. you will die during dry season so that the grave diggers will not be able to dig your grave to 6 feet. i will search for your mother.I will like to feed my own crocodile with your mum for christmas.

***

I have just placed your name on the search web this morning and came out with result that you are not a human being, you are an animal, a beast. You are a beast of no nation. Infact, you are an anti-christ. How I wish you are in the WORLD TRADE CENTRE on that September 11.

NOTES

CHAPTER 1

p. 14
Cartoon by Trevor Dykes
Purveyor of quirky humor at "How To Become Rich Dot Com" (www.how-to-become-rich-dotcom.de).

Perhaps this should not be surprising, as bandits have been said to run cars off Nigerian expressways and loot the wreckage
B. C. Okagbare. "The twilight of Nigerian 419 fraudsters." Mbeyi & Associates Ltd., Lagos, 2003.

In 2003 I looked at the *headers* of one thousand e-mails...
E. Edelson, "The 419 Scam: information warfare on the scam front," Computers & Security, 2003.

p. 16
Others set up shop in nearby Ghana or Togo, or Dubai or increasingly South Africa
Mark Shaw. "Towards an understanding of West African criminal networks in Southern Africa." *African Security Review*, Vol. 10, No 4, 2001. Available online [www.iss.co.za/Pubs/ASR/10No4/Shaw.html].

"Nigerian 419 scam: 419 racket is turning SA into extortion capital of the world." Available online [www.swazi.com/scamcentre/419scam.html].

"Go south, con man: Why Nigerian fraudsters now like working in South Africa." For *The Economist*, August 12, 2004. Available online [www.economist.com/displayStory.cfm?story_id=3096850].

People have begun receiving scam letters after making inquiries to legitimate Nigerian business organizations
Bolaji Ojo. "Inside The Letter-Scam Industry." Available online [http://members.tripod.com/~orgcrime/niginside.htm].

Some victims claim they were taken through government offices by government employees
The Project 419 Coalition (home.rica.net/alphae/419coal/) maintains a comprehensive news collection on this subject.

According to Nuhu Ribadu, the head of Nigeria's Economic and Financial Crimes Commission, up to 100,000 Nigerians are involved
Tracey Logan. "Nigerian scammers in line of fire." March 3, 2004. Available online [http://news.bbc.co.uk/2/hi/technology/3526209.stm].

A former deputy superintendent of police felt the number is "less than one percent of Nigerians", which would mean 1.2 million people!
Charles Tive. *419 Scam: Exploits of the Nigerian con man*. Chicha Favours, 2002.

...Anecdotally, 419 seems like a successful business for some and a widespread hobby
Dulue Mbachu. "Internet Scammers Keep Working in Nigeria." Associated Press, August 6, 2005. Available online [news.yahoo.com/s/ap/20050806/ap_on_hi_te/internet_scammers].

p. 18
Between August and November 1998, the Sydney postal service alone confiscated 1.8 million pieces of '419' letters stamped with counterfeit postage
R. G. Smith, M. N. Holmes and P. Kaufman. "Nigerian advance fee fraud." No. 121, *Trends & Issues in Crime and Criminal Justice*, Australian Institute of Criminology, July 1999. Available online [www.aic.gov.au/publications/tandi/tandi121.html].

Some have been held for ransom and even killed
Philip de Bruin. "SA cops, Interpol probe murder." December 12, 2004. Available online [www.news24.com/News24/South_Africa/News/0,,2-7-1442_1641875,00.html].

Chris Abani's beautiful and tragic novel, *Graceland*
Chris Abani, *Graceland*. Farrar, Straus and Giroux, 2004.

419 scams cost Americans an estimated $250 million a year
Jonathan Winer, Deputy Assistant Secretary for International Narcotics and Law Enforcement Affairs. "Statement before the Subcommittee on Africa of the House International Relations Committee." Washington, D.C. September 11, 1996.

p. 21
They delivered the package and arrested Ken, also known as Adebayo Adedimila
Torsten Ove. "Nigerians running lucrative swindles; Trail leads to man in North Versailles." For *Pittsburgh Post-Gazette*. January 18, 2004.

This has brought suspicion on the service itself and caused resentment among relay operators, who know what is going on but are not (officially) free to intervene
Deaf relay operators discuss the issue online [http://ip_relay_scams.aimoo.com/].

CHAPTER 2

p. 27
The quote from Mackay
Charles Mackay. *Extraordinary Popular Delusions and the Madness of Crowds* (1841). Three Rivers Press, reprint ed. 1995.

The French version of the letter described by Vidocq was published in this book:
Eugène-François Vidocq. Dictionnaire argot-français, in *Mémoires/Les Voleurs*. Editions Robert Laffont, 1998.

CHAPTER 3

p. 35
"This is the period when we started hearing about 419..."
Nuhu Ribadu. "EFCC has recovered over N500bn so far." January 20, 2006. Available online [www.efccnigeria.org].

"The more destruction there is everywhere..."
Nikolai Gogol. *The Inspector General*, 1836. Kessinger Pubishing, 2004

Transparency International rates Nigeria one of the most corrupt countries.
Transparency International [www.transparency.org]: International non-governmental organization devoted to combating corruption.

The level of corruption in government and society is widely documented in the published literature, a vigorous Nigerian press, and online, with just a few sources cited here
G. B. N. Ayittey. *Africa Betrayed*. St. Martin's Press, 1992.
Karl Maier. *This House Has Fallen*. Westview Press, 2000.
Robert Guest. *The Shackled Continent*. Smithsonian Books, 2004.

Bribery is common in everyday transactions, extortion for spare change at police roadblocks being just one example
Niyi Oniororo. *Letter to Nigeria Police*. Ororo Publications, 1989

p. 36
People have been shot for holding out
"Policing a Democracy: a survey report on the role and functions of the Nigeria police force in a post military era." Center for Law Enforcement Education, Lagos and National Human Rights Commission, Abuja, 1999.

Bank employees siphon off money from accounts
"Nigerian bank fraud up 40%." For BBC News. Available online [news.bbc.co.uk/1/hi/business/3051247.stm].

Instead, there is widespread poverty, very high unemployment even for technically trained graduates, a crumbling infrastructure, and huge debt

The police are widely considered corrupt and brutal
Human Rights Watch, July 2005 Vol. 17, No. 11(A). "Rest in Pieces: Police Torture and Deaths in Custody in Nigeria." Available online [http://hrw.org/].

Niyi Oniororo, *Letter to Nigeria Police*. Ororo Publications, 1989.

A senior officer himself described the ranks as extremely poorly paid, trained and housed
Kayode Oseni. *Inside Out (The Circumstance of the Nigeria Police Force)*. Raose Nig. Ltd., 1993.

...and are finding vigilantes serious competition
E. E. Obioha. "Public perception of the role of Nigeria police force and civil society based security operatives in urban crime management in Nigeria: A study in Onitsha, Anambra State, Nigerian Institute of Social and Economic Research." Ibadan, Monograph Series No. 1, 2004.

p. 37
... which floods the market and drives local companies under
N. Ribadu. "Implication of Economic and Financial Crimes on the Nation's Economy, Defence Adviser Conference in Abuja." September 10, 2004. Available online [www.efccnigeria.org].

President Obasanjo has fired some high-level bureaucrats for financial irregularities, including managers of the Nigerian National Petroleum Corporation
"Nigerian oilmen sacked over scam." April 19, 2004. Available online [news.bbc.co.uk/2/hi/africa/3640053.stm].

one of the few foreigners to have testified in a Nigerian court on the matter
Victor Efeizomor. "Man jailed 376 years for defrauding American of $1.9m." For the *Daily Independent*. January 16, 2006. Available online [www.independentng.com/news/nnjan160607.htm].

In 2005, the EFCC forced 419ers to return $4.5 million stolen from a Chinese family
"Nigeria conmen repay scam victim." October 7, 2005. Available online [news.bbc.co.uk/2/hi/africa/4320984.stm].

spurred the Nigerian Bar Association to a two-day boycott of the court system in 2006
"Boycott shuts down Nigeria courts." For BBC News. Available online [http://news.bbc.co.uk/2/hi/africa/4800824.stm].

These crimes sometimes make use of knowledge gained while employed in banks
T. Catán and M. Peel. "Bogus websites, stolen corporate identities: how Nigerian fraudsters steal millions from western banks." For the *Financial Times*. March 3, 2003.

In 2002, South African police arrested 22 Nigerians for running fake bank web sites
Nicki Padayachee. "Scorpions bust website scammers." For the South Africa *Sunday Times*. August 18, 2002. Available online [www.suntimes.co.za/2002/08/18/news/news20.asp].

p. 38
In 2003, six 419ers in Amsterdam were sentenced to prison and ordered to compensate their victims
Lester Haines. "419 gang scam themselves into the slammer." June 2, 2003. Available online [www.theregister.co.uk/2003/06/02/419_gang_scam_themselves_into/].

In 2004, two Nigerians were arrested in Dubai
Hani M. Bathish. "Justice meted out to crooks who tricked Saudi national."
For *Khaleej Times Online*. February 16, 2004. Available online [www.khaleejtimes.com/DisplayArticle.asp ?xfile=data/theuae/2004/February/theuae_February285.xml&section=theuae].

In 2004, Nigerians were arrested in India and Pakistan for running the "wash wash" scam
Sanjay Sharma. "Four Nigerians Arrested In Delhi For Trying To Pull The 'Black Dollar Scam.'" December 18, 2004. Available online [www.gurgaonscoop.com/story/2004/12/18/233718/80].

"Nigerians arrested with fake dollars." For *Daily Times of Pakistan*. May 29, 2004. Available online [www.dailytimes.com.pk/default.asp?page=story_29-5-2004_pg7_23].

In 2004, a Nigerian was sentenced in Wales
"Nigerian jailed for email scam." For BBC News. April 2, 2004. Available online [news.bbc.co.uk/1/hi/wales/north_west/3594043.stm].

They were also running a 419 scam on a Ghanaian businessman
"$48.6 m Fraud Busted." Available online [www.ghanapolice.org/news/13jan04_48mil.htm].

In 2005, six Nigerians and two Senegalese
Tidiane Sy. "Senegal swoop on email scammers." May 3, 2005. Available online [news.bbc.co.uk/go/pr/fr/-/2/hi/africa/4509837.stm].

...18,000 letters by mail each week
"Spanish police arrest 300 over 'multinational' scam." For *The Guardian*. July 23, 2005.

In 2004, a Nigerian immigrant in Texas...
Matt Stiles. "Nigerian charged in US money order 419 scam." For the *Dallas Morning News*. December 29, 2004.

... the scammers invested the proceeds in cars, clothes, and gadgets
Kimball Perry. "Oops: ID thief targets a Lindner." For the *Cincinnati Post*. November 11, 2004. Availble online [www.cincypost.com/2004/11/24/sent112404.html].

...has worked with a number of potential victims to set up sting operations
J. Buchanan and A. J. Grant. "Investigating and Prosecuting Nigerian Fraud." For *US ATTORNEYS' BULLETIN*, Nov. 2001 (Vol. 49, No. 6). Available online [www.usdoj.gov:80/USo/eoUS/foia_reading_room/USb4906.pdf].

p. 39
... merchandise ordered with phony credit cards
Edward Ericson Jr. "FBI Agent Heads Sting that Brings Down 16 People Involved in Nigerian IP Relay Fraud Operations." For *Baltimore City Paper Online*. June 16, 2004. Available online [www.citypaper.com/news/story.asp?id=7811].

... unlikely to be vindicated through the justice system
Bank fraud examiners may be able to produce results, depending on the circumstances, for instance in cases of unauthorized wire transfers.

She got a settlement, but the scam took over her life
Uwe Buse. "Africa's City of Cyber Gangsters." For *Der Spiegel* 45/2005. November 7, 2005. Available online [www.spiegel.de/international/spiegel/0,1518,384317,00.html].

CHAPTER 4

p. 49
Candide
Lillian Hellman, score by Leonard Bernstein, lyrics by Richard Wilbur, John Latouche and Dorothy Parker. *Candide*, 1956.

p. 50
Then e-mails began arriving from people all over the world who'd received similar letters
To date, Argentina, Australia, Austria, Belgium, Bolivia, Bulgaria, Canada, Costa Rica, the Czech Republic, Denmark, England, Finland, France, Germany, Hong Kong, Hungary, India, Indonesia, Ireland, Israel, Italy, Kenya, Latvia, Lithuania, Mali, Mexico, Nigeria, the Netherlands, Pakistan, the Philippines, Poland, Portugal, New Zealand, Russia, Sierra Leone, Slovenia, South Africa, Spain, Sweden, Thailand, Turkey, Vietnam, the United Arab Emirates, the UK, the US, and Yugoslavia.

CHAPTER 5

p. 65
I seen my opportunities and I took 'em.
George Washington Plunkitt. *Plunkitt of Tammany Hall, A Series of Very Plain Talks on Very Practical Politics.* Recorded by William L. Riordon in 1963. Available online from The Gutenberg Project [www.gutenberg.org] as well as in paperback by William J. Riordan and Peter Quinn, from Signet Classics, 1995.

CHAPTER 6

p. 84
outright breaking into insecure bank systems (which did happen to a Nigerian bank)
Jerry Amah. "What Nigerians do in cyber cafes." For *The Sun*. July 26, 2004. Available online [africa.rights.apc.org/index.shtml?apc=21862se_1&x=22475].

Femi Oyesanya, who writes on Nigerian IT issues, calls Nigeria the "Wild Wild West of Internet Crime"
Femi Oyesanya, Nigeria. "Haven for Terrorist Internet Communication?" August 4, 2004. Available online from

[www.nigeriavillagesquare1.com/Articles/oyesanya/2004/08/nigeria-haven-for-terrorist-internet.html].

...Turkey, Nigeria and Pakistan to pass messages
"A suspect reveals communication strategy." For CNN. August 4, 2004. Available online
[http://www.cnn.com/2004/US/08/03/terror.threat/].

... coded plans for assassinations in West Africa
Wayne Madsen. "US intelligence links 419s to terrorist attacks." For *Compsec Online*. January 21, 2004. Available
online [www.compseconline.com/analysis/040121419fraud.html].

CHAPTER 8

p. 141
...Others are specific—quality of service, unreliable power, maintaining computers
E. Amaefule. "The rise and fall of cyber cafes." For *Daily Times of Nigeria*. April 7, 2003.
Available online [http://www.dailytimesofnigeria.com/DailyTimes/2003/April/7/The.asp].

O. Kanu. "Issues Nigerian ISPs Contend With." For *This Day Online*. October 24, 2002.
Available online [http://www.thisdayonline.com/archive/2002/10/24/20021024e-b01.html].

p. 142
... causing indiscriminate damage
"Cyber-café operators in Festac having problems with police (419)." Available online
[www.nairaland.com/Nigeria/topic2522.0.html].

... Internet Exchange Points—multi-ISP hubs
Femi Oyesanya. "A Technical Solution for Nigerian 419 Emails." April 5, 2004. Available online [www.nigeriavil-
lagesquare1.com/Articles/oyesanya/2004/04/technical-solution-for-nigerian-419.html].

p. 144
To be vigilant over calls received on their telephone lines
Jidaw Systems Limited IT News. Available online [www.jidaw.com/itnewsoctoberfull.html].

CHAPTER 9

p. 153
Fiorello:
"Little Tin Box," a song from the beautiful 1959 musical *Fiorello* (lyrics Sheldon Harnick, music Jerry Bock, book by
Jerome Wiedman and George Abbott). Fiorello LaGuardia was a Real Person, a Republican who ran against the
Democratic "Tammany Hall" political establishment to become mayor of New York City in the 1930s. To his backers'
surprise and annoyance, he was serious about reform.

CHAPTER 10

p. 177
Nkem Owoh:
Nkem Owoh. Usuofia is a Nigerian comic actor who has released some hit songs about 419 scams. More information
available online [http://people.africadatabase.org/en/person/16076.html].

p. 182
... uses a local radio show to warn people about fraud
Seth Schiesel. "Turning the Tables on Email Swindlers." For *New York Times*. June 17, 2004. Available online [http://www.nytimes.com/2004/06/17/technology/circuits/17hoax.html?ex=1402891200&en=c41168a8fa42945f&ei=5007&partner=USERLAND].

Its description of such groups fits both scammers and anti-scammers.
J. Arquilla and D. Ronfeldt (eds.). *Networks and Netwars: the future of terror, crime, and militancy*. Rand, 2001. Available online [http://www.rand.org/pubs/monograph_reports/MR1382/index.html].

THE END (ALMOST)

p. 195
Anakin Skywalker
"Anakin Skywalker meets Russian Bride Nastya." Available online [members.419eater.com/~padme/iloveyoumore.htm].

P. 203
Ken Saro Wiwa
Ken Wiwa. *In the Shadow of a Saint*. Steerforth, 2001.

disinformation®